beginner's
FRENCH
grammar

Wendy Bourbon with
Duncan Sidwell and Elaine Haviland

TEACH YOURSELF BOOKS

For UK orders: please contact Bookpoint Ltd, 39 Milton Park, Abingdon, Oxon OX14 4TD. Telephone: (44) 01235 400414, Fax: (44) 01235 400454. Lines are open from 9.00–6.00, Monday to Saturday, with a 24-hour message answering service. Email address: orders@bookpoint.co.uk

For U.S.A. & Canada orders: please contact NTC/Contemporary Publishing, 4255 West Touhy Avenue, Lincolnwood, Illinois 60646–1975, U.S.A. Telephone: (847) 679 5500, Fax: (847) 679 2494.

Long-renowned as the authoritative source for self-guided learning – with more than 30 million copies sold worldwide – the *Teach Yourself* series includes over 200 titles in the fields of languages, crafts, hobbies, business and education.

British Library Cataloguing in Publication Data
A catalogue entry for this title is available from The British Library.

Library of Congress Catalog Card Number: On file.

First published in UK 1999 Hodder Headline Plc, 338 Euston Road, London, NW1 3BH.

First published in US 1999 by NTC/Contemporary Publishing, 4255 West Touhy Avenue, Lincolnwood (Chicago), Illinois 60646–1975, U.S.A.

Typeset by Transet Limited, Coventry, England.
Printed in Great Britain for Hodder & Stoughton Educational, a division of Hodder Headline Plc, 338 Euston Road, London NW1 3BH by Cox & Wyman Ltd, Reading, Berkshire.

Impression number   10 9 8 7 6 5 4
Year   2004 2003 2002 2001 2000

CONTENTS

Introduction _____ 1

NOUNS AND ARTICLES

1	Nouns: the definite article	le cinéma, la voiture, les livres _____	2
2	Nouns: the indefinite article	un journal, une veste, des documents __	4
3	Uses of the articles	Elle a les cheveux longs._____	6
4	Gender of nouns (1)	le russe, la banane _____	8
5	Gender of nouns (2)	-âge (m), -eau (m), -euse (f), -ère (f)__	10
6	Nouns with two genders and meanings	le poste, la poste _____	12
7	Compound nouns	la belle-fille, le wagon-lit _____	14
8	**Il est** and **C'est**	Il est tard. C'est moi. _____	16
9	The partitive article	du vin, de la confiture_____	18

PREPOSITIONS

10	Simple prepositions (1)	après, avant, avec, chez, contre, dans	20
11	Simple prepositions (2)	depuis, derrière, devant, en, entre, envers, malgré_____	22
12	Simple prepositions (3)	par, parmi, pendant, pour, sans, sauf, sous, sur, vers _____	24
13	The preposition **de**	la voiture de Paul, un verre de vin __	26
14	The preposition **à**	au cinéma, à l'heure _____	28
15	Complex prepositions	grâce à, à côté de_____	30

ADJECTIVES AND ADVERBS

16	Possessive adjectives	mon livre, notre maison _____	32
17	Adjectives: agreement (1)	amusant, amusante _____	34
18	Adjectives: agreement (2)	heureux, heureuse _____	36
19	Adjectives: position	une jolie maison, un livre intéressant	38
20	Demonstrative adjectives	ce, cet, cette, ces _____	40
21	Adverbs (1): regular forms	sérieusement, absolument _____	42
22	Adverbs (2): irregular forms	gentiment, bien _____	44
23	Adverbs (3): position	Il travaille vite. J'ai trop mangé.____	46
24	Adjectives: comparison	plus … que, moins … que _____	48
25	Adverbs: comparison	plus … que _____	50

iii

26 Adjectives: superlative   le/la plus…, le/la moins,
                              le/la meilleur(e), etc. _____ 52
27 Adverbs: superlative   le plus…, le moins…, le pis, etc. __ 54
28 Indefinite adjectives and
   pronouns (1)   autre, certain, quelque, etc. _____ 56
29 Indefinite adjectives and
   pronouns (2)   chaque, quelque chose, etc._____ 58

VERBS (1)

30 The verb   infinitive, regular, irregular_____ 60
31 Present tense (1) regular
   -er verbs   je porte, tu portes, il porte, etc. ____ 62
32 Present tense (2): -er verbs
   with changes in the stem   j'achète, nous achetons, etc. _____ 64
33 Present tense (3): regular
   -ir verbs   je finis, tu finis, il finit, etc. _____ 66
34 Present tense (4): regular
   -re verbs   je vends, tu vends, il vend, etc. ____ 68
35 Present tense (5): reflexive
   verbs   je me lève, tu te lèves, il se lève, etc.__ 70

PRONOUNS

36 Subject pronouns   je, tu, il, elle, on, nous, vous, ils, elles__ 72
37 Subject pronoun: on   On va en ville? On est fatigués. ____ 74
38 Emphatic pronouns   moi, toi, lui, elle, etc. _____ 76
39 Possessive pronouns   le mien, la mienne, les miens,
                              les miennes, etc. _____ 78
40 Demonstrative pronouns   celui, celle, ceux, celles _____ 80
41 Relative pronouns (1)   qui, que _____ 82
42 Relative pronouns (2)   dont, où _____ 84
43 Relative pronouns (3)   lequel, lesquels, laquelle, lesquelles 86
44 Relative pronouns (4)   ce qui, ce que, ce dont _____ 88
45 Object pronouns (1)   me, te, le, la, les, lui, leur, etc. ____ 90
46 Object pronouns (2)   y, en_____ 92
47 Object pronouns (3):
   position   Elle les aide. Les aide-t-elle? _____ 94

VERBS (2)

48 Irregular verbs: avoir   j'ai, tu as, il a, elle a, etc. _____ 96
49 Irregular verbs: être   je suis, tu es, il est, elle est, etc. ____ 98

50	Irregular verbs: **aller** and **faire**	je vais, je fais	100
51	Irregular verbs: **mettre** and **prendre**	je mets, je prends	102
52	Irregular verbs: **pouvoir** and **vouloir**	je peux, je veux	104
53	Irregular verbs: **devoir** and **savoir**	je dois, je sais	106
54	Verbs with more than one subject	ma sœur et moi sortons	108
55	The present participle	trouvant, sortant	110
56	The imperative	Continue. Levez-vous.	112
57	The infinitive (1)	J'aime chanter. Il veut venir.	114
58	The infinitive (2)	Elle commence à le préparer.	116
59	Verb constructions with objects	J'attends Paul. Je joue au golf.	118
60	The perfect tense (1)	j'ai acheté	120
61	The perfect tense (2): with **être**	je suis allé(e)	122
62	The perfect tense (3): reflexive verbs	Je me suis levé(e).	124
63	The perfect tense (4): preceding direct objects	Je les ai vus.	126
64	The imperfect tense	j'allais, il était	128
65	Past tenses: perfect or imperfect?	Quand il est arrivé, elle mangeait.	130
66	The pluperfect tense	j'avais fini, elle était sortie	132
67	The past historic tense	je parlai, il mangea	134
68	The future tense	j'arriverai, il finira	136
69	The future perfect tense	j'aurai acheté, vous aurez fait	138
70	The conditional	je trouverais, il irait	140
71	The conditional perfect	j'aurais acheté, vous auriez fait	142
72	Using **si**	Si tu viens, nous irons au cinéma.	144
73	The perfect infinitive	après avoir fini, après être tombé(e)	146
74	The passive	La pièce a été repeinte.	148
75	The present subjunctive	que j'attende	150
76	The perfect subjunctive	que j'aie attendu	152
77	When to use the subjunctive (1)	je veux que…	154
78	When to use the subjunctive (2)	avant que … (ne), il faut que…	156

79 When to use the   rien qui…, personne qui…,
    subjunctive (3)   quel que… _____ 158

CONJUNCTIONS

80 Conjunctions (1)   donc, et, mais, ou, pourtant, etc. __ 160
81 Conjunctions (2)   afin que, bien que, parce que, etc. __ 162

NEGATIVES

82 Negatives (1)   ne … pas, ne … rien, ne … jamais __ 164
83 Negatives (2)   Je n'ai pas compris. _____ 166

QUESTION FORMS

84 Asking questions (1)   Est-ce qu'il vient? _____ 168
85 Asking questions (2)   Où? Quand? Comment? Combien?
                           Pourquoi? Quel…? _____ 170
86 Asking questions (3)   Lequel? Qui…? Que…?, etc. _____ 172

NUMBERS, DATES AND TIME

87 Numbers (1)   un, deux, vingt, cent, etc. _____ 174
88 Numbers (2)   premier, une dizaine _____ 176
89 Fractions and decimals une demie, la moitié, un quart ____ 178
90 Dimensions and distance haut de…, long de…, profond de… etc. 180
91 Telling the time   huit heures et demie,
                           vingt heures trente _____ 182
92 Days, dates and years lundi le 15 février 1999 _____ 184

MISCELLANEOUS

93 **Depuis**, **il y a** and depuis dix mois, il y a un an,
    venir de   il vient de… _____ 186
94 **Il y a**   Il y a un sandwich pour toi. _____ 188
95 Saying yes and no   oui, si, non _____ 190
96 Countries, nationalities
    and languages   la France, un Français, français ____ 192
97 Inversion   dit-il, a-t-il dit _____ 194
98 Faux amis   assister à _____ 196
99 Expressions of quantity assez de, trop de _____ 198
    Verbs followed by **à/de** _____ 200
    Glossary   _____ 201
    Key to exercises   _____ 203

Introduction

The purpose of this book

This book is designed to help you learn about the French language and how it is structured. It is divided into 99 units, each of which explains a particular grammar point. You will find related exercises on the practice pages which are located opposite the explanations for ease of reference. Answers to each of the exercises are provided at the end of the book, and the glossary explains the main grammatical terms used.

How to use this book

The contents page will help you to identify a grammar point you wish to practise. You do not need to work through the book in any particular order – you will find that each unit can be used independently as an introduction to new learning or for revision or reference. You may find it helpful to revisit a unit several times until you are able to complete the exercises without referring to the explanation. Writing the answers down and repeating them out loud can often aid learning.

Examples of more advanced grammar have been included to help you to develop your understanding of how the language works. As you progress, you will encounter many such points which you will find useful as your ability to manipulate the language grows.

Studying the grammar of a language can help you to identify the specific patterns and structures it contains. As a result, you will gradually be able to build up your understanding of how the language works, which will help you to use it effectively.

Bonne chance!

1 UNiT | Nouns: the definite article

Nouns are words that name a person, an object or a concept. They can be singular or plural, and in French they have a gender.

A In French, nouns have a gender: they are either masculine or feminine. In dictionaries gender is shown by *nm* and *nf*. (*m*) or (*f*) are also used.

Masculine		Feminine	
le cinéma	*the cinema*	**la** voiture	*the car*
le dictionnaire	*the dictionary*	**la** liberté	*freedom*

B There are two words for *the* in the singular – **le** and **la**. These are called definite articles. Masculine nouns take **le**, feminine nouns take **la**.

- For all nouns beginning with a vowel (a, e, i, o, u) and most nouns beginning with an unsounded **h**, **le** and **la** are shortened to **l'**.

  l'hôpital (*nm*)   *the hospital*   **l'**église (*nf*)   *the church*

To talk about more than one thing (masculine or feminine) you use **les**.

Masculine		Feminine	
les cinémas	*the cinemas*	**les** voitures	*the cars*
les livres	*the books*	**les** circonstances	*the circumstances*

C To make a noun plural an **-s** is usually added to it (not usually pronounced).

  le document   *the document*   les documents   *the documents*

However, some nouns have irregular plurals, and others do not change at all:

- Nouns ending in **-s**, **-x** or **-z** remain unchanged.

le bras	*the arm*	les bras	*the arms*
le prix	*the prize/price*	les prix	*the prizes/prices*

- Nouns ending in **-au** or **-eu** add an **-x**.

le bateau	*the boat*	les bateaux	*the boats*
le jeu	*the game*	les jeux	*the games*

- Nouns ending in **-al** or **-ail** drop their singular ending and add **-aux**.

le cheval	*the horse*	les chevaux	*the horses*
le travail	*the work*	les travaux	*the works*

But note **le festival** (*the festival*), **les festivals** (*the festivals*).

2 ⚠ un œil   *an eye*   les yeux   *the eyes*

1 Put *le*, *la*, or *l'* in front of the following nouns according to whether they are masculine (*nm*) or feminine (*nf*).
E.g. piscine (*nf*) *la* piscine → *swimming pool*

a supermarché (*nm*) *supermarket*
b banque (*nf*) *bank*
c image (*nf*) *picture*
d pâtisserie (*nf*) *cake shop*

e fromage (*nm*) *cheese*
f office de tourisme (*nm*) *tourist office*
g téléviseur (*nm*) *television set*
h patron (*nm*) *boss*

2 Spot the nouns and their genders in the following wordsearch grid. The nouns in the grid are in the box beside it.

```
l e v i n o s t f m
p t l m y r l n y p
s l e l a i t q r b
l a c h e m i s e t
i r h f l e p l a n
m a i l a c r è m e
a d e e l' h o m m e
g i n p v x a n l n
e o c r p l a r u e
o l a v o i t u r e
```

rue	crème
chemise	vin
plan	lait
homme	voiture
chien	radio
image	

3 Insert the appropriate nouns from the box into the postcard below.

l'hôtel (*the hotel*); les vins (*the wines*); la piscine (*the swimming pool*);
le petit déjeuner (*the breakfast*); les repas (*the meals*)

Cher André,
......................est formidable! Je vais (*go*) à..................
tous les matins avant de prendre........ ....sont délicieux,
et..............de la région sont excellents!

À bientôt
Jeanne

4 Give the plural forms of these singular nouns, remembering to include the plural of the definite article as well.
E.g. bras → les bras

a journal *newspaper*
b banque *bank*
c voix *voice*

d fromage *cheese*
e bateau *boat*
f cinéma *cinema*

3

Nouns: the indefinite article

Like the word for the, the words for a/an, some or any vary according to the number and gender of the noun they relate to.

A The two words for *a* (or *an* before a vowel) are **un** and **une**. These are called indefinite articles. **Un** is used with masculine nouns, and **une** with feminine ones.

un journal	*a newspaper*
une veste	*a jacket*
une église	*a church*

B If you want to say *some books*, *any books* or even just *books* (rather than *a book*), you will need to use the word **des**. **Des** is used for both masculine and feminine nouns in the plural.

un journal	*a newspaper*	**des** journaux	*(some/any) newspapers*
une secrétaire	*a secretary*	**des** secrétaires	*(some/any) secretaries*
une école	*a school*	**des** écoles	*(some/any) schools*

Unlike **les**, **des** refers to an unspecified group of people, things or ideas. Compare:

J'ai vu **les** documents sur le bureau. *I saw **the** documents on the desk.*

J'ai vu **des** documents sur le bureau. *I saw documents (or some documents) on the desk.*

The word **des** cannot be left out, as *some* often is in English.

J'ai acheté des sandwichs au supermarché. *I bought sandwiches (or some sandwiches) at the supermarket.*

C In English, we often use *any* after a question. This is expressed in French by **des**.

Vous avez des enfants? *Have you got any children?*

D **Des** is replaced by **de** (or by **d'** before a noun beginning with a vowel or an unsounded **h**):

- after a negative:
  Je n'ai pas d'enfants. *I haven't got any children.*

- when an adjective precedes a plural noun:
  Ils vendent de belles voitures. *They sell (some) beautiful cars.*
  Ils ont de vieux meubles. *They've got (some) old furniture.*

➤ See the partitive article in Unit 9, position of adjectives in Unit 19, negatives in Unit 82.

1 Put *un* or *une* before the following nouns.

E.g. bateau (*nm*) → *un* bateau

a patron (*nm*) *boss*

b poste (*nf*) *post office*

c dîner (*nm*) *dinner*

d chambre (*nf*) *room*

e piano (*nm*) *piano*

f timbre (*nm*) *stamp*

g boisson (*nf*) *drink*

h journal (*nm*) *newspaper*

i savon (*nm*) *soap*

j sandwich (*nm*) *sandwich*

2 Complete the following table by inserting the indefinite article, *des* and the nouns as appropriate, as in the example.

E.g.	une	voiture	des	voitures
a	un			bureaux
b		pullover (*nm*)		
c				plantes
d		veste		
e		journal		
f				églises
g				yeux

3 Complete the following dialogues using *un, une* or *des, de* or *d'*.

E.g. Il y a _____ supermarché par ici, s'il vous plaît? →

Il y a *un* supermarché par ici, s'il vous plaît?

a Vous avez _____ stylo, s'il vous plaît?

Oui, il y a (*there are*) _____ stylos dans mon bureau.

b Je peux avoir _____ boisson?

Oui, il y a _____ boissons dans le frigo.

c Vous avez _____ pommes?

Non, je n'ai pas _____ pommes, mais j'ai _____ bananes et _____ oranges.

4 Choose the correct article to complete the sentences.

E.g. Il n'a pas de/des livres. → Il n'a pas *de* livres.

a J'ai acheté les/des œufs à la ferme.   *I bought (some) eggs at the farm.*

b Il n'a pas d'/des animaux familiers.   *He hasn't any pets.*

c Vous avez de/des journaux?   *Have you got any newspapers?*

d J'ai vu les/des feux d'artifice hier soir. *I saw the fireworks last night.*

e Ils vendent de/des belles choses.   *They sell (some) nice things.*

3 UNIT | Uses of the articles

French usage of the definite and indefinite articles differs in some ways from English usage.

A The French definite article is used as follows:

* with nouns being used in a general way

Il s'intéresse à **la** pêche.	*He's interested in fishing.*
Le poisson est délicieux.	*Fish is delicious.*

* to express price, rate or quantity

C'est 12 F **le** kilo	*It's 12 francs a kilo.*

* with parts of the body (rather than **son/sa**, etc.)

Elle a **les** cheveux longs.	*She has long hair.*
Il s'est cassé **le** bras.	*He broke his arm.*

⚠ However, the possessive adjective (**mon, ma, mes**, etc.) is used when an adjective qualifies the noun (except with **avoir** indicating possession, which always needs the definite article in sentences like those above).

> Elle a ouvert ses beaux yeux bleus. *She opened her lovely blue eyes.*

* with proper names used with an adjective, or with titles, ranks and professions

La petite Marie s'est endormie.	*Little Marie went to sleep.*
C'est **le** colonel Chabart.	*It's Colonel Chabart.*
Le docteur Michelet est venu me voir.	*Dr Michelet came to see me.*

* with the names of some festivals

La Toussaint *All Saints' Day*   **La** Pentecôte *Whitsun*

⚠ The definite article is not used with **Pâques** *Easter* and **Noël** *Christmas*.

* with nouns when they refer to a particular thing

C'est à **la** page 5.	*It's on page 5.*
C'est **la** chambre numéro 18.	*It's room 18.*

* with continents, countries, lakes, mountains, rivers, oceans, seas

Le lac Léman est beau.	*Lac Léman is beautiful.*

B The indefinite article means *a* or *an* and is used much as in English. Its plural form is **des** (*some, any* when plural). This is never omitted in French, although it can be in English.

Elle a **un** nouveau bureau.	*She's got a new office.*
Des policiers l'ont arrêté.	*Police officers arrested him.*

➤ See also partitive articles in Unit 9, de in Unit 13, à in Unit 14, possessive adjectives in Unit 16, countries in Unit 96.

1 Match the two parts of each sentence, using the English as a guide.

E.g. **Elle a + les cheveux longs et blonds.** → *She has long, blond hair.*

a Elle a	**i** 50 F le kilo.
b Il s'est cassé	**j** à 250 kilomètres à l'heure.
c Les mains sur	**k** les cheveux longs et blonds.
d Elle décide d'aller voir	**l** le docteur Balesta.
e La Loire est	**m** la rivère la plus longue de France.
f Le prix est de	**n** la tête, il l'a regardée.
g Le train roule	**o** à 40 F le mètre.
h Le bois se vend	**p** le bras.

1 *She decides to go and see Dr Balesta.*
2 *The train goes at 250 kilometres an hour.*
3 *The Loire is the longest river in France.*
4 *With his hands on his head he looked at her.*
5 *The wood sells at 40 francs a metre.*
6 *He broke his arm.*
7 *She has long, blond hair.*
8 *The price is 50 francs a kilo.*

2 Put the correct article in front of each noun, using the English sentence as a guide to meaning.

E.g. _____ **vieux Paul est en Italie.** *Le* **vieux Paul est en Italie.**
Old Paul's in Italy.

a _____ mont (*nm*) Everest est très dangereux. *Mount Everest is very dangerous.*
b _____ lac Windermere est en Angleterre. *Lake Windermere is in England.*
c _____ duc d'Orléans est mort. *The Duc d'Orléans is dead.*
d _____ docteur Chabas est ici. *Dr Chabas is here.*
e Il a _____ cheveux blonds. *He's got fair hair.*
f _____ France est un grand pays. *France is a big country.*
g C'est 10 F _____ kilo. *It's 10 francs a kilo.*
h Elle s'est cassé _____ bras. *She's broken her arm.*
i Je trouve que _____ fromage est cher. *I find that cheese is expensive.*
j Demain, c'est _____ Toussaint. *Tomorrow is All Saints' Day.*
k _____ général de Gaulle était président de France. *General de Gaulle was President of France.*
l Je vais en France à _____ Pentecôte. *I'm going to France at Whitsun.*
m _____vin blanc va bien avec _____ poulet. *White wine goes well with chicken.*

4 UNIT | Gender of nouns (1)

There are general rules that govern whether a noun is masculine or feminine in French. There are also exceptions to these rules.

A Most nouns falling into the following categories are *masculine*:
- human and animal males: **l'homme** (*man*), **le fermier** (*farmer*), **le tigre** (*tiger*)
- days, months, seasons, points of the compass: **le mardi** (*Tuesday*), **le mai** (*May*), **l'automne** (*autumn*), **l'ouest** (*west*)
- countries and rivers not ending in -e: **le Danemark** (*Denmark*), **le Lot** (*the Lot*) (but **le Rhône**, **le Danube** and **le Mexique**)
- languages: **le français** (*French*), **le russe** (*Russian*)
- colours: **le bleu** (*blue*), **le jaune** (*yellow*)
- metric weights and measures, cardinal numbers, fractions, letters: **le litre** (*litre*), **le trois** (*the number three*), **un quart** (*a quarter*), **le S** (*the letter S*)
- trees and shrubs: **le pommier** (*apple tree*); **le lilas** (*lilac*)
- fruits and vegetables not ending in -e: **le citron** (*lemon*), **le melon** (*melon*)
- metals and minerals: **le fer** (*iron*), **le sel** (*salt*)

B Nouns in the following categories are *feminine*:
- human and animal females: **la femme** (*woman*), **la lionne** (*lioness*)
- female roles or occupational names: **l'actrice** (*actress*), **la reine** (*queen*). Many traditionally male roles and occupations can now be used with a feminine definite article for females where there is no female form of the noun: **la ministre** (*minister*), **la docteur** (*doctor*), **la professeur** (*teacher*), **la médecin**
- countries and rivers ending in -e: **la Suisse** (*Switzerland*), **la Loire** (*the Loire*)
- most fruit, flowers and vegetables: **la banane** (*banana*), **la carotte** (*carrot*)
- school subjects, apart from specific languages (see above): **les langues** (*fpl*) (*languages*), **la science** (*science*)
- arts, trades and sciences: **la sculpture** (*sculpture*), **la physique** (*physics*)
- festivals: **la Toussaint** (*All Saints' Day*) (but **Pâques** (*nm*) (*Easter*) and the masculine expression **Joyeux Noël** (*Happy Christmas*))

C Words for people can in some cases take either gender: **un(e) enfant** (*child*), **un(e) élève** (*pupil*), **le/la sans-emploi** (*unemployed person*).

➤ *See countries, nationalities and languages in Unit 96.*

4 UNIT Gender of nouns (1) – Exercises

1 Give the gender of the following nouns.

E.g. banque *bank* → *la* banque

a lundi *Monday*
b arbre *tree*
c bouleau *silver birch*
d Danemark *Denmark*
e musique *music*
f Seine *Seine*
g rose *rose*
h chêne *oak*
i physique *physics*
j rouge *red*

k pomme *apple*
l science *science*
m Chine *China*
n Pérou *Peru*
o six *six*
p mètre *metre*
q acier *steel*
r cinq *five*
s betterave *beetroot*
t été *summer*

2 Which of the following words are masculine?

E.g. pommier *apple tree* ✔

a Japon *Japan*
b or *gold*
c jeudi *Thursday*
d Rhône *River Rhône*
e peinture *painting*
f hiver *winter*
g lion *lion*
h Seine *Seine*

3 Which of the following words are feminine?

E.g. banane *banana* ✔

a St-Jean *St John's Day*
b japonais *Japanese*
c marguerite *daisy*
d Bolivie *Bolivia*
e pêche *peach*
f histoire *history*
g tigresse *tigress*
h Garonne *River Garonne*

5 UNIT | Gender of nouns (2)

The gender of a noun can also often be inferred from its ending. There are certain masculine and feminine forms for living things.

A Some noun endings for living creatures or people have a masculine form and a feminine form: **un chat** is a male cat, while **une chatte** is a female cat. Here is a table of these endings.

Masculine form		Feminine form	
-at	chat	-atte	chatte
-eur	vendeur	-euse	vendeuse
-eur	acteur	-rice	actrice
-er	épicier	-ère	épicière
-an	paysan	-anne	paysanne
-en	canadien	-enne	canadienne
-on	lion	-onne	lionne
-f	veuf	-ve	veuve
-x	époux	-se	épouse

B Some other endings are either distinctly masculine or distinctly feminine.

Masculine endings		Feminine endings	
-er, -ier	fer, acier	-ière	bière *but not* le cimetière
-eau	chapeau *but not* l'eau (*f*), la peau	-lle	ville
-et	billet	-té, -tte	difficulté, fourchette
-c, -d	sac, pied	-èche, -èque	crèche, bibliothèque
-ail, -eil	travail, soleil	-ffe, -ppe	étoffe, enveloppe
-oir	soir	-sse, -nne	caisse, personne
-age	fromage *but not* la cage, la page, la rage, l'image, la plage	-ace	glace
		-aine, -eine, -oine	semaine, reine, macédoine *but not* le moine
-ède, ège, -ème	remède, collège, problème	-ance, -anse	ambulance, distance
		-ence, -ense	essence, défense *but not* le silence
-isme	tourisme	-ure	blessure
-ment	bâtiment	-sion, -tion	télévision, question
-ou	genou	-ée	l'armée, la journée *but not* le musée, le lycée

10

5 UNIT Gender of nouns (2) - Exercises

1 Give the gender of the following nouns.

E.g. fromage *cheese* → *le* fromage

a cage *cage*

b problème *problem*

c vendeur *seller*

d glace *ice/mirror*

e semaine *week*

f ambulance *ambulance*

g tourisme *tourism*

h billet *ticket*

i difficulté *difficulty*

j plage *beach*

k caisse *cash desk*

l question *question*

m sac *bag*

n reine *queen*

o bâtiment *building*

2 Complete the following sentences using le, la, l' or les, un or une, using the English as a guide.

E.g. Tu as _____ voiture? *Have you got the car?* → Tu as *la* voiture?

a C'est _____ bon chanteur.   *He's a good singer.*

b _____ situation n'est pas claire.   *The situation isn't clear.*

c _____ soleil est faible aujourd'hui.   *The sun's weak today.*

d _____ lunettes qu'il vend sont coûteuses. *The glasses he sells are expensive.*

e _____ distance n'est pas grande.   *The distance is not great.*

f Tu as _____ enveloppe?   *Have you got an envelope?*

g C'est _____ bateau qu'il a acheté.   *It's the boat he bought.*

h Vous voulez _____ couchette?   *Do you want a couchette?*

i Où sont _____ gâteaux?   *Where are the cakes?*

j _____ épouse de Paul s'appelle Marie.   *Paul's wife is called Marie.*

3 What are the following in French? Use un, une or des as appropriate in your answer. Refer to earlier units if necessary.

a *a foot*

b *an arm*

c *a nose*

d *a horse*

e *a book*

f *television sets*

g *lamps*

h *a cinema*

i *a church*

j *a female doctor*

6 UNIT | Nouns with two genders and meanings

There are a number of French nouns that are identical in spelling and pronunciation, but different in gender and meaning.

A The following list gives examples of nouns whose meanings change according to their gender.

Masculine		Feminine	
l'aide	*male assistant*	l'aide	*help, assistance; female assistant*
le crêpe	*crape fabric*	la crêpe	*pancake*
le critique	*critic*	la critique	*criticism*
le faune	*faun*	la faune	*fauna*
le livre	*book*	la livre	*pound (sterling/weight)*
le manche	*handle (e.g. of broom)*	la manche	*sleeve*
le mémoire	*memorandum; dissertation*	la mémoire	*memory*
le merci	*thanks*	la merci	*mercy*
le mode	*method, way*	la mode	*fashion*
le mort	*dead male*	la mort	*death*
le page	*page(-boy)*	la page	*page (of book)*
le pendule	*pendulum*	la pendule	*clock*
le poêle	*stove*	la poêle	*frying pan*
le poste	*position, job; station (e.g. police); radio/TV set; telephone extension*	la poste	*post (postal service); post office*
le rose	*pink (colour)*	la rose	*rose (flower)*
le somme	*nap, sleep*	la somme	*sum, sum total*
le tour	*(guided) tour; turn; walk; trick*	la tour	*tower*
le vague	*vagueness*	la vague	*wave*
le vapeur	*steamship*	la vapeur	*steam, vapour*
le vase	*vase*	la vase	*silt, mud*
le voile	*veil*	la voile	*sail*

B Some anomalies:

Chose *thing* is feminine but **quelque chose** *something* is masculine.

Délice *delight* is masculine in the singular but feminine in the plural.

Personne *person* used as a noun is feminine, but as a pronoun (*no one*) it is masculine.

➤ See gender of nouns (1) and (2) in Units 4 and 5.

1 Choose the correct option to complete the following sentences.

E.g. Il a acheté un/*une* livre de pommes. *He bought a pound of apples.*

a Le/la critique a lu l'article. *The critic read the article.*

b Ce/cette poêle a un/une manche cassé. *This frying pan has a broken handle.*

c La robe que j'ai achetée n'est pas du tout au/à la mode. *The dress I bought is not at all in fashion.*

d Elle est entrée dans la/le poste pour acheter des timbres. *She went into the post office to buy some stamps.*

2 Complete the following sentences with the definite article *le* or *la*.

E.g. *La* manche droite est trop courte. *The right sleeve is too short.*

a Il a cassé _____ vase. *He has broken the vase.*

b Elle a mis les œufs dans _____ poêle. *She put the eggs into the frying pan.*

c Ils ont offert _____ poste à M. Dupont, qui a toujours voulu travailler à _____ poste. *They offered the job to M. Dupont, who has always wanted to work at the post office.*

d Vous avez vu _____ tour Eiffel? *Have you seen the Eiffel Tower?*

3 Complete the following sentences using a word from the box, with the appropriate article. Some words are used more than once.

somme	poste	livre	voile	tour	mémoire

E.g. Je n'ai plus de francs et je n'ai qu'*une livre* sterling. *I don't have any francs left and I've only got £1.*

a _____ de cet ordinateur est trop faible. *The memory of this computer is too small.*

b Elle a écrit _____ au sujet de la Grande Guerre. *She wrote a book about the Great War.*

c Elle portait _____ au visage. *She wore a veil over her face.*

d Je n'ai pas assez d'argent. _____ demandée est trop grande. *I don't have enough money. The sum requested is too big.*

e Tu veux faire _____ dans le parc avec moi? *Do you want to go for a walk in the park with me?*

f Pourrais-je avoir _____ numéro 5892? *Could I have extension number 5892?*

g Pendant le voyage le bateau avait perdu _____ . *During the journey the boat had lost a sail.*

13

7 UNIT | Compound nouns

Compound nouns are made up of two or more words and fall into categories. Their gender and plurals are governed by certain rules.

Compound nouns can be divided into the following categories.

A Adjective + noun

le grand-père	*grandfather*	les grands-pères	*grandfathers*
la grand-mère	*grandmother*	les grands-mères	*grandmothers*

The gender normally follows that of the noun part. Both parts become plural.

B Noun + noun

le chou-fleur	*cauliflower*	les choux-fleurs	*cauliflowers*
le wagon-lit	*sleeper*	les wagons-lits	*sleepers*

The gender follows that of the main noun, usually the first one. Both nouns become plural.

⚠ **le timbre-poste** *postage stamp* becomes **les timbres-poste** *postage stamps* in the plural (no **-s** on the end of **poste**).

C Noun + preposition + noun

l'arc-en-ciel (*nm*) *rainbow*		les arcs-en-ciel	*rainbows*
le chef-d'œuvre	*masterpiece*	les chefs-d'œuvre	*masterpieces*

With some notable exceptions, the gender is that of the first noun. That noun alone becomes plural. Certain of these nouns remain invariable in the plural, e.g. **le tête-à-tête**, **les tête-à-tête**.

D Prefix + noun

la mini-jupe	*mini-skirt*	les mini-jupes	*mini-skirts*

The gender is that of the simple noun. The noun alone becomes plural.

E Adverb + noun

un haut-parleur	*loudspeaker*	les haut-parleurs	*loudspeakers*
un avant-goût	*foretaste*	les avant-goûts	*foretastes*

The noun alone becomes plural.

F Preposition + noun

le/la sans-emploi *unemployed person*	les sans-emploi *unemployed people*	
le sous-titre *subtitle*	les sous-titres *subtitles*	

These are usually masculine, unless they refer specifically to a female person. The plural varies depending on the sense of the word.

G Verb + noun

le tire-bouchon	*corkscrew*	les tire-bouchon	*corkscrews*
le porte-clefs	*key-ring*	les porte-clefs	*key-rings*

These are usually masculine. The plural is as for preposition + noun.

H Generally, the plural form is added to noun and adjective components.

7 UNIT Compound nouns – Exercises

1 Give the gender of the following nouns.

E.g. grand-mère (*grandmother*) → la grand-mère

a belle-mère *mother-in-law*

b mot-clé *crossword*

c demi-tarif *half-fare*

d pare-brise *windscreen*

e gratte-ciel *skyscaper*

f wagon-restaurant *dining car*

2 Form the plurals of the following nouns.

E.g. la grand-mère (*grandmother*) → les grands-mères

a le chef-lieu *county town*

b un porte-bagages *luggage rack*

c le timbre-poste *postage stamp*

d la demi-heure *half-hour*

e le sous-sol *basement, subsoil*

f le tête-à-tête *tête-à-tête, private discussion*

g le vice-président *vice president*

3 Form singular nouns from the following plurals.

E.g. les grands-mères (*grandmothers*) → la grand-mère

a les beaux-pères *fathers-in-law*

b les haut-parleurs *loudspeakers*

c les porte-clefs *key-rings*

d les chefs d'œuvre *masterpieces*

e les rouges-gorges *robins*

f les oiseaux-mouches *humming birds*

4 Complete the sentences using the family tree, and words from the box to guide you.

```
Claudette = divorcée
           = Pierre
    |
Martine   Anne=Paul   Hélène=Henri   André = divorcé
                                            = Ghislaine
                                               \
                                              Marcel
```

E.g. Anne et Hélène sont _____ de Martine. → Anne et Hélène sont *les belles-sœurs* de Martine.

a Paul est _____ de Ghislaine.

b Martine est _____ de Pierre.

c Marcel est _____ de Ghislaine.

d Claudette est _____ d'Henri.

e Pierre est le _____ de Paul.

f Martine est _____ d'André.

la belle-fille *daughter-in-law, stepdaughter*	le beau-fils *son-in-law, stepson*
le beau-père *father-in-law, stepfather*	la belle-mère *mother-in-law, stepmother*
la belle-sœur *sister-in-law, stepsister*	le beau-frère *brother-in-law, stepbrother*

15

8 UNIT | *Il est* and *c'est*

Il and **elle** and their plural forms are used to refer back to specific nouns, as in these examples:

Tu connais Marie? Elle est notaire. *Do you know Marie? She's a lawyer.*
Voici mon ami Paul. Il est canadien. *Here's my friend Paul. He's Canadian.*

In this unit you look at other uses of **il** and the uses of **ce**. (Note that in colloquial speech you may hear **ce** being used instead of **il** in some cases.)

A Il est

- **Il est** + time
  Il est sept heures.   *It's seven o'clock.*
  Il est tard.   *It's late.*
- **Il est** + adjective + **que**
  Il est évident qu'il est intelligent. *It's clear that he's intelligent.*
- **Il est** + adjective + **de** + infinitive
  Il est interdit de marcher sur   *It's forbidden to walk on*
    la pelouse.   *the grass.*
  Il est difficile de juger.   *It's difficult to judge.*

B C'est

- **C'est** + adjective alone, if the reference is to something that has already been mentioned or is otherwise understood
  C'est essentiel.   *It's/that's essential.*
  C'est ridicule.   *It's/that's ridiculous.*
- **C'est** + noun or pronouns (notice how many ways **ce** can be translated)
  C'est Barbara.   *It's Barbara.*
  C'est un fonctionnaire.   *He's a civil servant.*
  C'est un Américain.   *He's an American.*
  C'est mon amie.   *She's my friend.*
  C'est moi.   *It's me.*
  Ce sont mes frères.   *They're my brothers.*
  Qui est-ce?   *Who is it?*

⚠ Although the verb is **sont** when the subject is plural, as in **Ce sont des vélos tout terrain** (*They are mountain bikes*), this is not the case with **C'est nous** (*It's us*) or **C'est eux** (*It's them*), etc.

➤ See subject pronouns in Unit 36, emphatic pronouns in Unit 38, demonstrative pronouns in Unit 40, être in Unit 49, time in Unit 91.

8 UNIT | *Il est* and *c'est* – *Exercises*

1 Match the sentences to each other.

E.g. Il est sept heures. → *It's seven o'clock.*

1 C'est mon bureau.
2 Il est neuf heures.
3 Il est facile de faire cela.
4 Ce sont des lilas.
5 Il est vrai qu'il est tard.
6 Qui est-ce?

a *It's nine o'clock.*
b *Who's that?*
c *They're lilacs.*
d *It's true that it's late.*
e *It's my office/desk.*
f *It's easy to do that.*

2 Complete the gaps with either *c'est* or *ce sont*.

E.g. _____ mes amis. *They are my friends.* → *Ce sont* mes amis.

a _____ ma voiture. *It's my car.*
b _____ un de mes amis. *He is one of my friends.*
c _____ un professeur. *He's a teacher.*
d _____ des romans. *They are novels.*
e _____ une bonne idée. *It's a good idea.*
f _____ difficile. *It's difficult.*
g _____ mes clés. *They are my keys.*
h _____ une histoire intéressante. *It's an interesting story.*

3 Complete the following with *c'est, ce sont* or *il est*.

E.g. _____ facile? → *C'est* facile.

a _____ vrai que vous êtes malade? Oui, _____ vrai.
Is it true that you're ill? Yes, it's true.
b Elle est partie. _____ bizarre!
She's gone. That's strange!
c Quelle heure _____ ? _____ presque midi.
What time is it? It's almost midday.
d _____ évident qu'elle est fatiguée.
It's obvious that she's tired.
e _____ vos clés, n'est-ce pas?
These are your keys, aren't they?
f Qui est-ce? _____ mon fils.
Who's that? It's my son.
g _____ impossible de l'ouvrir.
It's impossible to open it.
h _____ trop tôt pour aller au café.
It's too early to go to the café.

17

9 UNIT | The partitive article

A Look at these examples of how French expresses the idea of *some*:

du pain *(some) bread*, de la viande *(some) meat*, des poires *(some) pears*

The word for *some* and *any* varies in French according to the gender and number of the noun that follows it. It is made up of **de** + the definite article and is called the partitive article.

Masculine	de + le → **du**	de + le vin	→ **du vin**	*(some/any)* wine
Feminine	de + la → **de la**	de + la confiture	→ **de la confiture**	*(some/any)* jam
Masculine and Feminine	de + l' → **de l'**	de + l'eau *(nf)*	→ **de l'eau**	*(some/any)* water
Plural	de + les → **des**	de + les ordinateurs	→ **des ordinateurs**	*(some/any)* computers

B In French the partitive article translates the English *some* and *any*. It is also used when in English neither of these would be used. In all the following cases a form of the partitive article is used in French.

J'ai de la bière.	*I've got some beer.*
Vous avez du vin?	*Have you got any wine?*
Vous voulez du thé ou du café?	*Would you like tea or coffee?*
Il y a des tomates dans la salade.	*There are tomatoes in the salad.*

C After a negative, **du, de la, de l'** and **des** become **de** when they indicate a lack or an absence of something.

J'ai des enfants.	*I've got children.*
Je n'ai pas d'enfants.	*I don't have any children.*

When no absence or lack is being indicated or a contrast is being made, then the normal form of the partitive article or another article is used:

Je n'ai pas acheté des oranges,	*I didn't buy oranges,*
j'ai acheté des poires.	*I bought pears.*
Ce n'est pas un long voyage,	*It's not a long journey.*

➤ See the preposition de in Units 13 and 15, negatives in Units 82 and 83, expressions of quantity in Unit 99.

9 UNIT The partitive article – Exercises

1 **Translate the following sentences into English.**

E.g. **Il y a des boissons dans le frigo.** → *There are some drinks in the fridge.*

a Je voudrais (*I would like*) des glaçons (*ice-cubes*) dans mon whisky.

b Vous avez des voitures à louer (*hire*)?

c Donnez-moi du café, s'il vous plaît.

d L'ordinateur a beaucoup de capacité.

e Vous avez des enveloppes?

2 **Complete the following sentences with the appropriate form of the partitive article.**

E.g. **Tu as _____ billets?** → **Tu as *des* billets?**

a Je n'ai pas _____ limonade.

b Il y a _____ documents sur ton bureau.

c Aujourd'hui, il passe la journée avec _____ amis américains.

d C'est une rue très dangereuse. Il y a toujours _____ accidents.

e Vous avez _____ encre, s'il vous plaît?

f J'ai acheté _____ lait (*nm*).

g Tu peux me donner _____ argent?

3 **Compile a shopping list of the following items. The gender of each item is given with its illustration.**

E.g. **du lait, …**

10 | Simple prepositions (1)

Simple prepositions are single words like à (to or at), avec (with) or sans (without).

The following list gives examples of some of the more common prepositions and how they are used. Note the way English and French sometimes use prepositions differently.

A après (*after*)

Elle est partie après moi.   *She left after me.*

B avant (*before (time)*)

Il va arriver avant moi.   *He will arrive before me.*
Il a mangé avant de partir.   *He ate before leaving.*

C avec (*with*)

Jeanne est allée avec Marc.   *Jeanne went with Marc.*
Il mangeait avec son couteau.   *He ate with his knife.*

D chez (*to/at the home of, among*)

Je vais chez le médecin cet après-midi.   *I'm going to the doctor's this afternoon.*
Je vais rester chez moi ce soir.   *I'm going to stay at home this evening.*
La cuisine est importante chez les Français.   *Cooking is important for the French.*

E contre (*against, with*)

J'ai laissé mon vélo contre le mur.   *I left my bike against the wall.*
Vous pouvez échanger cette voiture contre une nouvelle.   *You can exchange this car for a new one.*
Il s'est fâché contre elle.   *He got annoyed with her.*

F dans (*on, in, from, until, out of*)

- Position
  Il est dans le salon.   *He's in the living room.*
  J'ai laissé mon journal dans le train.   *I've left my newspaper on the train.*
  Elle a pris le café dans le placard.   *She took the coffee from/out of the cupboard.*

  Elle buvait dans la boîte.   *She drank from/out of the tin.*
- Time (*after/at the end of which*)
  On se retrouve dans une heure?   *Shall we meet in (after) an hour?*

➤ See also other prepositions in Units 11–15.

10 UNIT Simple prepositions (1) – Exercises

1 Match the following to make translations of the English sentences below.

E.g. Le train part + après le bus. → *The train leaves after the bus.*

a Il va arriver
b Le train part
c J'ai laissé mon vélo
d Le chien est
e Elle a pris une tasse
f Il est venu
g Je serai chez vous
h Elle a pris le costume

i avec son chien.
j contre le mur.
k chez mon père.
l avant deux heures.
m après ses parents.
n dans le placard.
o dans l'armoire.
p dans une heure.

1 *He will arrive after his parents.*
2 *The train leaves before two.*
3 *I've left my bike against the wall.*
4 *The dog is at my father's.*
5 *She took a cup out of the cupboard.*
6 *He came with his dog.*
7 *I'll be at your place in an hour.*
8 *She took the suit out of the wardrobe.*

2 Complete each sentence with an appropriate preposition from the box. Then match it with its translation.

E.g. Je vais _____ Marcel. *I'm going to Marcel's.* → Je vais *chez* Marcel.

contre	avec	chez	après	dans	avant

a Ils sont arrivés _____ 10 heures.
b Je n'ai rien _____ elle.
c Il a laissé son manteau _____ le train.
d Elle a lu un livre _____ le dîner.
e Elle va _____ le dentiste _____ son fils.

1 *He left his coat on the train.*
2 *They arrived after ten o'clock.*
3 *She read a book before dinner.*
4 *She is going to the dentist's with her son.*
5 *I have nothing against her.*

11 UNIT Simple prepositions (2)

A depuis (*since, from, for*)

Il est là depuis ce matin.	*He's been here since this morning.*
Je travaille ici depuis quatre ans.	*I've worked here for four years.*
Je n'ai pas eu de ses nouvelles depuis des années.	*I haven't had any news from him/her for years.*

B derrière (*behind*)

Le parking se trouve derrière les bureaux.	*The car park is behind the offices.*

C devant (*in front of, before (location)*)

Elle attend devant le cinéma.	*She is waiting in front of the cinema.*
Il passe devant moi.	*He goes before me.*

D en (*in, by, whilst*)

Ils sont en vacances en France.	*They're on holiday in France.*
Il est allé en ville.	*He's gone into town.*
Elle est en ville.	*She's in town.*
Il va à Paris en avion.	*He is going to Paris by plane.*
Ils sont venus en voiture.	*They came by car.*

⚠ But **à pied** *on foot*, **envoyer par avion** *to send by air*

J'ai fait mes courses en dix minutes.	*I did my shopping in ten minutes. (i.e it took me ten minutes)*
Il buvait du café en travaillant.	*He drank coffee whilst working.*
C'était en quelle année? En 1987.	*It was in which year? In 1987.*
Le texte est en espagnol.	*The text is in Spanish.*
Ma chambre est peinte en bleu.	*My room's painted blue.*
Il était en costume.	*He was in a suit.*

E entre (*between*)

Il est entre le cinéma et l'église.	*It's between the cinema and the church.*

F envers (*towards (with regard to)*)

Je n'aime pas son attitude envers moi.	I don't like his attitude towards me.

G malgré (*in spite of, despite*)

Malgré l'heure ils continuaient.	*In spite of the time they went on.*

➤ See also other prepositions in Units 10 and 12–15, use of tenses with depuis in Unit 93, countries in Unit 96.

1 Match the sentence halves in French to translate the English sentences below.

E.g. **Elle est ici + depuis une heure.** → *She's been here since one o'clock.*

a Elle est partie
b Il est écrit
c Il va à Moscou
d Ils travaillent ici
e C'est
f Votre sac est
g C'est
h Je le ferai

i malgré tout.
j depuis trois mois.
k derrière le fauteuil.
l devant le cinéma.
m entre le musée et l'église.
n entre six et sept heures.
o en russe.
p en avion.

1 *She left between six and seven o'clock.*
2 *It's written in Russian.*
3 *He's going to Moscow by plane.*
4 *They've worked here for three months.*
5 *It's in front of the cinema.*
6 *Your bag is behind the armchair.*
7 *It's between the museum and the church.*
8 *I'll do it in spite of everything.*

2 Complete the following with appropriate prepositions using the English as a guide.

E.g. **Elle est _____ ville.** *She is in town.* → **Elle est *en* ville.**

a La librairie est _____ la poste et la boulangerie. *The bookshop is between the post office and the bakery.*
b _____ la pluie, ils sont sortis. *In spite of the rain they went out.*
c Il est mort _____ 1982. *He died in 1982.*
d Je suis allé _____ France pour la première fois _____ 1992. *I went to France for the first time in 1992.*
e Cette chaise est _____ métal – l'autre est _____ bois. *This chair is in metal – the other is in wood.*

3 Complete the following sentences using the English as a guide.

E.g. **Je me suis garé _____.** *I've parked behind the offices.*
 Je me suis garé *derrière les bureaux*.

a Je vous vois _____.   *I'll see you in July.*
b Il y a voyagé _____.   *He travelled there by plane.*
c Je préfère aller _____.   *I prefer to go by car.*

12 UNIT Simple prepositions (3)

A Par (*by, in, per*)

Ils sont venus par le train.	*They came by train.*
Je l'ai appris par cœur.	*I learnt it by heart.*
L'article a été écrit par un expert.	*The article was written by an expert.*
C'est 5 F par personne.	*It's 5 francs per person.*
On se retrouve deux fois par an.	*We meet twice a year.*
Elle l'a vu par la fenêtre.	*She saw him out of the window.*
Je suis passé par Andorre.	*I went through Andorra.*

B parmi (*among*)

Vous trouverez des exemples parmi ces chiffres.
You'll find some examples among these figures.

C pendant (*during*)

Pendant les vacances j'ai beaucoup lu. *I read a lot during the holidays.*

D pour (*for, in order to*)

Ce cadeau est pour toi.	*This present is for you.*
Je suis là pour te voir.	*I'm here to see you.*

E sans (*without*)

Je ne peux pas le faire sans lui. *I can't do it without him.*

F sauf (*except*)

Ils sont tous là sauf elle. *They're all there except her.*

G sous (*under*)

Le chat est sous la table. *The cat's under the table.*

H sur (*on, by, in, from, off, over, about*)

Les documents sont sur le bureau.	*The documents are on the desk.*
Il a pris la casserole sur la cuisinière.	*He took the saucepan off the cooker.*
La pièce fait cinq mètres sur quatre.	*The room is five metres by four.*
C'est un livre sur la physique.	*It's a book about physics.*

I vers (*towards (direction), approximate time*)

Il est parti vers Tours.	*He set off towards Tours.*
Je suis parti vers la fin du film.	*I left towards the end of the film.*

➤ See also other prepositions in Units 10, 11, 13–15, the passive in Unit 74, dimensions in Unit 90.

24

1 Match the French half-sentences, using the English as a guide.

E.g. **Ils sont + parmi les documents.** *They are among the documents.*

a La fenêtre mesure

b Elle a voulu payer

c Il m'a vu

d Elle a appris ses verbes

e Il a mangé

f Je suis parti

g par la fenêtre.

h par cœur.

i pendant l'émission.

j un mètre sur un mètre cinquante.

k par chèque.

l sans argent.

1 *He saw me out of the window.*

2 *I left without any money.*

3 *She learnt her verbs by heart.*

4 *The window measures one metre by one metre fifty.*

5 *He ate during the programme.*

6 *She wanted to pay by cheque.*

2 Complete the following using the appropriate preposition.

E.g. **Je mange _____ la pause.** *during* → **Je mange** *pendant* **la pause.**

a Vous payez 5 F _____ personne. *per*

b Elle a été examinée _____ un spécialiste. *by*

c Votre manteau est _____ les autres sur la chaise. *among*

d La lettre est _____ Mme Dubois. *for*

e Le spectacle commence _____ 22 heures. *at about*

f Je suis passé _____ Paris. *via*

g Je passe mes vacances en France deux fois _____ an. *a/per*

h C'est une brochure _____ les Antilles. *about*

3 Complete the following using the English as a guide.

E.g. **Pourriez-vous le confirmer _____?** *Could you confirm it in writing?*
→ **Pourriez-vous le confirmer** *par écrit?*

a Il a voyagé _____.   *He travelled by train.*

b Elle va voir sa mère _____.   *She goes to see her mother twice a week.*

c Vous pouvez venir _____?   *Can you come this way?*

d Le train _____.   *The train arrives at about six o'clock.*

13 UNIT | The preposition *de*

The preposition *de* has a wide range of uses and combines where necessary with the definite article le, la, l' and les to produce du, de la, de l' and des.

A possession – expressing *of* or *belonging to* (often *'s* in English):

J'ai perdu la clé de la voiture.	*I've lost the car key.*
Ce sont les vêtements de Michel.	*Those are Michel's clothes.*

B meaning *of* or *from*:

Je voudrais une tasse de thé.	*I'd like a cup of tea.*
Je viens de Belgique.	*I'm from Belgium.*
Je dors de 22 heures à 7 heures.	*I sleep from 10 pm until 7 am.*
Elle habite à cinq minutes de l'hôpital.	*She lives five minutes from the hospital.*
J'ai besoin d'un feutre.	*I need a felt-tipped pen. ('have need of')*

C with measurements:

La pièce fait trois mètres de long.	*The room is three metres long.*

D with certain expressions of time:

Il est six heures du matin.	*It's six o'clock in the morning.*
Il est parti à sept heures du soir.	*He left at seven in the evening.*

E after certain adjectives or **il** + adjective + **de** + infinitive:

Il est facile de réserver une place.	*It's easy to reserve a seat.*
Elle était ravie de me voir.	*She was delighted to see me.*

F with comparatives **plus** (*more*) and **moins** (*less*), and after a superlative:

Elle gagne plus de 10.000 F.	*She earns more than 10,000 francs.*
C'est le plus grand bâtiment de Paris.	*It's the biggest building in Paris.*

G to show the cause of something:

Ils meurent de faim.	*They're dying of hunger.*
Il souffre de la grippe.	*He's suffering from the flu.*

H with specific verbs

Elle joue du piano.	*She's playing the piano.*

➤ See the partitive article in Unit 9, also other prepositions in Units 10–12, 14, 15, comparative adjectives in Unit 24, superlative adjectives and adverbs in Units 26 and 27, the infinitive (2) in Unit 58, dimensions in Unit 90, telling the time in Unit 91, countries in Unit 96, expressions of quantity in Unit 99.

13 The preposition *de* – Exercises

1 **Match the French sentences to the appropriate English ones.**

E.g. Il vient de Pologne. → *He comes from Poland.*

a Je vais à la piscine de six à sept heures.

b Il est difficile de juger.

c Il part à six heures du matin.

d Elle travaille à cinq minutes de chez lui.

e Elle joue très bien du piano.

f C'est la plus grande cathédrale de France.

g Ce sont les enfants de mon ami.

h Il a perdu plus d'un million à la bourse.

1 *She plays the piano very well.*

2 *He lost more than a million on the stock exchange.*

3 *It's the biggest cathedral in France.*

4 *I go to the swimming pool from six to seven o'clock.*

5 *They are my friend's children.*

6 *She works five minutes from his place.*

7 *It's difficult to judge.*

8 *He's leaving at six o'clock in the morning.*

2 **Complete the following using *du, de la, de l', des* or *de.***

E.g. **Prenez un verre** _____ **bière.** *Have a glass of beer.* → **Prenez un verre de bière.**

a C'est le chat _____ voisin. *It's the neighbour's cat.*

b Il est l'ami _____ Pauline. *He's Pauline's friend.*

c Elle est propriétaire _____ trois cafés. *She's the owner of three cafés.*

d J'ai la brochure _____ hôtel. *I've got the hotel brochure.*

e Ce train va _____ Bruxelles à Paris. *This train goes from Brussels to Paris.*

f Il a gagné plus _____ 100.000 F. *He won more than 100,000 francs.*

g Le spectacle commence à huit heures _____ soir. *The show starts at 8 pm.*

h Est-ce que tu as les clés _____ appartement? *Have you got the keys to the flat?*

3 **Translate the following sentences into French.**

E.g. *These are the hotel keys.* → **Ce sont les clés de l'hôtel.**

a *Here's Hélène's case.* (**la valise**)

b *It's Jean's flat.*

c *The train arrives at six in the evening.*

d *I like the colour of the bikes.*

14 | UNIT | The preposition à

> The preposition à can combine with the definite article le, la, l',
> or les to produce au, à la, à l' and aux.

A

Masculine	à + le → **au**	à + le cinéma → **au cinéma** *at/to the cinema*
Feminine	à + la → **à la**	à + la gare → **à la gare** *at/to the station*
Masculine and Feminine	à + l' → **à l'**	à + l'aéroport (*nm*) → **à l'aéroport** *at/to the airport*
Plural	à + les → **aux**	à + les magasins → **aux magasins** *at/to the shops*

B The uses of **à**:

- location (*to, on, in*)

  Elle va à Paris demain. — *She's going to Paris tomorrow.*

  J'habite au troisième étage. — *I live on the third floor.*

  La photo est à la page 16. — *The photo is on page 16.*

  Qu'est-ce qu'il y a à la télé? — *What's on TV?*

  Elle est au téléphone. — *She's on the phone.*

  J'ai mal à la tête/au dos. — *I've got a headache/back ache.*

  Ils habitent au Japon/aux États-Unis. — *They live in Japan/the United States.*

- time (*at, to*)

  J'arrive à dix heures. — *I arrive at ten o'clock.*

  Nous partons du 3 au 8 mars. — *We're away from 3 to 8 March.*

- distance (*from*)

  Caen se trouve à 40 kilomètres d'ici. — *Caen is 40 kilometres from here.*

- transport (*by, on*)

  Je suis venu à vélo/à bicyclette/à pied. — *I came by bike/on foot.*

- description

  Il cherche un homme aux yeux bleus. — *He's looking for a man with blue eyes.*

  Je prends un sandwich au fromage. — *I'll have a cheese sandwich.*

  Je prends le slip à 40 F. — *I'll take the briefs that cost 40 francs.*

  Ce manteau n'est pas à moi. — *This coat isn't mine.*

  Il est facile à ouvrir. — *It's easy to open.*

- after certain verbs

  Pierre joue au football. — *Pierre's playing football.*

➤ See prepositions in Units 10–13 and 15, the infinitive (2) in Unit 58, distances in Unit 90, time in Unit 91, countries in Unit 96.

1 How many sentences can you make from the following table? Translate all those you find.

E.g. **Pierre va à l'église.** *Pierre is going to church.*

Pierre va	à	pâtisserie (*nf*)
Nous allons	à la	école (*nf*)
Je travaille	au	cinéma (*nm*)
Mes enfants vont	à l'	pharmacie (*nf*)
On achète des gâteaux	aux	magasins (*nmpl*)
Elle va		église (*nf*)
Vous travaillez		café (*nm*)
Je vais		Montpellier

2 Give the French for the following, using the vocabulary in brackets.

E.g. *She has a headache.* (**la tête**) → **Elle a mal à la tête.**

a *His hand is hurting.* (**la main**)

b *She's got a toothache.* (**les dents**) (*nfpl*)

c *He's got a bad foot.* (**le pied**)

d *His knee is hurting.* (**le genou**)

e *She's got a sore throat.* (**la gorge**)

3 Complete the sentences describing the following illustrations.

E.g.

Il joue _____. → **Il joue au football.**

a Une personne _____ et une personne _____.

b Il va _____.

quatrième

c Marie habite _____.

15 UNIT Complex prepositions

Complex prepositions consist of two or more words e.g. grâce à. The most commonly used ones include à or de.

A The following are examples of prepositions that include **à**:

grâce à *thanks to*	jusqu'à *up to, as far as, until*
par rapport à *with regard to, in relation to*	quant à *as for*

Je reste ici jusqu'à vendredi.　*I'll stay here till Friday.*

As usual when **à** is used with **le, la, l'** and **les**, these words combine and agree with the gender and number of the following word:

Ils sont montés jusqu'au sommet.　*They went as far as the summit.*
Allez jusqu'aux feux.　*Go up to the traffic lights.*

B The following are examples of prepositions that include **de**:

autour de *around*	à cause de *because of*
à côté de *next to, beside*	au-delà de *beyond*
en dehors de *outside*	au-dessous de *below*
au-dessus de *above*	au lieu de *instead of*
en face de *opposite*	en haut de *at the top of*
au milieu de *in the middle of*	loin de *far from*
en bas de *at the bottom of*	au sujet de *about*
près de *near*	

Il s'est assis à côté de moi.　*He sat down next to me.*
Si on sortait au restaurant au lieu de manger à la maison?　*How about going to a restaurant instead of eating at home?*

As usual when **de** is used with **le, la, l'** and **les**, these words combine and agree with the gender and number of the following word:

C'est en face du cinéma.　*It's opposite the cinema.*
J'habite près de la poste.　*I live near the post office.*

C The following are examples of complex prepositions that do not end in **à** or **de**:

d'après *according to, in the style of*	par-dessus *over*
à travers *through, across*	par-dessous *under*

Son second service est passé juste par-dessus le filet.　*His second service went just over the net.*

➤ See the prepositions de in Unit 13 and à in Unit 14.

15 UNIT Complex prepositions – Exercises

1 Match the French with the English.

E.g. en dehors du bâtiment → *outside the building*

a quant à lui
b par-dessus le mur
c en haut de l'arbre
d à travers le terrain de football
e jusqu'à la gare
f au milieu de la place

1 *as far as the station*
2 *as for him*
3 *at the top of the tree*
4 *over the wall*
5 *in the middle of the square*
6 *across the football pitch*

2 Match the French sentences with their English translations.

E.g. Le supermarché est en face du parking. → *The supermarket is opposite the car park.*

a Allez jusqu'aux feux.
b Il met un pullover par-dessus sa chemise.
c Elle a regardé autour d'elle.
d L'hôpital n'est pas loin de l'église.
e Grâce à lui, j'ai fini mon travail.

1 *He puts a pullover on over his shirt.*
2 *Thanks to him I finished my work.*
3 *The hospital is not far from the church.*
4 *Go up to the traffic lights.*
5 *She looked around.*

3 Complete the gaps in the following sentences with words from the box.

E.g. J'ai lu un article _____ la guerre. *I have read an article about the war.* → J'ai un article au sujet de la guerre.

| à travers | ~~au sujet de~~ | d'après | à cause de | en face de | près de |

a La poste est _____ supermarché. *The post office is opposite the supermarket.*
b _____ ma montre, nous sommes en retard. *According to my watch, we're late.*
c Il a couru _____ le parking. *He ran across the car park.*
d Il habite _____ son travail. *He lives near his work.*
e Les trains sont en retard _____ la neige. *The trains are late because of the snow.*

31

16 UNIT | Possessive adjectives

> *Possessive adjectives indicate possession or a relationship, for example* ma voiture *my car,* mon oncle *my uncle,* ma tante *my aunt.*

A The form of the French possessive adjective is determined by the person owning (*my, his, her, our, your, their*) and by the number and, in some cases, the gender of the noun that follows.

B

	Masculine	Feminine	Masculine/feminine plural
my	mon	ma	mes
your	ton	ta	tes
his/her/ its/one's	son	sa	ses
our	notre		nos
your	votre		vos
their	leur		leurs

C *My*: **mon** is used for masculine nouns, **ma** for feminine nouns, **mes** for all plural nouns. **Mon** is also used before feminine nouns beginning with a vowel (**a, e, i, o, u**) and an unsounded **h**.

  (le bureau) mon bureau *my desk*   (les dossiers) mes dossiers *my files*
  (la veste) ma veste *my jacket*   (l'amie) mon amie *my (female) friend*

D *Your*: **ton, ta, tes** are used when referring to someone who is a close friend, a relative or a child. **Ton, ta, tes** behave in the same way as **mon, ma, mes**.

  ton stylo *your pen*   ta maison *your house*   tes manteaux *your coats*

E *His/her*: **son, sa**, and **ses** each mean *his* or *her* – which one is usually clear from the context. **Son** tells you the gender of **livre**, not the gender of the owner. They behave in the same way as **mon, ma, mes**.

  son costume *his/her suit*   ses documents *his/her documents*
  sa voiture *his/her car*

F *Our*: **notre** (masculine and feminine singular nouns) and **nos** (plural nouns).
  notre fils *our son*   notre fille *our daughter*   nos enfants *our children*

G *Your*: **votre** (masculine and feminine singular nouns) and **vos** (plural nouns) when referring to someone with whom you are not on familiar terms.
  votre ami *your (male) friend*   vos amis *your friends*
  votre amie *your (female) friend*

H *Their*: **leur** (masculine and feminine singular) and **leurs** (plural).
  leur journal *their newspaper*   leurs journaux *their newspapers*

➤ *See also possessive pronouns in Unit 39.*

16 Possessive adjectives – Exercises

1 Complete the following questions with *ton*, *ta*, or *tes* and the corresponding answers with *mon*, *ma*, or *mes*.

E.g. Où est _____ bureau?   _____ bureau est dans la rue Lemaître.
→ Où est **ton** bureau?   *Mon* bureau est dans la rue Lemaître.

a Où est _____ passeport? (*nm*) _____ passeport est dans _____ valise. (*nf*)
b Tu as _____ manteau? (*nm*) Oui, _____ manteau est là.
c Où habitent _____ parents? (*nmpl*) _____ parents habitent en Sologne.
d Où travaille _____ sœur? (*nf*) _____ sœur travaille à Caen.
e Tu peux me présenter _____ amie? (*nf*) Voici _____ amie Claire.
f Comment s'appelle _____ chien? (*nm*) _____ chien s'appelle Max.

2 Complete the following conversation using the appropriate words for *your* and *our*.

E.g. Réceptionniste: **Vos** passeports, monsieur. _____ chambre est au premier étage. Où sont _____ bagages? (*nmpl*)
M. Leclerc: _____ bagages sont dans la voiture.
Réceptionniste: Voici _____ clé (*nf*). Antoine va monter _____ valises à la chambre.
M. Leclerc: Merci. _____ passeports, s'il vous plaît.
Réceptionniste: Voilà, monsieur. _____ passeports.

3 Complete the following sentences using the appropriate possessive adjectives.

E.g. _____ clé est dans ma poche. → *Ma* clé est dans ma poche.

a Dans _____ valise, Maurice a _____ vêtements (*nmpl*), _____ affaires de toilette (*nfpl*) et _____ permis de conduire (*nm*).
b Quand elle part en vacances elle prend toujours _____ raquette (*nf*) et _____ chaussures (*nfpl*) de tennis.
c Vous avez _____ passeport?
d Tu as passé _____ vacances (*nfpl*) en Italie?
e Jeanne est arrivée portant _____ nouvelle robe (*nf*).
f Ils veulent _____ journaux? Ils sont sur la table.
g Nous avons acheté des fleurs pour _____ grand-mère.
h Il a envoyé un courrier électronique à _____ collègues (*nmpl*).

4 Translate the following into French. (Look at Units 10–15 on prepositions if you need to.)

a *You've got my pen.*
b *It's her jacket.*
c *These are your documents.*
d *The hospital is near my church.*

33

17 UNIT | Adjectives: agreement (1)

In French, adjectives reflect the gender and number of the noun or pronoun they relate to, i.e. masculine or feminine, singular or plural.

A Basic agreement

The basic form of the adjective (as it is found in the dictionary) is used with masculine nouns and pronouns.

Mon ami est espagnol. Il est amusant. *My friend is Spanish. He's amusing.*

● Most adjectives add an **-e** when relating to a feminine noun or pronoun.
Mon amie est espagnole. *My (female) friend is Spanish.*

● When it relates to a plural noun or pronoun the adjective adds an **-s**. (Exceptions to this rule are shown in the next unit.)
Mes amis sont espagnols. *My friends are Spanish.*
Mes amies sont espagnoles. *My (female) friends are Spanish.*

B Other patterns to note

● Adjectives ending in **-e** with no accent do not add an extra **-e** in the feminine form.
jeune (*m*) jeune (*f*) jeunes (*m/fpl*) *young*

● The following table shows how the feminine endings of various adjectives are formed. You will see that adjectives ending in **-n, -l, -s** and **-t** generally double the final consonant in the feminine.

Adjective ending	Masculine	Feminine	
-on	bon	bonne	*good*
	mignon	mignonne	*sweet, pretty*
-en	ancien	ancienne	*ancient, former*
-el	cruel	cruelle	*cruel*
-er	cher	chère	*dear, expensive*
-eil	pareil	pareille	*similar, same*
-as	gras	grasse	*fatty*
-et ⎫ see	net	nette	*clear*
-eur ⎬ Unit	menteur	menteuse	*lying*
-eur ⎭ 18	protecteur	protectrice	*protective*
-f	actif	active	*active*
-g	long	longue	*long*
-c	blanc	blanche	*white*
	public	publique	*public*
	sec	sèche	*dry*

 ➤ *See Unit 18 for irregular forms.*

17 Adjectives: agreement (1) – Exercises

1 Complete the following with the feminine forms of the adjectives.

E.g. Il est grand. Elle est *grande*.

a Il est petit.   Elle est _____.

b Le chien est mignon.   La souris est _____.

c Le pantalon est rouge.   La jupe est _____.

d Il est actif.   Elle est _____.

e Il est intelligent.   Elle est _____.

f Il est français.   Elle est _____.

2 Look at the following descriptions and choose the correct adjective from the options available.

E.g. Anne-Marie est très grand/*grande*.

a Elle a les cheveux court/courts et les yeux verts/vertes.

b Le chien de Jean est méchant/méchante, mais il est aussi timide/timides.

c André porte un pantalon grise/gris, une chemise bleu/bleue, une cravate jaune/jaunes, des chaussettes bleu/bleues et des chaussures (*nfpl*) noirs/noires.

3 Complete the following conversations with the appropriate form of the adjectives in brackets.

E.g. Vous avez les documents (récent)? → Vous avez les documents *récents*?

a Simone   Vous avez les tasses (blanc) (*nfpl*)?

   Danielle   Non. Elles sont sur la (petit) table dans le salon.

b Paul   C'est un (bon) hôtel.

   Jean   Oui. Mais ma chambre est (cher).

   Paul   Mais elle est (grand).

c Henri   Mon amie (espagnol) arrive aujourd'hui.

   Hélène   Comment est-elle?

   Henri   Elle est très (joli). Elle a les cheveux (*nmpl*) (long) et (noir). Et les yeux (brun).

18 UNIT | Adjective: agreement (2)

A Adjectives ending in **-x** replace the **-x** with **-se** in the feminine, and do not take an **-s** in the masculine plural:

heureux (*m*) heureux (*mpl*) heureuse (*f*) heureuses (*fpl*)　　*happy*

The following are exceptions to this feminine pattern:

| doux | doux | douce | douces | *sweet, mild, gentle* |
| faux | faux | fausse | fausses | *false* |

B Adjectives ending in **-s** do not add another **-s** in the masculine plural:

français　français　française　françaises　*French*

C Adjectives ending in **-et** change the ending to **-ète** in the feminine:

secret　secrets　secrète　secrètes　*secret*

also **complet** *full*, **inquiet** *worried*

D A group of adjectives ending in **-eur** add an **-e** in the feminine and do not change the ending to **-euse**:

meilleur　meilleurs　meilleure　meilleures　*better*

also **supérieur** *superior*, **inférieur** *inferior*, **extérieur** *exterior* and **intérieur** *interior*.

E Adjectives ending in **-al** have irregular masculine plural forms:

| normal | normaux | normale | normales | *normal* |

BUT

| final | finals | finale | finales | *final* |
| fatal | fatals | fatale | fatales | *fatal* |

F A small group of adjectives have two masculine forms and an irregular feminine form. The second masculine form given below is used before vowels and an unsounded **h**:

le vieux château　*the old chateau*　le vieil hôtel　*the old hotel*

beau/bel	beaux	belle	belles	*beautiful*
fou/fol	fous	folle	folles	*mad*
nouveau/nouvel	nouveaux	nouvelle	nouvelles	*new*
vieux/vieil	vieux	vieille	vieilles	*old*

G The following adjectives are irregular:

bref	brefs	brève	brèves	*brief*
gentil	gentils	gentille	gentilles	*kind*
frais	frais	fraîche	fraîches	*fresh*

18 — Adjective: agreement (2) – Exercises

1 **Choose the appropriate form of the adjective in each of these sentences.**

E.g. Il possède un très beau/bel cheval. → Il possède un très *beau* cheval.

a C'est la décision final/finale.

b Le vieux/vieil monsieur est très gentil/gentille.

c Est-ce que le lait est frais/fraîche?

d Madeleine est très heureux/heureuse aujourd hui.

e Le nouveau/nouvel hôtel est très beau/belle.

f C'est un café tout à fait normal/normale.

g Ils ont eu une conversation très bref/brève.

h Jacqueline semble très inquiet/inquiète.

2 **Complete the following with the feminine form of the adjective.**

E.g. Il est vieux; elle est _____. → Il est vieux; elle est *vieille*.

a Il est doux; elle est _____.

b Il est gentil; elle est _____.

c Il est beau; elle est _____.

d Il est discret (*discreet*); elle est _____.

3 **Complete the following sentences using the adjective in brackets.**

E.g. C'est une (vieux) amie. C'est une *vieille* amie.

a Cette voiture est (inférieur).

b Les bâtiments (extérieur) sont très (ancien).

c Les enfants ne sont pas très (heureux).

d Ce (vieux) monsieur est son père.

e Elle arrive avec un (vieux) ami.

f Il y a une (bref) pause dans le spectacle.

g Il y avait des accidents (*nmpl*) (fatal).

h Ce sont des enfants tout à fait (*completely*) (normal).

i Ce sont mes (nouveau) amies (français).

4 **Translate the following into French. (You may need to look back to Unit 17.)**

a *The interior rooms* (**la pièce**) *are big.*

b *The cheese* (**le fromage**) *is fresh.*

c *The new hotel is open* (**ouvert**).

d *This house is old.*

e *The route* (**la route**) *is very long.*

19 UNIT | Adjectives: position

*In English adjectives go before the noun they relate to.
In French they go before or after.*

A The majority of adjectives in French go after the noun.

    C'est un livre intéressant.   *It's an interesting book.*

B However, the following commonly used adjectives go before the noun:
autre (*other*); **beau** (*beautiful*); **bon** (*good*); **court** (*short*); **gentil** (*kind, nice*); **grand** (*big, tall*); **gros** (*big, fat*); **haut** (*high*); **jeune** (*young*); **joli** (*pretty*); **long** (*long*); **mauvais** (*bad*); **même** (*same*); **meilleur** (*better*); **nouveau** (*new*); **petit** (*small*); **vieux** (*old*).

    Ce jeune homme est son fils.   *This young man is his son.*
Ordinal numbers also precede the noun.

    Le premier train va à Cherbourg.   *The first train goes to Cherbourg.*

⚠ When used as an adjective, **tout** (**tout, tous, toute, toutes**) stands before the definite article.

    Toutes les voitures sont vendues.   *All the cars are sold.*

C There are rules to follow when there is more than one adjective with a noun.
- When there are two adjectives they take their normal place before or after the noun.

    Un grand arbre mort.   *A big, dead tree.*
    Deux bons petits chats.   *Two good little cats.*

- If there is more than one adjective after the noun, they are joined by **et**.
Une femme amusante et intelligente. *An amusing and intelligent woman.*

D **Dernier** and **prochain** have different meanings before and after the noun.

la dernière semaine de l'année	*the last week of the year (i.e. last in a series)*
la semaine dernière	*last week (i.e. the one before this)*
la prochaine réunion	*the next meeting (i.e. next in a series)*
jeudi prochain	*next Thursday (i.e. the one after this)*

When used with a number **dernier** and **prochain** follow the number, unlike English.

    les deux derniers mois   *the last two months*
    les dix prochaines années   *the next ten years*

➤ *See indefinite adjectives (tout) in Unit 28,
ordinal numbers in Unit 88.*

19 UNIT Adjectives: position – Exercises

1 Write the words in the following sentences in the correct order. Use the English to guide you.

E.g. lait du J' du frais. *I have some milk.* → **J'ai du lait frais.**

a costume un Elle beau bleu a   *She has a lovely blue suit.*

b une C'est riche femme   *She's a rich woman.*

c grand gris un C'est bâtiment   *It's a big, grey building.*

d un C'est camarade bon   *He's a good friend.*

e écrivain vieux Ce célèbre est un monsieur   *This old man is a famous writer.*

f rouge la Je jupe longue préfère   *I prefer the long red skirt.*

g concours le du jour dernier C'est   *It's the last day of the competition.*

2 Put the adjective in brackets into the sentence in the correct position, making it agree in number and gender. (You may need to refer to an earlier unit.)

E.g. **C'est un centre commercial. (nouveau)** → **C'est un *nouveau* centre commercial.**

a J'ai de la bière. (français)

b Il a un ordinateur. (vieux)

c C'est une rue. (dangereux)

d Je lis un article. (intéressant)

e Les documents sont sur ton bureau. (tout, nouveau)

f Tu as de la crème? (frais)

g C'est un chemin. (beau)

h C'est une histoire. (bon, amusant)

3 Translate the following sentences into French.

a *My mother is Spanish.*

b *I have some fresh lemonade.*

c *It's an old hotel.*

d *It's a big room.*

e *He has a new red car.*

f *This is the last bottle.*

g *The first coach (**le car**) is in front of the white building.*

h *All the children are on the coach.*

> The demonstrative adjective **ce** and its forms mean
> *this, that, these* and *those.*

A Like any adjective, the demonstrative adjective agrees in gender and number
with the noun that follows it.

J'aime **ce** journal/**cette** plage.　　*I like this paper/this beach.*

	Singular	Plural
Masculine	ce, cet	ces
Feminine	cette	ces

- **Ce** is used before masculine singular nouns.
  J'ai acheté ce stylo hier.　　*I bought this/that pen yesterday.*

- **Cette** is used before feminine singular nouns.
  Tu aimes cette table?　　*Do you like this/that table?*

- **Cet** is used before masculine singular nouns beginning with a vowel or a
  silent **h**.
  Cet hôtel est excellent.　　*This/that hotel is excellent.*

- **Ces** is used before masculine and feminine plural nouns.
  Je n'ai plus besoin de ces vêtements. *I don't need these/those clothes any*
  more.

B If you need to differentiate more clearly between *this* and *that*, or *these* and
those, **-ci** can be added after the noun to express *this* or *these* (**-ci** comes from
ici *here*, so it indicates something nearer) and **-là** can be added to express *that*
or *those* (**là** means *there*, so it indicates something further away).

Je préfère ce costume-ci.　　*I prefer this suit.*
Vraiment? Moi, je préfère ce　　*Really? I prefer that suit.*
　costume-là.
Combien coûte cette chaise-ci?　　*How much is this chair?*
Je vais acheter cette chaise-là.　　*I'm going to buy that chair.*
Cet hôtel-ci est très bien.　　*This (particular) hotel is very good.*
Cet homme-là vend une voiture.　　*That man (there) is selling a car.*
Qu'est-ce qu'on prend? Ces　　*What shall we buy? These flowers*
　fleurs-ci ou ces fleurs-là?　　　*(here) or those flowers (there)?*
Prenons ces fleurs-là.　　*Let's take those flowers (there).*

> ➤ *See demonstrative pronouns in Unit 40.*

1 Match the following with their meanings.

E.g. ces vêtements-ci → *these clothes*

a cette chaise-ci
b ce livre-là
c ces voitures-ci
d cet homme-là
e ce livre-ci
f ces voitures-là
g cette chaise-là
h cet homme-ci

1 *that chair*
2 *that man*
3 *this chair*
4 *this man*
5 *those cars*
6 *that book*
7 *these cars*
8 *this book*

2 Write a sentence about each illustration using the words in the box.

E.g. Cette veste coûte 9.400 F.

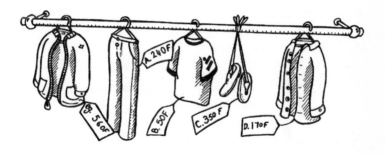

| le T-shirt | la chemise | le pantalon | les chaussures | l'anorak (*nm*) |

3 Complete the gaps in the conversation with either *ce, cet, cette* or *ces*, adding *-ci* or *-là* where appropriate. One example has been done for you in bold.

– Bonjour madame. Je voudrais des vêtements pour mes vacances. Vous avez des T-shirts?
– J'ai **ces** T-shirts**-ci** à 25 F et _____ T-shirts_____ à 55 F.
– Je préfère _____ T-shirts-là. Vous avez _____ jupe en bleu?
– Non madame, _____ jupe_____ est seulement en rouge ou en gris.
– Qu'est-ce que vous avez comme pulls? J'aime bien _____ pull_____ .
– Le bleu?
– Oui, et _____ short_____ . Je peux les essayer? (*Can I try them on?*)

21 UNIT | Adverbs (1): regular forms

> *An adverb is a word that adds to the meaning of a verb, an adjective or another adverb, for example carefully, loudly, mostly, extremely.*

In French, most adverbs are formed by adding **-ment** to a form of the adjective.

Elle a simplement refusé. *She simply refused.*

A For adjectives ending in a consonant the adverb is formed from the feminine form of the adjective. The table below shows a few examples.

Elle parle très doucement. *She speaks very quietly.*

Masculine adjective	Feminine adjective	Adverb
complet	complète	**complètement** *completely*
franc	franche	**franchement** *frankly*
heureux	heureuse	**heureusement** *happily*

B Adjectives ending in a vowel add **-ment** to the masculine form of the adjective.

Je trouve cela absolument absurde. *I find that absolutely absurd.*

Masculine adjective	Adverb
absolu	**absolument** *absolutely*
facile	**facilement** *easily*
vrai	**vraiment** *truly*

Exceptions to this rule are **fou** (*mad*), **gai** (*gay, happy*) and **nouveau** (*new*), which form the adverb from the feminine form of the adjective.

Il se battait follement. *He struggled madly.*

C Two groups of adverbs are exceptions to the general rules.

- Adjectives ending in **-ant** and **-ent** change the **-nt** to **-mment**.

Il parle italien couramment. *He speaks Italian fluently.*

courant → **couramment** *fluently*   évident → **évidemment** *evidently*

⚠ **Lent** is an exception to this rule and becomes **lentement**.

- A small number of adverbs end in **-ément**, for example:

commun → **communément** *commonly*   énorme → **énormément** *hugely*

précis → **précisément** *precisely*   profond → **profondément** *profoundly*

▶ *See agreement of adjectives in Units 17 and 18.*

21 UNIT Adverbs (1): regular forms – *Exercises*

1 Form adverbs from the following adjectives.

E.g. énorme *enormous* → **énormément**

a joyeux *joyous*
b vrai *true*
c poli *polite*
d résolu *resolute*
e parfait *perfect*
f profond *profound*
g malheureux *unfortunate*
h certain *certain*
i bruyant *noisy*

2 Complete the following sentences with adverbs formed from the adjectives in brackets.

E.g. Il parle _____ . (franc) → **Il parle franchement.**

a Jouez ce passage plus _____, s'il vous plaît. (doux)
b Nous écoutons _____ . (attentif)
c Ils comprennent _____ . (final)
d Lui, il y va _____ . (régulier)
e Je suis _____ fatigué. (extrême)
f Il est _____ fou! (complet)

3 Select appropriate adjectives from the box and make them into adverbs to complete the following sentences.

E.g. Il travaille _____ . → **Il travaille rapidement.**

| confortable | lent | rare | ~~rapide~~ | doux | sûr | bruyant |

a Elle s'est _____ installée devant le téléviseur.
b Il parle trop _____ .
c Le train arrive _____ à l'heure.
d Les enfants jouent _____ dans leur chambre.
e Votre père, il marche toujours si _____ ?
f C'est un livre intéressant mais _____ difficile à lire.

43

22 UNIT Adverbs (2): irregular forms

A The adverbs in the table below are irregular.

Il parle brièvement	*He talks briefly.*
Elle écrit bien.	*She writes well.*
Je travaille peu en ce moment.	*I'm not working much at the moment.*
Il court très vite.	*He runs very quickly.*

Masculine adjective	Adverb
bon	**bien** *well*
bref	**brièvement** *briefly*
gentil	**gentiment** *kindly, nicely*
mauvais	**mal** *badly*
meilleur	**mieux** *better*
moindre	**moins** *less*
petit	**peu** *little*

⚠ **Vite**, meaning *quickly*, has no related adjective; use **rapide** *quick* instead.

B Some adjectives can be used as adverbs in particular expressions or with particular meanings.

bas	*low*	voler bas	*to fly low*
bon	*good*	sentir bon	*to smell good*
mauvais	*bad*	sentir mauvais	*to smell bad*
cher	*expensive*	coûter cher	*to be expensive*
fort	*loudly*	parler fort	*to speak loudly*
juste	*straight, precise*	viser juste	*to aim accurately*
dur	*hard*	travailler dur	*to work hard*
court	*short*	couper court	*to cut short*
clair	*clearly*	voir clair	*to see clearly*
faux	*false*	sonner faux	*to sound wrong*
haut	*loud*	chanter haut	*to sing loudly*
net	*short, clean*	s'arrêter net	*to stop dead*

1 Form adverbs from the following adjectives – you'll find a mixture of regular and irregular forms (look back to Unit 21 if you need to).

E.g. moindre → moins

a gentil   **d** petit   **g** précis

b sérieux   **e** lent   **h** courant

c patient   **f** absolu   **i** mauvais

2 Insert an appropriate word from the box and match the sentences.

E.g. Ça sent _____ . Ça sent bon. *That smells good.*

mauvais	bien	haut	brièvement	peu	cher	bien	mieux	~~bon~~

a Ils parlent _____ .   **1** *She sings well.*

b Ça sent _____ .   **2** *I'm better now.*

c Ces chaussures coûtent _____ .   **3** *That smells bad.*

d Elle chante _____ .   **4** *They speak loudly.*

e Il parle _____ .   **5** *He works well.*

f Je vais _____ maintenant.   **6** *He doesn't speak much.*

g Il travaille _____ .   **7** *These shoes are expensive.*

3 Complete each of the following sentences by using a word from the box in its correct form.

E.g. Il est _____ en route. Il est *certainement* en route.

bas	meilleur	mauvais	fort	net	haut	bon	cher	~~certain~~

a Je n'entends rien. Tu parles trop _____ .

b Ces chocolats coûtent _____ .

c Elle travaille _____ que lui.

d Ils parlent _____ le français.

e Ce livre est _____ écrit.

f Le ballon est monté très _____ .

g Ils crient _____ .

h Il s'arrête _____ .

4 Put the following into French.

a *He works very little at the moment.*   **c** *He plays well.*

b *She sings very loudly.*   **d** *He writes badly.*

23 UNIT Adverbs (3): position

A In simple tenses (the present, imperfect, future) and in conditional sentences the adverb usually comes straight after the verb it relates to.

Elle parle sérieusement.	*She talks seriously.*
Il travaille lentement.	*He works slowly.*

B Some adverbs may appear at the beginning of a sentence when qualifying the whole phrase. This can be done to give an element of emphasis.

Malheureusement, il était parti.	*Unfortunately, he had gone.*
Demain, elle va à Paris.	*Tomorrow, she's going to Paris.*

C When an adverb qualifies an adjective, the adverb goes first. Where adverbs occur together, **très** *very*, **trop** *too* and **bien** *really, very* go first.

Elle est extrêmement jolie.	*She's extremely pretty.*
Une maison très moderne.	*A very modern house.*
Je le vois trop rarement.	*I see him too rarely.*

D Note that *very much* is **beaucoup**. **Très** can never be used with it.

Il l'a beaucoup aimée.	*He loved her very much.*

E In compound tenses (e.g. the perfect and pluperfect tenses), some shorter adverbs come between the auxiliary verb (**avoir** or **être**) and the past participle.

Il a bien travaillé. *He has worked well.* Elle l'a vite fait. *She did it quickly.*

assez *enough*	jamais *never*
bien *well*	mal *badly*
beaucoup *a lot*	mieux *better*
bientôt *soon*	moins *less*
déjà *already*	souvent *often*
encore *yet*	toujours *always, still*
enfin *at last*	trop *too much*
vite *quickly*	tout à fait *completely*

F In compound tenses, adverbs of place, some adverbs of time, adverbs ending in **-ment** and other longer adverbs usually follow the past participle.

Je suis arrivé hier. *I arrived yesterday.* Il a voyagé rapidement. *He travelled quickly.*

aujourd'hui *today*	(avant-)hier *(the day before)*
demain *tomorrow*	*yesterday*
(après-)demain *(the day after) tomorrow*	autrefois *in former times*
hier *yesterday*	tard *late*

23 UNIT Adverbs (3): position – Exercises

1 **Insert the adverbs correctly in the following sentences.**

E.g. La lettre est *enfin* arrivée.

a Elle est partie. *déjà*
b J'ai voulu y aller. *toujours*
c Il est arrivé. *tard*
d Vous avez travaillé. *bien*
e Elle a attendu. *patiemment*
f Ils sont arrivés. *hier*
g Tu as bu. *trop*
h Il est parti. *vite*
i C'est impossible. *absolument*
j Je suis en retard. *souvent*
k Elle va arriver. *après-demain*
l Je parlais. *franchement*
m Vous avez mangé. *beaucoup*
n Elle a fini. *vite*
o Vous avez tort. *rarement*
p Tu as conduit. *prudemment*
q Vous êtes parti. *très tôt*

2 **Write answers to the following questions, inserting the adverbs appropriately.**

E.g. Est-elle heureuse? *certainement* → Oui, elle est certainement heureuse.

a Est-ce qu'il pleut? *naturellement*
b Il a raison? *toujours*
c Elles sont arrivées? *évidemment*
d Il a fini son travail? *vite*
e Elle va mieux? *heureusement*

3 **Complete the following passage using the adverbs from the box. One has been done for you.**

Aujourd'hui Pierre quitte le bureau _____ . Il est _____ fatigué. Il va _____ à la gare. _____ le train arrive _____ . Sa femme est _____ à la maison. Ils mangent _____ et puis ils s'installent _____ devant la télé.

à l'heure	~~aujourd'hui~~	confortablement	très	bien	tard
	heureusement	lentement	déjà		

47

24 UNIT | Adjectives: comparison

Comparison of adjectives is when you say something is more ... than, (bigger) than, less ... than or as ... as.

A Simple comparison

- To say *more ...* or *(bigg)-er* in French you use **plus** + adjective.
  Ce journal est plus sérieux.   *This newspaper is more serious.*

- To say *less ...* you use **moins** + adjective.
  Ce journal est moins sérieux.   *This newspaper is less serious.*

- To say *(just) as (big)* you use **aussi** + adjective (or **si** in the negative).
  Ce garçon est aussi grand.   *This boy is (just) as big.*
  Ce garçon n'est pas si/aussi grand.   *This boy isn't as big.*

B Comparing two things

- To say *more ... than* or *(bigg)-er than* you use **plus** + adjective + **que**.
  Mon frère est plus grand que son ami. *My brother is taller than his friend.*

- To say *less (big) than* you use **moins** + adjective + **que**.
  Il est moins riche que moi.   *He's less rich than I am.*

- To say *(just) as ... as* you use **aussi** + adjective + **que** (or **si ... que** in the negative).
  Claire est aussi grande que son frère. *Claire is (just) as tall as her brother.*
  Il n'est pas aussi/si riche que moi. *He's not as rich as me.*

C When used with a noun to indicate quantity (e.g. *more time, less wine*) **plus** or **moins** are followed by **de** before the noun.
  Il a plus d'argent (que moi).   *He's got more money (than me).*
  Elle fait moins de travail (que lui). *She does less work (than him).*

Note also the similar use of **autant de ... que** meaning *as much/many ... as*.
  Il y a autant de places libres ici   *There are as many free seats here*
  que là-bas.   *as over there.*

D Some adjectives have irregular comparative forms.

bon *good*	meilleur *better*
mauvais *bad*	pire/plus mauvais *worse*
petit *little*	moindre/plus petit *smaller, lesser*

⚠ **Plus mauvais** refers to quality, **pire** means 'morally worse'.
  Plus petit refers to size, **moindre** to significance.

In French you can say **moins bon** (*less good*) to mean *worse*.
  Ce film est moins bon que l'autre. *This film is worse than the other.*

1 Complete the following sentences, ensuring that the adjectives agree appropriately with their nouns.

E.g. Elle est _____ que moi (grand).
She is bigger than me. → Elle est plus grande que moi.

a Monique est _____ que son amie. (petit) *Monique is smaller than her friend.*

b Henri a _____ que sa sœur. (talent) *Henri has more talent than his sister.*

c Ce bureau est _____ que les autres. (grand) *This desk is as big as the others.*

d Cette maison est _____ que l'appartement à Paris. (cher) *This house is more expensive than the flat in Paris.*

e Ici les matins sont _____ que chez nous. (frais) *Here the mornings are fresher than at home.*

2 Look at the following sentence.

Georges est petit. (*more … than*) → Il est plus petit que son frère.

Now follow the same process with the following sentences, using *que son frère* at the end of each sentence.

a Colette est polie. (*more … than*)   **f** Hélène est active (*as … as*)

b Yves est patient. (*less … than*)   **g** Simone est paresseuse (*lazy*)

c Michel est fort (*strong*). (*as … as*)   (*less … than*)

d Anne-Marie est chic. (*less … than*) **h** Julien n'est pas intelligent. (*as … as*)

e Cécile est riche (*more … than*)

3 Complete the following sentences using the appropriate form of the adjective in brackets.

E.g. Cette maison est aussi *grande* que la mienne. (grand)

a Ce vin est _____ que le précédent. (bon)

b Cette voiture est plus _____ que la mienne. (puissant *powerful*)

c Ce café est moins _____ que l'autre. (fort)

d Je trouve ce plat (*dish*) moins _____ que l'autre. (bon)

e La plage de Bénodet est _____ que la plage de Dieppe. (bon)

f Cette veste est aussi _____ que la veste noire. (cher)

4 Translate the following into French.

a *This hotel is better than the other.*   **e** *Jules is smaller than his brother.*

b *Jean-Pierre has more money than Daniel.*   **f** *The beach is worse than the beach at Biarritz.*

c *Sylvie is younger than her sister.*   **g** *This film is more interesting than the other.*

d *This coffee is stronger than the other.*

49

25 UNIT | Adverbs: comparison

Comparison of adverbs is saying someone does something more (quickly) than, (faster) than, less (quickly) than or as (quickly) as.

A Simple comparison

- To say *more (quickly)* or *(fast)-er* in French you use **plus** + adverb.
  Il court plus vite.   *He runs faster.*

- To say *less (quickly)* you use **moins** + adverb.
  Il court moins vite.   *He runs less quickly.*

- To say *(just) as (quickly)* you use **aussi** + adverb.
  Ce garçon court aussi vite.   *This boy runs (just) as quickly.*
  Ce garçon ne court pas aussi vite.   *This boy doesn't run as fast.*

B Comparing two things

- To say *more (quickly) than* or *faster than* you use **plus** + adverb + **que**.
  Il écoute plus attentivement que moi. *He listens more attentively than me.*

- To say *less (quickly) than* you use **moins** + adverb + **que**.
  Anne travaille moins sérieusement   *Anne works less seriously*
  que sa sœur.   *than her sister.*

- To say *(just) as ... as* you use **aussi** + adverb + **que** (or **si ... que** in the negative).
  Il écoute aussi patiemment que   *He listens (just) as patiently as his*
  son père.   *father.*
  Il n'écrit pas aussi/si bien que Pierre. *He doesn't write as well as Pierre.*

To say *as much as* you use **autant que**.
  Cela m'irrite autant que toi.   *That irritates me as much as it*
                                       does you.

C Some adverbs have irregular comparative forms.

bien *well*	mieux *better*
mal *bad*	pis/plus mal *worse*
peu *little*	moins *less*

Ce matin on avait des problèmes,   *This morning there were problems*
  mais maintenant ça va mieux.   *but now it's going better.*

⚠ **Pis** is rarely used except in certain idiomatic expressions:

  Tant pis!   *Too bad!*

25 UNIT Adverbs: comparison – Exercises

1 Match the French and English sentences.

E.g. Il parle plus couramment que moi. → *He speaks more fluently than me.*

a Il court plus vite que moi.

b Il parle plus rapidement que Sylvie.

c Il va au cinéma plus régulièrement que nous.

d Il court moins vite que moi.

e Elle écoute plus attentivement que vous.

f Il parle moins vite que Sylvie.

g Elle chante mieux que moi.

1 *He goes to the cinema more regularly than us.*

2 *He speaks more quickly than Sylvie.*

3 *He runs more slowly than me.*

4 *He speaks more slowly than Sylvie.*

5 *She listens more attentively than you.*

6 *She sings better than me.*

7 *He runs faster than me.*

2 Complete the following sentences using the English as a guide.

E.g. Elle parle _____ que toi. (doucement) *She speaks more softly than you.* → Elle parle plus doucement que toi.

a Henri travaille _____ que vous. (sérieusement)
Henri works harder than you.

b On mange ici _____ que chez Gaston. (souvent)
We eat here less often than at Gaston's.

c Il conduit _____ que son père. (prudemment)
He drives more carefully than his father.

3 Complete the following sentences, inserting in the correct form of the adverb in the comparative.

E.g. Elle écoute _____ que vous. *She listens more attentively than you.* → Elle écoute plus attentivement que vous.

a Il travaille _____ que nous.
He works less regularly than us.

b Ici on mange _____ que chez Maurice.
Here you eat better than at Maurice's.

c Laurence écoute _____ que vous.
Laurence listens less attentively than you.

d Je viens ici _____ que vous.
I come here as regularly as you.

4 Translate the following into French.

a *I go to the cinema more regularly now.*

b *He plays the piano as well as Charles.*

c *She speaks French faster now.*

d *He works more slowly than Jean.*

51

26 UNIT | Adjectives: superlative

The fastest, the most expensive *are examples of superlative adjectives. They are formed by using the comparative preceded by* **le, la,** *or* **les.**

A To form the superlative of an adjective you put the definite article (**le, la,** or **les**) in front of the simple comparative form.

Cet hôtel est **le plus cher**.	*This hotel is the most expensive.*
Ces hôtels sont **les moins chers**.	*These hotels are the least expensive.*

With two superlative adjectives the definite article is repeated.

Cet hôtel est le plus cher et le plus confortable.	*This hotel is the most expensive and the most comfortable.*

• Both the adjective and the definite article must agree in gender and number with the noun.

le plus **grand** jardin	*the biggest garden*
la région **la** moins **importante**	*the least important region*

• The superlative adjective takes its normal place in relation to the noun.

Sarah est la plus jeune infirmière.	*Sarah's the youngest nurse.*
Sarah est l'infirmière la plus patiente.	*Sarah's the most patient nurse.*

When the adjective comes after the noun the definite article is repeated.

B Superlatives of irregular adjectives

bon	le meilleur	*the best*
mauvais	le plus mauvais/le pire	*the worst*
petit	le moindre	*the least, the slightest*
	le plus petit	*the smallest*

Ce vin est le plus mauvais de tous les vins.	*This wine is the worst of all the wines.*
Ceci est le plus petit sac.	*This is the smallest bag.*
Cela n'a pas la moindre importance.	*That doesn't have the least importance.*

C After the superlative **de** is used to mean *in* or *of*.

C'est l'hôtel le moins cher de la ville.	*It's the cheapest hotel in town.*
Il est le plus doué de tous.	*He's the most gifted of them all.*

D **Le plus ... que**. After this construction the subjunctive is used.

C'est la plus belle région que je connaisse.	*It's the loveliest region I know.*

➤ *See when to use the subjunctive in Unit 79.*

1 **Complete the sentences using superlative forms. Remember that the adjectives must agree with the nouns.**

E.g. Elle a acheté la bague (*ring*) la _____ (cher) → Elle a acheté la bague la plus chère.

a C'est le _____ festival de France. (grand)

b Ils ont la _____ maison de la ville. (beau)

c C'est la _____ montagne d'Europe. (haut)

d C'était l'expérience la _____ de ma vie. (mauvais)

e Elle est la _____ musicienne de tous. (bon)

f Cette ville est la _____ de la région. (important)

g C'est la raison la _____ . (stupide)

2 **Choose nouns from the box to match the superlatives in order to make the phrases below, using the English to guide you. Remember to put the adjective in the appropriate position in relation to the noun.**

E.g. la plus haute + la montagne → la plus haute montagne

> l'église   la dame   le musée   la fille   les films   ~~la montagne~~
> les enfants   l'homme   le garçon

a le plus grand   *the tallest boy*

b la plus amusante   *the most amusing girl*

c les plus intelligents   *the most intelligent children*

d la plus vieille   *the oldest lady*

3 **Complete the gaps with the appropriate comparative or superlative from the box below.**

E.g. Ce livre est *meilleur* que l'autre, mais ces livres sont *les meilleurs*. *This book is better than the other, but these books are the best.*

> mieux   la moindre   le meilleur   pire   le plus mauvais
> la moins importante   la plus petite   plus mauvais

a Ce jardin est _____ et a gagné le prix.
   This garden is the best and has won the prize.

b Ce restaurant est _____ que l'autre.
   This restaurant is worse than the other.

c Je n'ai pas _____ idée.
   I haven't the slightest idea.

27 | UNIT | Adverbs: superlative

The fastest, the best, etc. are examples of superlative adverbs. They are formed by using the comparative preceded by le, la, *or* les.

A To form the superlative of an adverb you put the masculine definite article **le** in front of the comparative form. The definite article is invariable; it is always **le**.

Il court le plus vite de tous les athlètes. *He runs the fastest of all the athletes.*

Elle travaille le moins régulièrement de tous les employés. *She works the least regularly of all the employees.*

Elle travaille le moins régulièrement et le moins sérieusement de tous les employés. *She works the least regularly and the least seriously of all the employees.*

With two superlative adverbs **le** has to be repeated.

B The superlative adverb always comes after the verb.

Il mange le plus vite de tous. *He eats the fastest of them all.*

C Superlatives of irregular adverbs

bien	le mieux	*the best*
mal	le plus mal	*the worst*
	le pis	*the worst*
peu	le moins	*the least*

Il tape le moins rapidement. *He types the most slowly.*

D After the superlative, **de** is used to mean *in* or *of*.

Il travaille le plus dur de tous. *He works the hardest of them all.*

E In French the expression *as (quickly) as possible* is said with **le plus** + adverb + **possible**, or **aussi** + adverb + **que possible**.

Faites cela, s'il vous plaît, le plus vite possible. *Please do that as quickly as possible.*

Faites cela, s'il vous plaît, aussi vite que possible. *Please do that as quickly as possible.*

Il a ouvert la porte le plus doucement possible. *He opened the door as quietly as possible.*

Il a ouvert la porte aussi doucement que possible. *He opened the door as quietly as possible.*

27 UNIT Adverbs superlative – Exercises

1 Match the parts of the French sentences using the English as a guide.

E.g. Il fait la vaisselle + le plus rarement de tous. → *He washes up the least often of all.*

a Il joue
b Elle joue
c Elle parle l'espagnol
d C'est lui qui manque
e Elle fait la cuisine
f Il prépare les rapports

g le mieux de la classe.
h le moins de tous les enfants.
i le mieux de tous.
j le mieux au tennis.
k le plus lentement de tous les employés.
l le plus souvent.

1 *He plays tennis best.*
2 *She cooks best of all.*
3 *He prepares reports the slowest of all the employees.*
4 *She speaks Spanish the best in the class.*
5 *She plays the least of all the children.*
6 *It's him who's most often missing.*

2 Complete the following sentences using a superlative adverb formed from the word in brackets.

E.g. Parlez _____ possible. (doux) → Parlez *le plus doucement* possible.

a Il chante _____ de tous. (bien)
b Ce train roule _____ vite. (peu)
c Il travaille _____ du groupe. (patient)
d Elle crie _____ de tous les bébés. (fort)
e Il calcule _____ de tous les étudiants. (rapide)

3 Complete the sentences using appropriate adverbs from the box.

E.g. Moi, je conduis _____ Pierre, mais toi, tu conduis _____ . *I drive worse than Pierre, but you drive the worst.* → Moi, je conduis *pire que* Pierre, mais toi, tu conduis *le plus mal.*

mieux	pire	le plus mal	le plus fréquemment	plus mal

a Sophie travaille _____ que Nadine, mais Pascale travaille _____ de tous. *Sophie works better than Nadine, but Pascale works the best of all.*
b Henri chante _____ que Pierre, mais Yves chante _____ de tous. *Henri sings worse than Pierre, but Yves sings worst of all.*
c Elle va au cinéma _____ de la famille. *She goes to the cinema the most frequently in the family.*

55

28 UNIT
Indefinite adjectives and pronouns (1)

Indefinite adjectives and pronouns include words like each, such, other and someone.

A The indefinite adjectives and pronouns are as follows:

Adjectives		Pronouns	
aucun(s), aucune(s)	*none, not any*	aucun(s), aucune(s)	*none, not any*
autre(s)	*other*	autre(s)	*other(s)*
certain(s), certaine(s)	*certain*	certain(s), certaine(s)	*certain (ones), some*
même(s)	*same*	même(s)	*same*
tout, tous, toute, toutes	*all*	tout, tous, toute, toutes	*all*
plusieurs	*several*	plusieurs	*several*
		personne	*no one*
chaque	*each*	chacun(e)	*each one*
quelque(s)	*some, a few*	quelqu'un, quelques-uns, quelques-unes	*someone some (people)*
		quelque chose	*something, anything*
tel(s), telle(s)	*such*		

B A number of indefinites have the same form and can be used both as adjectives and pronouns, as shown in the table above.

● As adjectives

Il arrivera sans **aucun** doute.	*He'll arrive without any doubt.*
On prend le **même** bus tous les jours.	*We take the same bus every day.*
Nous avons **plusieurs** pièces à côté.	*We have several rooms next door.*
On remet ça à un autre jour.	*We'll postpone that to another day.*

⚠ **plusieurs** does not add an **-e** in the feminine.

● As pronouns

Je ne vois **aucun** des deux.	*I can't see either of them.*
Les autres sont au troisième étage.	*The others are on the third floor.*
Certains préfèrent travailler ici.	*Some prefer to work here.*
Plusieurs des pièces sont délabrées.	*Several of the rooms are dilapidated.*
Toutes sont à décorer.	*All have to be decorated.*
J'en ai vu **plusieurs**.	*I saw several.*

➤ See agreement of adjectives (1) in Unit 17, negatives in Units 82 and 83.

1 **Match the two halves of each sentence, then find the English translation below.**

E.g. Toutes + les pièces sont déjà réservées. *All the rooms are already reserved.*

a Toutes   **i** ont été repeints.

b Les autres ont   **j** pris le bus.

c Certaines   **k** les chambres sont déjà réservées.

d Tous les projets   **l** des voyageurs n'est arrivé.

e Tous les bureaux   **m** des voitures ont été réparées.

f Plusieurs   **n** sont terminés.

g Les autres   **o** personnes ont acheté des billets.

h Aucun   **p** voitures sont déjà vendues.

1 *Some of the cars have been repaired.*

2 *All the rooms are already reserved.*

3 *The others took the bus.*

4 *None of the travellers has arrived.*

5 *The other cars are already sold.*

6 *Several people have bought tickets.*

7 *All the projects are finished.*

8 *All the offices have been repainted.*

2 **Complete the following using the appropriate form of the word in brackets.**

E.g. Il a préparé (tout) les brochures (*nf*). → Il a préparé toutes les brochures.

a Il y a (plusieurs) voitures (*nf*) à vendre.

b (Tout) les employés (*nm*) sont arrivés.

c Tu as l'(autre) dépliant (*nm*)?

d (Tout) les détails (*nm*) du projet ont été expliqués.

e J'ai (certain) idées (*nf*) à discuter avec vous.

3 **Complete the gaps with an appropriate word from the box using the English as a guide.**

E.g. **Tous** les étudiants sont arrivés. *All the students have arrived.*

plusieurs	autre	certaines	autres	tous	plusieurs

a Les _____ spectateurs sont arrivés. *The other spectators have arrived.*

b _____ personnes disent que c'est trop tard. *Certain people say it's too late.*

c Il y a _____ documents à préparer. *There are several documents to prepare.*

d J'ai rangé _____ les papiers. *I've tidied all the papers.*

e Il a réparé l' _____ voiture. *He's repaired the other car.*

f _____ demandent à vous voir. *Several are asking to see you.*

29 UNIT | Indefinite adjectives and pronouns (2)

A The following indefinites can be used only as adjectives.

chaque	*each*
quelque(s)	*some, a few*
tel(s), telle(s)	*such*

Chaque élève a reçu un stylo.	*Each pupil received a pen.*
Quelque temps après, il est arrivé.	*Some time later, he arrived.*
Il a fait quelques commentaires.	*He made a few comments.*
Cela nous a fait un tel problème!	*That caused us such a problem!*
Vous voyez la question telle qu'elle est.	*You see the question as it is.*

B The following indefinites can be used only as pronouns.

chacun, chacun(e)	*each one*
personne	*no one*
quelque chose	*something*
quelqu'un	*someone*
quelques-uns, quelques-unes	*some (people)*

● **Chacun, chacune**

Chacun peut prendre un stylo.	*Everyone can take a pen.*

● **Personne** can be used on its own or as part of a negative.

Qui est là? Personne.	*Who's there? No one.*
Il n'y a personne là.	*There's no one there.*

● **Quelque chose**

J'ai acheté quelque chose au marché.	*I bought something at the market.*

● **Quelqu'un, quelques-un(e)s**

⚠ The plural of this is formed with a hyphen.

Il y a quelqu'un à la porte.	*There's someone at the door.*
Quelques-uns désirent partir plus tôt.	*Some want to leave earlier.*

➤ See agreement of adjectives (1) in Unit 17, negatives in Units 82 and 83.

1 **Match the sentence halves, then find their English translation.**

E.g. **Il veut + quelque chose.** *He wants something.*

a J'ai perdu
b Elle a donné un projet
c J'en ai vu
d J'ai vu
e Tu veux
f Il parle de

g quelqu'un.
h quelque chose à boire?
i quelqu'un.
j quelque chose.
k quelques-uns en bas.
l à chacun des employés.

1 *She's given a project to each employee.*
2 *I've lost something.*
3 *I saw some downstairs.*
4 *He's talking about someone.*
5 *I saw someone.*
6 *Would you like something to drink?*

2 **Complete the gaps with an appropriate word from the box, using the English as a guide.**

E.g. **J'ai perdu** _____ . **J'ai perdu quelque chose.** *I've lost something.*

chaque	chacune	quelque chose	quelqu'un	quelqu'un
	chacun	personne	quelques-unes	

a _____ a téléphoné. *Someone has telephoned.*
b _____ doit prendre un billet. *Each (one) must take a ticket.*
c Le bureau est vide. _____ n'y travaille. *The office is empty. No one works in there.*
d _____ voyageur porte une valise. *Each traveller is carrying one case.*
e Vous avez des brochures? Oui, j'en ai _____ . *Do you have brochures? Yes, I've got a few.*
f Il reste encore _____ à faire. *There's still something to do.*
g _____ vous attend. *Someone is waiting for you.*
h J'ai parlé avec _____ des infirmières. *I have spoken with each of the nurses.*

3 **Translate into French, referring to the previous unit where necessary.**

a *Some work hard.*
b *Brochures? There are a few on the table.*
c *Every day I arrive at 6 o'clock.*
d *Each eats in his room.*
e *I have all the documents.*
f *She has several (women) friends.*

30 UNIT | The verb

A Verbs are words that show an *action* or a *state* of affairs and are often called 'doing words'.

B Verbs have a basic form that is called the *infinitive* (in English *to ...*). In French the infinitive is indicated by the end of the word: *to carry* = **porter**, *to finish* = **finir**, *to sell* = **vendre**.

C Verbs can be classified into groups. There are two big groups – *regular* verbs and *irregular* verbs. Regular verbs have a common pattern of change (see E below) and are classified into three main types according to the ending of their infinitive: the **-er** verbs, the **-ir** verbs and the **-re** verbs. Irregular verbs each have an individual pattern.

D When a verb is used it has a *subject* which shows who is doing the action. The subject can be a noun or a pronoun: *the women work, he runs*.

E When a verb is shown in its pattern it is shown with the *subject pronouns* (*I*, *you*, etc.). Changing the infinitive to match its subject is called *conjugating* the verb, for example:

je porte	I carry	nous portons	we carry
tu portes	you carry	vous portez	you carry
il porte	he carries	ils portent	they carry
elle porte	she carries	elles portent	they carry

F Verbs also change because of their *tense*. Different tenses indicate that an action occurs in the present, in the future or in the past, for example:

present tense	je travaille	I work, I am working
future tense	je travaillerai	I will work
perfect tense	j'ai travaillé	I have worked, I worked
imperfect tense	je travaillais	I used to work, I was working

G The perfect tense is an example of a *compound tense*. That means it is made up of two verbs, the *auxiliary* (**ai** above) and the *main verb* (**travaillé** above).

H Verbs can be used
   - in the *indicative*: the normal everyday use, as those shown in F above
   - in the *conditional*: **je préférerais** *I would like*
   - in the *imperative*: for giving orders or instructions. *Come here.* **Venez ici.**
   - in the *subjunctive*: used in French to show, for example, doubt or emotion.

30 UNIT | The verb – *Exercises*

1 **Underline the verbs in the following passage. One has been done for you.**

We usually <u>arrive</u> at work at about 8.30. We go by train, unless one of us needs the car during the day for some reason. When we get there Angela goes off to the offices, where she has a job in the dispatch department, and I go to the production unit, which is the main part of the plant of course.

2 **Now underline the verbs in this French passage. Again, one has been done for you.**

Ma journée typique <u>commence</u> à six heures, quand je me lève. Je pars pour le bureau vers sept heures et demie. Je prends le train. Je mange à midi à la cantine. Je finis vers cinq heures. Le soir, on mange à sept heures et après je regarde la télévision ou je lis un peu. Quelquefois j'ai du travail à faire.

3 **Underline the infinitive in each of the following sentences.**

E.g. Je sais <u>nager</u>. *I can swim.*

a Je voudrais manger maintenant. *I'd like to eat now.*
b Vous pouvez venir avec nous. *You can come with us.*
c Je vais prendre des vacances. *I am going to take a holiday.*
d Est-ce que tu peux acheter une bouteille de vin? *Can you buy a bottle of wine?*
e Il commence à travailler vers neuf heures. *He starts working at about nine o'clock.*

4 **Underline the subject of each verb in the following passage. One has been done for you.**

<u>Elle</u> s'appelle Josie et elle travaille à Paris. Le bureau de Josie est dans le nord de la ville. Il est près de la gare du Nord. Elle travaille avec huit collègues. Ils sont très aimables, et ils s'entendent bien. La patronne s'appelle Madame André. Son père a fondé (*founded*) l'entreprise (*company*) en 1977.

5 **Match the subject pronouns to the correct part of the verb.**

E.g. ils + portent

| 1 nous | 2 vous | **a** portes | **b** portons |
| 3 tu | 4 elles | **c** portent | **d** portez |

6 **Say whether the following phrases refer to the present, the past or the future.**

E.g. *he had been* → past

a We were.
b They'll be.
c You have worked.
d She went.
e They are waiting.
f They can stay.

61

31 UNIT | Present tense (1): regular -er verbs

A large number of French verbs follow a regular pattern. The largest group are those whose infinitive ends in -er.

A To use a regular **-er** verb in the present tense firstly remove the **-er** from the infinitive, which will leave you with the stem of the verb.

travail**er** *to work* → **travaill-** = stem

You then add the appropriate ending to this stem, as follows.

Singular endings			Plural endings		
I	je	**-e**	*we*	nous	**-ons**
you	tu	**-es**	*you*	vous	**-ez**
he	il	**-e**	*they*	ils	**-ent**
she	elle	**-e**	*they*	elles	**-ent**

⚠ The pronunciation of the verb is the same for all the endings, apart from the **nous** and **vous** forms.

B Here is an example.

TRAVAILLER *to work*	
je travaille	nous travaillons
tu travailles	vous travaillez
il travaille	ils travaillent
elle travaille	elles travaillent

C Here are some common **-er** verbs.

aimer *to like, to love*
arriver *to arrive*
chanter *to sing*
chercher *to look for*
écouter *to listen to*
fermer *to close*
jouer *to play*

parler *to speak*
porter *to carry, to wear*
préparer *to prepare*
regarder *to watch*
rester *to stay*
traverser *to cross*
trouver *to find*

D In French there is no equivalent to the English continuous present tense: *I speak* and *I am speaking* are both translated by **je parle**. Here are some more examples.

Elle écoute la radio.
Nous jouons aux cartes.
Il cherche son portable.

She listens/She's listening to the radio.
We play/We're playing cards.
He's looking for his mobile phone.

1 **By looking at the endings of the following verbs, and at the English sentences, fill in the correct subject pronoun (*je, tu*, etc.).**

E.g. *Nous* préparons un repas. *We are preparing a meal.*

a _____ arrive à la gare. *He arrives at the station.*
b _____ aimons le vin. *We like wine.*
c _____ préparez les papiers. *You prepare the papers.*
d _____ travaille au centre de Paris. *I work in the centre of Paris.*
e _____ joues au tennis? *Do you play tennis?*

2 **Complete the following sentences by filling in the correct verb endings.**

E.g. *Vous regard_____ la télévision. You're watching television.* **Vous** *regardez* **la télévision.**

a Elle port_____ une jupe. *She's wearing a skirt.*
b Ils écout_____ la radio. *They're listening to the radio.*
c Je prépar_____ le déjeuner. *I'm preparing lunch.*
d Tu cherch_____ quelque chose? *Are you looking for something?*
e Vous rest _____ chez vous? *Are you staying at home*

3 **Say what the following people are doing using the present tense of the verbs in the box.**

E.g. **a Elle travaille.**

jouer	travailler	parler

a

b

c

32 Present tense (2): -er verbs with changes in the stem

Some -er verbs have the same endings as regular -er verbs, but the spelling changes slightly in the stem.

A Most verbs ending in **-eter** and **-eler** double the consonant before an unsounded **-e**, that is in all but the **nous** and **vous** forms.

JETER *to throw*		APPELER *to call*	
je jette	nous jetons	j'appelle	nous appelons
tu jettes	vous jetez	tu appelles	vous appelez
il/elle jette	ils/elles jettent	il/elle appelle	ils/elles appellent

Similarly **geler** *to freeze*, **peler** *to peel*.

B Some verbs ending in **e** + consonant + **er**, or **é** + consonant + **er** take a grave accent before an unsounded **-e**, that is in all but the **nous** and **vous** forms.

ACHETER *to buy*		ESPÉRER *to hope*	
j'achète	nous achetons	j'espère	nous espérons
tu achètes	vous achetez	tu espères	vous espérez
il/elle achète	ils/elles achètent	il/elle espère	ils/elles espèrent

Similarly **lever** *to lift, to raise*, **préférer** *to prefer*.

C Verbs ending in **-oyer** or **-uyer** change the **y** to an **i** except in the **nous** and **vous** forms.

ENVOYER *to send*		S'ENNUYER *to be bored*	
j'envoie	nous envoyons	je m'ennuie	nous nous ennuyons
tu envoies	vous envoyez	tu t'ennuies	vous vous ennuyez
il/elle envoie	ils/elles envoient	il/elle s'ennuie	ils/elles s'ennuient

Similarly **employer** *to use*.

⚠ The same change occurs but is optional in the present tense of verbs that end in **-ayer** (**payer** *to pay*, **essayer** *to try*).

D -er verbs that end in **-ger** take an **-e** after the **-g-** in the **nous** form, and verbs ending in **-cer** change the **-c** to **-ç** in the **nous** form. This is in order to retain the soft **g** or **c** sound.

> manger *to eat* nous mangeons *we eat/we are eating*
> commencer *to begin* nous commençons *we begin/we are beginning*

Insert the correct subject to match the verb. (For some verbs there is more than one possible subject.)

E.g. _____ essayons. → **Nous essayons.**

a _____ commencez.

b _____ jette.

c _____ achètent.

d _____ mangeons.

e _____ emploie.

f _____ répètes.

g _____ partagez.

h _____ jetons.

i _____ avance.

j _____ espère.

Fill in the correct part of the missing verb.

E.g. Tu _____ . (jeter) → **Tu jettes.**

a J' _____ . (appeler)

b Nous _____ dans la mer. (nager)

c Ils _____ de dormir. (essayer)

d Tu _____ souvent des spaghetti? (manger)

e Elle _____ des cadeaux. (acheter)

f Nous _____ le repas à huit heures. (commencer)

g Il _____ toujours la même chose. (répéter)

h Elles _____ des cartes postales à leurs amis. (envoyer)

Find answers to the following questions using the jumbled sentences.

E.g. **Vous vous levez à quelle heure?** heures lève me je sept à → **Je me lève à sept heures.**

a Vous préférez le cinéma ou le théâtre?

b Vous achetez quelque chose pour Léon?

c Vous mangez souvent au restaurant?

d Vous espérez aller où en vacances?

1 mangeons au beaucoup oui nous restaurant

2 le préfère je théâtre

3 en aller j' France espère

4 je livre un achète lui

33 UNIT | Present tense (3): regular -ir verbs

A To use a regular **-ir** verb in the present tense remove the **-ir** from the infinitive, which will leave you with the stem of the verb.

remp**lir** *to fill* → **rempl-** = stem

You then add the appropriate ending to this stem as follows.

	Singular endings			Plural endings	
I	je	**-is**	*we*	nous	**-issons**
you	tu	**-is**	*you*	vous	**-issez**
he	il	**-it**	*they*	ils	**-issent**
she	elle	**-it**	*they*	elles	**-issent**

⚠ The **je**, **tu**, **il** and **elle** forms are pronounced in the same way: the final **-s** and **-t** are not pronounced.

B Here is an example.

FINIR *to finish*	
je finis	nous finissons
tu finis	vous finissez
il finit	ils finissent
elle finit	elles finissent

C Here are some common **-ir** verbs.

applaudir *to applaud, to clap*   obéir *to obey*
choisir *to choose*   réfléchir *to think about*
grandir *to grow*   réussir *to succeed*
maigrir *to lose weight*   rougir *to blush*

D There are a small number of **-ir** verbs that take the endings of **-er** verbs in the present tense.

OUVRIR *to open*	
j'ouvre	nous ouvrons
tu ouvres	vous ouvrez
il ouvre	ils ouvrent
elle ouvre	elles ouvrent

Other verbs in this group include **offrir** *to offer*, **souffrir** *to suffer* and **cueillir** *to pick, to gather*.

33 UNIT — Present tense (3) regular -ir verbs – *Exercises*

1 Unscramble the verbs in the following sentences.

E.g. Elle veoru. → Elle ouvre. *She opens.*

a Nous snsfonisi. *We finish.*
b Elle ogrtui. *She is blushing.*
c Je smgairi. *I'm losing weight.*
d Vous zuéssisers. *You succeed.*
e Tu asgnrdi. *You are growing.*

2 Match the words in the left-hand list with those on the right to make the English sentences below.

E.g. Je + finis vers six heures. *I finish at about six o'clock.*

a J'
b Elles
c Il
d Nous
e Vous
f Tu
g Ils
h Elle
i Je
j Vous
k Je

l offrons un cadeau.
m cueillent des fleurs.
n remplissez la fiche.
o attends un bus.
p ouvre la porte.
q choisit une chemise rouge.
r grossissent.
s maigrissez, Michel!
t rougit.
u réussis.
v finis vers six heures.

1 *They are picking flowers.*
2 *We give a gift.*
3 *I am succeeding.*
4 *You wait for a bus.*
5 *I open the door.*
6 *She is blushing.*
7 *He chooses a red shirt.*
8 *They are putting on weight.*
9 *You are losing weight, Michel!*
10 *You fill in the form.*
11 *I finish at about six o'clock.*

3 Replace the infinitive in brackets with the correct form of the verb.

E.g. Je (rougir) *I blush.* → Je rougis.

a Il (obéir) *He obeys.*
b Ils (applaudir) *They are clapping.*
c Nous (réussir) *We are succeeding.*
d Elle (finir) *She finishes.*
e Vous (ouvrir) *You open.*
f Elles (souffrir) *They are suffering.*
g Tu (offrir) *You offer.*
h Je (cueillir) *I am picking.*

4 Translate the following into French.

a *She is opening the present.*
b *He chooses a pen.*
c *Everyone applauds.*
d *They fill the bottles.*
e *It's suffering.*
f *I'm thinking about it.*

67

A third category of verbs end in -re in the infinitive, and many follow a common pattern.

A To use an **-re** verb in the present tense remove the **-re** from the infinitive, which will leave you with the stem of the verb.

vend**re** *to sell* → **vend-** = stem

You then add the appropriate ending to this stem as follows.

	Singular endings			Plural endings	
I	je	**-s**	*we*	nous	**-ons**
you	tu	**-s**	*you*	vous	**-ez**
he	il	**–**	*they*	ils	**-ent**
she	elle	**–**	*they*	elles	**-ent**

You will notice that the latter half of the verb (plural endings) follows the same pattern as regular **-er** verbs.

⚠ Pronunciation of the **je**, **tu**, **il** and **elle** forms is the same. Although the **-ent** ending isn't pronounced, for **ils** and **elles** it does cause the preceding consonant to be pronounced (e.g. in **ils vendent** you pronounce the **d**).

B Here is an example.

PERDRE *to lose*	
je perds	nous perdons
tu perds	vous perdez
il perd	ils perdent
elle perd	elles perdent

C Further examples of **-re** verbs that follow this pattern in the present tense are:

vendre *to sell*
attendre *to wait (for)*
répondre *to reply, to answer*
descendre *to descend, to go down*

fondre *to melt*
entendre *to hear*
rendre *to give back, to return*
correspondre *to correspond*

Je vends des voitures.	*I sell cars.*
Tu attends le bus, Michel?	*Are you waiting for the bus, Michel?*
Il répond à la question.	*He replies to the question.*
Nous descendons maintenant.	*We are coming down now.*
Ils rendent l'argent.	*They return the money.*
Elles entendent un bruit.	*They hear a noise.*

Present tense (4): regular -re verbs – *Exercises*

1 Match the words in the left-hand list with those on the right. In some cases more than one combination is possible.

E.g. Ils + entendent

a elle
b je
c il
d nous
e tu
f ils
g vous
h elles

i rends
j vend
k correspondez
l perdent
m répond
n entends
o attendons
p descendent

2 Insert the correct form of the verb into the gap provided.

E.g. il _____ , vous _____ (rendre) → **il rend, vous rendez**

a j' _____ , ils _____ (attendre)
b vous _____ , elle _____ (vendre)
c je _____ , il _____ (répondre)
d tu _____ , elles _____ (entendre)
e ils _____ , nous _____ (perdre)
f nous _____ , il _____ (descendre)
g elles _____ , elle _____ (correspondre)
h il _____ , ils _____ (fondre)

3 Unscramble the verbs to complete the sentences.

E.g. J' _____ quelque chose (nstdene) *I can hear something.* → **J'entends quelque chose.**

a Je _____ toujours. (psornéd) *I always answer.*
b Mes amis _____ le bus. (dteatnten) *My friends are waiting for the bus.*
c Vous _____ des cartes postales? (nzvdee) *Do you sell postcards?*
d Elle _____ le livre à sa tante. (ndre) *She returns the book to her aunt.*
e Nous _____ avec des amis français. (rdcnonssropoe) *We correspond with French friends.*

4 Translate the following into French.

a *I'm selling this bike.*
b *They're waiting for the train.*
c *He's coming down the mountain now.*
d *She replies to the letter.*

35 Present tense (5): reflexive verbs

Reflexive verbs express an action that reflects back to the subject. Their infinitives include the reflexive pronoun se.

A Reflexive verbs are recognisable in the infinitive by the reflexive pronoun **se**. They can be **-er**, **-ir**, or **-re** verbs and are conjugated in the same way as other verbs. The reflexive pronoun **se** changes according to the subject.

Common reflexive verbs include **s'amuser** *to enjoy oneself*, **se promener** *to go for a walk*, **s'appeler** *to be called*, **se doucher** *to shower*, **se raser** *to shave*, **s'arrêter** *to stop*, **s'habiller** *to get dressed*, **se reposer** *to rest*, **se coucher** *to go to bed*, **se lever** *to get up*, **se réveiller** *to wake up*.

B Here is an example of a reflexive verb, showing conjugation and all the reflexive pronouns.

SE LAVER *to wash (oneself)*	
je **me** lave	nous **nous** lavons
tu **te** laves	vous **vous** lavez
il/elle **se** lave	ils/elles **se** lavent

C Reflexive verbs are also used to describe action to parts of the body.

Je me brosse les dents.	*I brush my teeth.*
Elle se casse la jambe.	*She breaks her leg.*

D Two common reflexive verbs are **se passer** *to happen* and **se trouver** *to be situated*.

Qu'est-ce qui se passe?	*What is happening?*
Le village se trouve au sud de Paris.	*The village is south of Paris.*

E A number of verbs that are not normally reflexive can be used reflexively to include the meaning *each other, oneself, themselves,* or *to each other*.

Je me demande où il est?	*I wonder ('ask myself') where he is?*
Ils se téléphonent chaque jour.	*They telephone each other every day.*

When used in such cases with **on** meaning *we*, the reflexive pronoun **se** means *(to) ourselves* or *(to) each other/one another*.

On s'écrit souvent.	*We often write to each other.*

Non-reflexive verbs can be used reflexively where in English we might use a passive to say how things are done, or how they happen, or how they are.

Ça s'écrit avec un S.	*It's written/spelt with an S.*
Ça se dit.	*It's said like that./You hear that.*
Ce vin se boit avec le poisson.	*This wine is drunk with fish.*

➤ See uses of the articles in Unit 3, the imperative in Unit 56, reflexives in the perfect tense in Unit 62, the passive in Unit 74.

Unscramble the following sentences.

E.g. douche matin je me le. *I shower in the morning.* → **Je me douche le matin.**

a il à lève se heures sept. *He gets up at seven o'clock.*

b les brossent elles dents se. *They brush their teeth.*

c nous à heures couchons nous onze. *We go to bed at eleven o'clock.*

d les me cheveux lave je. *I wash my hair.*

e réveillez à vous heures vous six. *You wake up at six o'clock.*

f elle huit s' à habille heures. *She gets dressed at eight o'clock.*

g promènent se ensemble ils. *They go for a walk together.*

h le car s' devant arrête cinéma le. *The coach stops in front of the cinema.*

Fill in the missing words.

E.g. Elles **se lèvent** à six heures et demie.   **a** Elle _____ à sept heures.

b Je _____ à sept heures et demie.   **c** Il _____ à minuit.

Fill in the missing words. The translation below may help you.

Je **me réveille** à sept heures. Je _____ dix minutes plus tard, puis je _____ dans la salle de bains. Je _____ . Puis je bois une tasse de café dans la cuisine. En général, je mange des toasts, puis je _____ les dents. Le weekend je _____ à neuf heures, et quelquefois je _____ en ville.

I wake up at seven o'clock. I get up ten minutes later, then I get washed in the bathroom. I get dressed. Then I drink a cup of coffee in the kitchen. Usually I eat some toast, then I brush my teeth. At the weekend I get up at nine o'clock, and sometimes I go for a walk in town.

36 UNIT | Subject pronouns

Subject pronouns can stand in place of a noun to indicate who is performing the action of a verb. They are words such as I, you, he, she, etc.

A

Singular	Grammatical name	Plural	Grammatical name
je *I*	first-person singular	nous *we*	first-person plural
tu *you*	second-person singular	vous *you*	second-person plural
il *he, it*	third-person singular	ils *they*	third-person plural
elle *she, it*	third-person singular	elles *they*	third-person plural
on *one (they)*	third-person singular		

B The subject pronoun goes before the verb in a statement (or in a statement used as a question), or after the verb in a question. **Je** becomes **j'** before a vowel.

J'apprends le français.	*I'm learning French.*
Allez-vous en France cette année?	*Are you going to France this year?*
Elle ne va pas au musée.	*She's not going to the museum.*

C The second-person singular **tu** is familiar and used when addressing people you are close to, children and pets. **Vous** is formal and is used with all other individuals. **Vous** is also used when addressing more than one person, whether you know them closely or not.

D **Il**, **elle**, **ils** and **elles** are used for both people and things and mean *he, she, it* and *they*. These must always be the same in number and gender as the noun they are referring to.

Paul? Il est ici. Anne? Elle est là-bas.	*Paul? He's here. Anne? She's over there.*
Cette église? Elle est très vieille.	*This church? It's very old.*
Les poires? Elles sont dans la cuisine.	*The pears? They're in the kitchen.*

E Several masculine nouns together, or several feminine nouns together, are referred to by the appropriate gender of pronoun in the plural.

Paul et Henri, où sont-ils?	*Where are Paul and Henri?*
Ghislaine et Marie, où sont-elles?	*Where are Ghislaine and Marie?*

When a mixed group of males and females, or of masculine and feminine objects, are referred to together with one pronoun, that pronoun is masculine plural.

Paul et Ghislaine, où sont-ils?	*Where are Paul and Ghislaine?*
La cathédrale et le château, ils datent du 15ème siècle.	*The cathedral and the château date from the 15th century.*

➤ See the subject pronoun on in Unit 37, verbs with more than one subject in Unit 54.

1 **Give the correct subject pronoun as shown by the form of the verb and by the English.**

E.g. _____ allons. *We go.* → **Nous allons.**

a _____ porte. *I carry.*

b _____ mangent. *They eat.* (feminine)

c _____ travaillons. *We work.*

d _____ part. *She leaves.*

e _____ finit. *He finishes.*

f _____ finis. *You finish.* (familiar)

g _____ arrive. *He arrives.*

h _____ partez. *You leave.* (plural)

i _____ vont. *They go.* (masculine)

j _____ changez. *You change.* (formal)

k _____ mange. *One eats.*

l _____ tombe. *It's falling.*

2 **Give the English for the following phrases.**

E.g. **Je mange.** → *I eat/am eating.*

a Il travaille.

b Elles portent.

c Vous mangez.

d Je finis.

e Ils arrivent.

f Nous mangeons.

g Tu arrives.

h Elle change.

3 **Give the French for the following phrases.**

E.g. *She dances.* → **Elle danse.**

a *He eats.*

b *They change.* (feminine)

c *She finishes.*

d *They sell.* (masculine)

e *We carry.*

f *I arrive.*

g *You work.* (formal)

h *You work.* (familiar)

4 **Complete the sentences with the correct subject pronoun, using the English and the words in brackets as a guide.**

E.g. _____ sont en vacances. (**Marie et Hélène**) *They are on holiday.* → **Elles sont en vacances.**

a _____ sont sur le bureau. (la disquette et les documents) *They're on the desk.*

b _____ travaillent très dur. (Jeannette et Claire) *They work very hard.*

c _____ vont au cinéma. (Pierre et Marc) *They're going to the cinema.*

d _____ commencent à huit heures. (le spectacle et le film) *They start at eight o'clock.*

37 UNIT | Subject pronoun: *on*

The subject pronoun **on** *is used frequently in French. It refers to an unspecified person or people and is generally translated by one, people, someone, we or they.*

On can refer to one person or several, its meaning depending on the context in which it is used. It is always used with the third-person singular part of the verb.

On m'a dit qu'il pleut.	*Someone told me it's raining.*
On se retrouve au cinéma?	*Shall we meet at the cinema?*

A **On** can mean *one*, non-specific *you*, *they* or *people*.

En général on va en vacances en été.	*People usually go on holiday in summer.*
On mange quand on a faim.	*You eat when you are hungry./One eats when one is hungry.*
On ne sait jamais.	*You never know./One never knows.*
En France on boit du vin pendant le repas.	*In France they drink wine with meals.*

B **On** can mean *someone* or non-specific *they*, and is often used in French when a passive form is used in English.

On m'a donné un plan de la ville.	*Someone gave me/I was given a town map.*
On va demander une pièce d'identité.	*Someone/They will ask/You'll be asked for a means of identification.*
On m'a dit que tu étais au théâtre hier soir.	*Someone told me/I was told you were at the theatre last night.*

C In informal French **on** is often used to mean *we* instead of **nous**.

On t'a vu au théâtre hier soir.	*We saw you at the theatre last night.*
Qu'est-ce qu'on va faire?	*What shall we do?*
On va en ville?	*Shall we go to town?*

- When **on** replaces **nous**, any adjective used is usually in the plural, although the verb remains in the singular.

Nous sommes fatigués.	*We are tired.*
On est fatigués.	*We are tired.*

- In compound tenses with **être** the past participle can be singular or plural.

On est rentré(-s/-es) à minuit.	*We came home at midnight.*
On est arrivé(-s/-es) trop tard.	*We arrived too late.*

➤ See agreement of adjectives in Units 17 and 18, avoidance of the passive in Unit 74, compound tenses in Units 60–63 (perfect), 66 (pluperfect), 69 (future perfect), 71 (conditional perfect).

1 Match the French and English sentences.

E.g. On va à la piscine? → *Shall we go to the swimming pool?*

a On mange au restaurant ce soir?   1 *Are you eating out this evening?*

b Il regarde la télé ce soir.   2 *In England we drive on the left.*

c Tu manges au restaurant ce soir?   3 *Have you got some money?*

d En Angleterre on roule à gauche.   4 *Have we got any money?*

e On a de l'argent?   5 *He's watching TV this evening.*

f Tu as de l'argent?   6 *Shall we eat out tonight?*

2 Replace the *nous* form with *on* in the following sentences, choosing the verb from among those in the box.

E.g. Nous partons bientôt? *Shall we leave soon?* → On part bientôt?

| prend | lit | ~~part~~ | aime | fait | va | sort | choisit |

a Nous aimons bien le vin rouge. *We really like red wine.*

b Nous allons au cinéma plus tard. *We're going to the cinema later.*

c Nous prenons du poisson. *We'll have fish.*

d Nous faisons du vélo cet après-midi? *Shall we go for a cycle ride this afternoon?*

3 Complete the following sentences using the correct form of the adjective or past participle given in brackets.

E.g. Marc et moi, on est (satisfait). *Marc and I – we're satisfied.* → Marc et moi, on est satisfaits.

a Jacques et moi, on est si (fatigué). *Jacques and I – we're so tired.*

b Les Jacquelin? On est (allé) les voir hier soir. *The Jacquelins? We went to see them last night.*

c Nous, on est (venu) à midi. *We left at midday.*

d Hélène et moi, on est très (content) de te voir. *Helen and I are very pleased to see you.*

e Oui, on est (arrivé) ensemble. *Yes, we arrived together.*

f On est (parti) en vacances avec les enfants. *We went on holiday with the children.*

4 Translate the following using *on*.

a *We're going to France at Easter.*

b *We eat at eight.*

c *Shall we meet tomorrow?*

d *Sometimes we prefer the cinema to the theatre.*

38 UNIT Emphatic pronouns

Emphatic pronouns are usually used for emphasis or after a preposition, as in the examples I don't know, It's me!, Go with him.

A Here is a full list of emphatic pronouns.

Singular		Plural	
moi	*me*	nous	*us*
toi	*you*	vous	*you*
lui	*him*	eux	*them*
elle	*her*	elles	*them*
soi	*oneself*		

B These pronouns are often used for emphasis of the subject or object.

Moi, j'aime voyager en voiture.   *I like travelling by car.*

Tu m'énerves, toi!   *You get on my nerves, you do!*

C They are also used with **c'est** or **ce sont** (in any tense) and with **qui** and **que**.

C'est moi.   *It's me.*

C'est moi qui vais en ville.   *I'm the one who's going into town.*

C'est elle que je vois régulièrement.   *She's the one I see regularly.*

D They can be used in answer to a question and after **pas**.

Qui a-t-elle rencontré? Lui!   *Who did she meet? Him!*

Qui veut faire la vaisselle? Pas moi!   *Who wants to wash up? Not me!*

E Emphatic pronouns are used after prepositions, including: **après** *after*, **avant** *before*, **avec** *with*, **chez** *at the home of*, **derrière** *behind*, **devant** *in front of*, **pour** *for*, **sans** *without*, **vers** *towards*.

chez moi *at my place, at home*   derrière lui *behind him*

They are used after the preposition **à** to show possession.

Cette veste est à moi.   *This jacket is mine.*

F After **comme**.

Elle travaille à Paris comme moi.   *She works in Paris like me.*

G With comparisons.

Il court plus vite que moi.   *He runs faster than me.*

H With a double subject or object.

Mon mari et moi y seront.   *My husband and I will be there.*

➤ See c'est in Unit 8, prepositions in Units 10–15, comparison of adjectives and of adverbs in Units 24 and 25, object pronouns y and en in Unit 46, verbs with more than one subject in Unit 54.

1 Complete the gaps with an appropriate emphatic pronoun.

– Le poisson est pour qui?   – Après _____
– Pour _____ s'il vous plaît.

2 Choose the appropriate emphatic pronoun to complete the sentences.

a J'arrive avant moi/vous.

b Vous voulez manger avec moi/vous?

c Henri, je prépare un repas pour toi/lui.

d Anne est ici. Voici une tasse de café pour elle/lui.

e Pierre et Sylvie arrivent à cinq heures. Je pars en vacances avec nous/eux.

3 Complete the following conversation using suitable emphatic pronouns from the box. One has been done for you in bold.

– Qu'est qu'on fait ce soir?

| ~~toi~~ | moi | nous | moi | elle |

– _____ , je voudrais regarder un
film à la télé. Et **toi**?

– _____ , je veux sortir avec les autres. Tu ne veux pas venir avec _____ ?

– Non, mon amie ne va pas très bien. Je vais rester avec _____ .

4 Match the following sentences and then insert an appropriate emphatic pronoun.

E.g. Ce stylo est à _____ . *This pen is mine.* → Ce stylo est à *moi.*

a Ce journal est à _____ , l'autre
est à _____ .

b J'ai écrit la lettre pour _____ .

c Ils partent sans _____ !

d Ce porte-clés n'est pas à _____ .

1 *I wrote the letter for them.*

2 *This newspaper is mine, the other is his.*

3 *This key-ring is not ours.*

4 *They are leaving without us!*

5 Translate the following into French.

a *I prefer red wine.*

b *He works here, not me.*

c *Her? She's got a headache.*

d *Me, I'm going with them.*

39 UNIT **Possessive pronouns**

Possessive pronouns are words such as mine, yours, his, hers *and* theirs, *which stand in place of a possessive adjective + noun.*

The form of the possessive pronoun, like the possessive adjective (**mon, ma, mes**, etc.) is determined by the person owning (*mine, yours*, etc.) and by the gender and number of the noun it stands for.

| Tu peux me prêter ton journal? J'ai oublié le mien. | *Can you lend me your newspaper? I've forgotten mine.* |

A

	Masculine singular	Feminine singular	Masculine plural	Feminine plural
mine	le mien	la mienne	les miens	les miennes
yours	le tien	la tienne	les tiens	les tiennes
his/hers/its/one's	le sien	la sienne	les siens	les siennes
ours	le nôtre	la nôtre	les nôtres	
yours	le vôtre	la vôtre	les vôtres	
theirs	le leur	la leur	les leurs	

Merci bien. Ça c'est ma tasse, à côté de la sienne. (*i.e. feminine singular for* tasse)	*Thank you very much. That's my cup next to his/hers.*
Voici un stylo. C'est le tien? (*i.e. masculine singular for* stylo)	*Here's a pen. Is it yours?*
J'ai mes papiers. Vous avez les vôtres? (*i.e. masculine plural for* papiers)	*I've got my papers. Have you got yours?*

B The definite article (**le, la, les**) is an integral part of the possessive pronoun. When occurring with **à** or **de** it combines with them in the usual way.

J'aime bien ta robe – je la préfère à la mienne.	*I like your dress – I prefer it to mine.*
Votre bureau est à côté du mien.	*Your office is next to mine.*
Nos chambres sont en face des leurs.	*Our rooms are opposite theirs.*

C **À** + an emphatic pronoun (**moi, toi**, etc.) is used to indicate who something belongs to.

| Cette photo est à qui? Elle est à moi/nous. | *Whose is this photo? It's mine/ours.* |
| À qui est ce foulard? C'est à elle. | *Whose is this scarf? It's hers.* |

➤ *See the preposition* à *in Unit 14, the partitive article (for declension of* de*) in Unit 9, possessive adjectives in Unit 16, emphatic pronouns in Unit 38.*

39 UNIT Possessive pronouns – Exercises

1 **Choose the correct option in the following sentences and translate them into English.**

E.g. Ce journal est **le mien**/la mienne. *This paper is mine.*

a Voici ma tasse. Où est **le vôtre/la tienne**?

b Elle préfère sa voiture **au nôtre/à la tienne**.

c J'ai mon porte-monnaie. Elle a **le sien/les siens**.

d Je donne ces bonbons à mes enfants, donnez les glaces **aux tiennes /aux vôtres**.

e Ma clé est dans la voiture. Tu as **le tien/la tienne**?

f Notre jardin est plus petit que **la sienne/le tien**.

2 **Replace the phrase in italics with an appropriate possessive pronoun.**

E.g. Il a son journal et *mon journal.* → Il a son journal et **le mien.**

a Ce sont mes gants. Où sont *tes gants*?

b Je préfère ta voiture à *sa voiture*.

c Paul va chercher ses clés et *mes clés*.

d J'ai téléphoné à ma mère. Tu as téléphoné à *ta mère*?

e Nous avons nos passeports. Avez-vous *vos passeports*?

f Ta maison est plus grande que *ma maison*.

3 **Choose suitable possessive pronouns from the box to complete the sentences, using the English as a guide.**

E.g. **Louis a une nouvelle bicyclette. Moi aussi – tu as vu *la mienne*?** *Louis has a new bicycle. Me too – have you seen mine?*

les miennes	les miens	les nôtres	~~la mienne~~	au tien
les nôtres	les vôtres	des siens	aux miennes	les leurs
le leur	la tienne	aux tiennes	à la tienne	

a Voici tes disquettes – où sont _____ ? *Here are your discs – where are mine?*

b Il a besoin de ses livres. A-t-elle besoin _____ ? *He needs his books. Does she need hers?*

c Ils ont leurs valises. Où sont _____? *They've got their suitcases. Where are yours?*

d Elle a son passeport. Où sont _____? *She's got her passport. Where are ours?*

e Je l'ai expliqué à mon frère. Tu l'as expliqué _____? *I have explained it to my brother. Have you explained it to yours?*

40 UNIT | Demonstrative pronouns

Demonstrative pronouns replace a demonstrative adjective + noun, and mean the one(s), this/that one *and* these/those.

A Celui, celle, ceux, celles

The form of the demonstrative pronoun changes according to the gender and number of the noun it relates to.

	Singular	Plural
Masculine	celui	ceux
Feminine	celle	celles

- When followed by **qui**, **que** or **dont**, the demonstrative pronouns mean *the one(s) that*, or, when referring to people, *the one(s)/he/she/those who*.

  Celui qui parle est mon frère.   *The one who's speaking is my brother.*

  Je n'aime pas ces chaussures. Je   *I don't like these shoes. I prefer the*
  préfère celles que vous avez là-bas.   *ones you have over there.*

- When followed by **de**, demonstrative pronouns can indicate possession.

  Ce n'est pas ma raquette, c'est   *It's not my racket, it's my father's.*
  celle de mon père.

- The suffixes **-ci** (for *this, these*) and **-là** (for *that, those*) can be added in order to reinforce the contrast between *this/that one*, *these/those (ones)*.

  celui-ci, celle-ci *this (one)*   ceux-ci, celles-ci *these (ones)*
  celui-là, celle-là *that (one)*   ceux-là, celles-là *those (ones)*

  Quel journal prenez-vous? Je   *Which newspaper will you have?*
  prends celui-ci/celui-là.   *I'll take this one/that one.*

B Ceci (*this*) and cela (*that*)

These do not refer to a specific noun that has been mentioned, but to an idea, event, fact or object. **Cela** is frequently shortened to **ça** in speech. Ça and cela are the most commonly used forms, and are both often used to mean *this* as well as *that*. **Ceci** is less common.

Je n'aime pas cela/ça.   *I don't like that.*
Ça suffit.   *That's enough.*

C Ce means *it* and *that*, and is mainly used with the verb **être**.

C'est mon ami.   *It's/That's my friend.*
Ce n'est pas juste.   *That's not fair.*

➤ *See the preposition* de *in Unit 13, demonstrative adjectives in Unit 20, relative pronouns (1) in Unit 41.*

40 UNIT Demonstrative pronouns – Exercises

1 **Match the French with the English.**

E.g. **C'est à moi, ça!** → *That's mine, that is!*

a Ceci est très amusant!

b Cela n'est pas vrai.

c Prenez ceci.

d Ce n'est pas facile.

e Écoutez cela!

1 *It isn't easy.*

2 *Take this.*

3 *This is very amusing!*

4 *Listen to that!*

5 *That's not true.*

2 **Combine sentences from (a) to (j) to match the English below.**

E.g. **Vous préférez quelle veste? + Je prends celle-ci.** *Which jacket do you prefer? I'll take this one.*

a J'ai acheté deux bouteilles de vin.

b Pouvez-vous me donner une autre tasse, s'il vous plaît?

c Tu préfères quelles cravates?

d Tu as choisi quel livre?

e J'ai eu du mal à choisir.

f Celle-ci est sale.

g Mais j'ai décidé de prendre ceci.

h Celle-ci est pour toi et celle-là est pour ta sœur.

i Moi, je préfère celles-ci.

j Je vais acheter celui-là.

1 *Could you give me another cup please? This one is dirty.*

2 *Which book have you chosen? I'm going to buy that one.*

3 *Which ties do you prefer? I prefer these.*

4 *It was hard to choose. But I've decided to take this.*

5 *I've bought two bottles of wine. This one is for you and that one is for your sister.*

3 **Follow the example to answer the questions below.**

E.g. **C'est votre bureau? (patron (*nm*))**
Non, c'est celui de mon patron.

a C'est ton stylo? (sœur)

b Ce sont vos papiers? (collègue (*nm*))

c C'est ta veste? (père (*nm*))

d C'est ton chat? (voisin (*nm*))

e Ce sont vos clés? (épouse)

41 UNIT | Relative pronouns (1)

Qui *means* who, which, *or* that. **Que** *means* whom, which, *or* that.

Qui and **que** and other relative pronouns introduce relative clauses. Both **qui** and **que** can refer to people and things. **Qui** is the subject of the verb that follows, whereas **que** is the object of the verb that follows.

La voiture **qui** est en panne est une Peugeot.	*The car that's broken down is a Peugeot.*
La voiture **que** vous voulez acheter est trop chère.	*The car that you want to buy is too expensive.*
Les brochures **qui** ont gagné le prix du meilleur dessin sont arrivées.	*The brochures that won the design award have arrived.*
Les brochures **que** nous avons préparées sont arrivées.	*The brochures that we prepared have arrived.*

A **Qui** is the *subject* of the following verb and means *who/that* for people and *which/that* for things.

Voici Alex, **qui** habite chez nous. *Here's Alex, who lives with us.*

In this sentence **qui** is the subject of the verb **habite**.

Le paquet **qui** est arrivé est pour toi. *The parcel that has arrived is for you.*

In this sentence **qui** is the subject of the verb **est arrivé**.

B **Que** is the *direct object* of the following verb and means *who(m)/that* for people and *which/that* for things. It is abbreviated to **qu'** before a vowel or unsounded **h**.

Le garçon que vous avez rencontré est mon fils. *The boy (whom/that) you met is my son.*

Que refers to **le garçon** and is the object of the verb **avez rencontré**. (The subject of the verb **avez rencontré** is **vous**.)

La table qu'il a réservée est pour quatre personnes. *The table (that) he reserved is for four people.*

Que refers to **la table** and is the object of **a réservée**. (The subject of the verb **a réservée** is **il**.)

⚠ A past participle following **que** agrees in gender and number with the word that **que** refers to.

⚠ Unlike its English equivalents, **que** can never be omitted in French.

➤ See preceding direct objects in the perfect and other compound tenses in Unit 63.

1 Choose the appropriate relative pronoun in each sentence.

E.g. C'est la femme qui/que est la patronne du café. → C'est la femme qui est la patronne du café. *It's the woman who runs the café.*

a Ça, c'est la voiture que/qui je veux acheter. *That's the car that I want to buy.*

b Il a la clé que/qui tu cherches. *He's got the key that you are looking for.*

c Elle parle des documents que/qui sont dans mon bureau. *She's talking about the documents that are in my office.*

d Les vacances que/qui nous avons passées au Maroc étaient fantastiques. *The holidays that we had in Morocco were wonderful.*

e Le client que/qui vient demain s'appelle Laclos. *The client who is coming tomorrow is called Laclos.*

2 Complete the following sentences with *qui* or *que*.

E.g. Le musée _____ nous allons visiter s'appelle le musée Grévin. → Le musée *que* nous allons visiter s'appelle le musée Grévin. *The museum that we are going to visit is called the musée Grévin.*

a La personne _____ travaille dans ce bureau s'appelle Madame Gilles. *The person who works in this office is called Madame Gilles.*

b Le film _____ j'ai vu hier soir était très bon. *The film that I saw last night was very good.*

c Les croissants _____ tu as achetés sont excellents. *The croissants that you bought are excellent.*

d Je travaille au musée, _____ est en face de la bibliothèque. *I work at the museum, which is opposite the library.*

e Le restaurant _____ je préfère est à dix minutes d'ici. *The restaurant that I like best is ten minutes from here.*

f L'équipe _____ a gagné le match était très forte. *The team that won the match was really good.*

g Le jeune homme _____ joue du piano est mon cousin. *The young man who is playing the piano is my cousin.*

h Le dépliant _____ je cherchais était dans le tiroir. *The leaflet, which I was looking for, was in the drawer.*

i Le porte-monnaie _____ elle a trouvé est vide. *The purse that she found is empty.*

j Les bureaux _____ nous avons achetés se trouvent au rez-de-chaussée. *The offices that we have bought are on the ground floor.*

42 UNIT | Relative pronouns (2)

A Dont is used for both people and things.

- It can mean *of whom, of which*. It may be used with a verb + **de** (**parler de** *to speak about*, **avoir besoin de** *to need, have need of*) or with an adjectival phrase + **de** (**être fier de** *to be proud of*).

Voici le livre dont j'ai besoin.   *Here's the book (that) I need.* (lit. *of which I have need*)

L'hôtel dont j'ai parlé est au coin.   *The hotel (that) I spoke about is on the corner.*

Voici le prix dont il est si fier.   *Here's the prize (that) he's so proud of.*

- It can indicate possession and mean *whose*.

J'ai rencontré un client dont j'ai oublié le nom. (J'ai oublié le nom **du** client.)   *I met a customer whose name I have forgotten.*

J'ai rencontré Michelle, dont tu m'as présenté le père. (le père **de** Michelle)   *I met Michelle, whose father you introduced to me.*

⚠ While in English you can sometimes leave out the relative pronoun, **dont** can never be omitted in French.

B Où generally means *where*.

Le parc où jouent les enfants va fermer.   *The park where the children play is going to close.*

- It can also replace a preposition + **lequel**.

La boîte où (= dans laquelle) vous trouverez les livres est dans le salon.   *The box you'll find the books in (in which you'll find…) is in the sitting room.*

- It is used to mean *when* after **le jour**, **le mois**, etc.

Il pleuvait le jour où tu es arrivé.   *It was raining on the day (when) you arrived.*

Les autres sont arrivés au moment où je partais.   *The others arrived at the moment when/just as I was leaving.*

C Dont cannot be used after a preposition – **lequel** etc. must be used instead.

C'est un joli lac, **au milieu duquel** il y a une petite île.   *It's a pretty lake, in the middle of which there's a little island.*

➤ See the preposition de in Unit 13, relative pronouns (3) lequel in Unit 43, verb constructions with objects in Unit 59.

42 Relative pronouns (2) – Exercises

1 Match the two parts of the sentences in French to correspond to the appropriate English sentences.

E.g. **C'est la personne + dont tu parles.** *It's the person you are talking about.*

a Ce sont les papiers
b C'est la maison
c C'est l'enfant
d C'est le jour
e C'est l'année

f où tu es allé en France.
g où nous sommes partis en vacances.
h dont je rêvais.
i dont il a besoin.
j dont il parle.

1 *It's the child he's talking about.*
2 *It's the day we went on holiday.*
3 *These are the papers he needs.*
4 *It's the house I dreamt of.*
5 *It's the year you went to France.*

2 Complete the following sentences using the relative pronoun.

E.g. **Le jour _____ il est arrivé, il neigeait.** *The day (when) he arrived, it was snowing.* **Le jour où il est arrivé, il neigeait.**

a Le film _____ tu parles s'appelle *Le Jour se lève*. *The film you're talking about is called* Le Jour se lève.
b Le dossier _____ j'ai besoin a disparu. *The folder that I need has disappeared.*
c L'hôtel _____ j'ai passé mes vacances se trouve sur la côte. *The hotel where I spent my holiday is on the coast.*
d Le mois _____ nous avons acheté l'appartement a été très chaud. *The month (when) we bought the flat was very hot.*
e La secrétaire _____ tu parlais s'appelle Alice. *The secretary you were talking about is called Alice.*

3 Replace the two French sentences with one, using the sentence in English as a guide.

E.g. **J'ai lu l'article. Il parlait de l'article.** *I have read the article that he was talking about.* → **J'ai lu l'article dont il parlait.**

a Voici les documents. Il a besoin des documents. *Here are the documents that he needs.*
b Toutes les personnes sont sur la liste. Nous avons le numéro de téléphone des personnes. *All the people whose telephone number we have are on the list.*

85

43 UNIT | Relative pronouns (3)

Lequel, laquelle, lesquels *and* lesquelles *are relative pronouns and are used after a preposition to mean* whom, that *or* which.

A The relative pronoun **lequel** agrees in gender and number with the noun it relates to, and has the following forms.

	Singular	Plural
Masculine	lequel	lesquels
Feminine	laquelle	lesquelles

These pronouns are used with prepositions to introduce a relative clause.

C'est la société pour laquelle je travaille.	*It's the company I work for (for which I work).*

B When used with the preposition **à**, or a complex preposition ending in **à**, the two combine to form **auquel**, **à laquelle**, **auxquels**, **auxquelles**. These replace **à** + noun. When referring to a person, **à qui** can also be used.

Le cinéma auquel il est allé est à dix minutes d'ici.	*The cinema he's gone to (to which he has gone) is ten minutes from here.*
Le client auquel/à qui j'ai donné les papiers est dans votre bureau.	*The client I gave the papers to (to whom I gave…) is in your office.*

C When used with the preposition **de**, or a complex preposition ending in **de**, the two combine to form **duquel**, **de laquelle**, **desquels**, **desquelles**. These replace **de** + noun. For people, **de qui** and **dont** are preferred.

Les résultats à propos desquels vous m'avez écrit sont inquiétants.	*The results you wrote to me about (about which…) are worrying.*
Les personnes dont/de qui on parlait n'étaient pas présentes.	*The people (who(m)) we were talking about weren't there.*

D After **parmi** and **entre**, only **lequel** and its forms can be used; **qui** is not used.

Nous avons 15 employés, parmi lesquels 8 sont des diplômés.	*We have 15 employees, of whom 8 have a higher qualification.*

Qui is used, however, with other prepositions when referring to people, as well as with **à** and **de** (above).

La femme avec qui je travaille est très gentille.	*The woman I work with is very kind.*

➤ *See prepositions in Units 10–15, relative pronouns* qui *and* dont *in Units 41 and 42, interrogative pronouns (*lequel *etc.) in Unit 86.*

43 UNIT Relative pronouns (3) – Exercises

1 **Choose the correct form of the relative pronoun.**

E.g. C'est l'agence avec lequel/laquelle il a négocié. *It's the agency he negotiated with.* → C'est l'agence avec laquelle il a négocié.

a Voici la femme avec lequel/laquelle j'ai dansé. *Here's the woman I danced with.*

b Ce sont les amies auxquels/auxquelles j'ai envoyé la carte. *These are the friends I sent the card to.*

c C'est le document à propos duquel/desquels j'ai eu un coup de téléphone. *It's the document I had a telephone call about.*

2 **Complete the gaps in the following sentences with *lequel, laquelle, lesquels* or *lesquelles*.**

E.g. Voici les ingrédients avec *lesquels* je vais faire un gâteau. *Here are the ingredients I'm going to make a cake with.*

a J'ai préparé le projet avec l'agence avec _____ tu as parlé. *I've prepared the project with the agency that you spoke with.*

b Les deux personnes entre _____ Paul se tient sont ses frères. *The two people Paul is standing between are his brothers.*

3 **Complete the gaps in these sentences using *auquel, à laquelle, auxquels, auxquelles* or *à qui* as appropriate.**

E.g. Je lui ai donné le numéro du bureau *auquel* il faut téléphoner. *I have given him the number of the office that he must telephone.*

a Vous avez posé des questions _____ je ne peux pas répondre. *You have asked questions that I can't answer.*

b Est-ce que c'est l'homme _____ vous avez parlé? *Is it the man you spoke to?*

c C'est la date avant _____ je dois rentrer. *That's the date that I must return by.*

4 **Complete the gaps in these sentences using *duquel, de laquelle, desquels, desquelles* or *de qui* as appropriate.**

E.g. Il possède un grand parc, au milieu *duquel* il y a un lac. *He owns a large park, in the middle of which there is a lake.*

a Voici l'usine à côté _____ je travaille. *Here's the factory I work next to (next to which I work).*

b Je voudrais lire les articles à propos _____ vous m'avez écrit. *I would like to read the articles you wrote to me about (about which you wrote to me).*

c Le bâtiment près _____ il a eu son accident est un peu plus loin. *The building near where (to which) he had his accident is a bit further on.*

> Ce qui and ce que *both mean what or which, in the sense of that which or the thing which. Ce dont means of which.*

A **Ce qui** is the subject of the verb that follows.

Je ne sais pas ce qui se passe.   *I don't know what is happening.*

Ce qui is the subject of the verb **se passe**.

Elle n'est pas encore arrivée, ce qui   *She's not arrived yet, which is*
est bizarre.   *strange.*

Notice that here **ce qui** is the subject of **est bizarre** and refers back to a whole clause (**elle n'est pas encore arrivée**).

B **Ce que** (**ce qu'** before a vowel or unsounded **h**) is the object of the verb that follows.

Je ne sais pas ce qu'il va faire.   *I don't know what he is going to do.*

Ce que is the object of the verb **(va) faire**.

Elle n'est pas retournée, ce que je   *She has not returned, which I don't*
ne comprends pas.   *understand.*

Ce que is the object of the verb **comprends** and refers back to the whole clause.

C **Ce dont** is the indirect object of the verb that follows.

- **parler de** *to speak of* or *about*

  Ce dont il parle est grave.   *What he's talking about is serious. (The thing of/about which he's talking)*

- **avoir besoin de** *to need ('have need of')*

  Il est malade. Je sais ce dont   *He's ill. I know what he needs*
  il a besoin.   *('has need of').*

- **avoir peur de** *to be afraid of*

  Il a perdu son emploi. C'est ce dont   *He's lost his job. That's what he was*
  il avait peur.   *afraid of (the thing of which he was afraid).*

D **Tout ce qui, tout ce que/qu'** and **tout ce dont** mean *all/everything/that/which/of which.*

Tout ce qu'il y a dans la valise est   *Everything in the suitcase is mine.*
à moi.

C'est tout ce qu'il a dit.   *That's all he said.*

➤ See Units 30 and 45 for explanation of the subject and objects of a verb, and verb constructions with objects in Unit 59.

1 Complete the gaps in the following sentences using *ce qui, ce que, ce qu'* or *ce dont.*

E.g. Ce n'est pas _____ j'ai dit. *That's not what I said.* → Ce n'est pas ce que j'ai dit.

a Je m'intéresse à _____ il parle. *I'm interested in what he's talking about.*

b Venez voir _____ j'ai fait. *Come and see what I've done.*

c Je ne comprends pas _____ elle a dit. *I don't understand what she said.*

d Dites-moi _____ se passe. *Tell me what's happening.*

2 Use *ce qui* or *ce que/ce qu'* to join the two halves of each sentence. The English translations are below.

E.g. Il veut savoir + nous avons écrit. → *He wants to know what we have written.*

a Vous devez décider	**g** est suprenant.
b Elle avait oublié	**h** elle allait dire.
c Je ne sais pas	**i** tu as fait en vacances.
d Il est en retard	**j** va se passer.
e Dis-moi	**k** il a fait.
f Je voudrais savoir	**l** vous voulez faire.

1 *You must decide what you want to do.*

2 *She had forgotten what she was going to say.*

3 *I don't know what is going to happen.*

4 *He's late, which is surprising.*

5 *Tell me what you did on holiday.*

6 *I'd like to know what he's done.*

3 *Tout ce qui* or *tout ce que/ce qu'*?

E.g. Il fait _____ il veut. *He does everything he wants.* → Il fait tout ce qu'il veut.

a Prenez _____ vous voulez. *Take everything you want.*

b Comprenez-vous _____ se passe? *Do you understand all that's happening?*

c Je vais vous montrer _____ il y a. *I'll show you everything there is.*

d J'ai compris _____ il a dit. *I understood everything he said.*

e Il est parti avec _____ il possédait. *He left with everything he owned.*

4 Translate the following into French.

a *I want* (**je veux**) *to know* (**savoir**) *what she will do.*

b *What he needs is a new office.*

c *He is not here, which is very strange.*

d *I'm eating all that there is.*

45 Unit | Object pronouns (1)

A The direct object of a verb can be replaced by a direct object pronoun:

Vous prenez **la chambre**?	*Will you take **the room**?*
Oui, je **la** prends.	*Yes, I'll take **it**.*

and the indirect object can be replaced by an indirect object pronoun:

Vous allez parler **à ce client**?	*Are you going to talk **to this customer**?*
Oui, je **lui** parle cet après-midi.	*Yes, I'm talking **to him** this afternoon.*

B The object pronoun can also have an abstract sense, in which case it is always masculine. In this usage there is not always an equivalent in English.

Je **le** sais. *I know (it).*   Je **l'**espère. *I hope so.*

C The form of these pronouns shows the gender and number of the object.

	Direct object	Indirect object	
je	me	me	*(to) me*
tu	te	te	*(to) you*
il	le	lui	*(to) him/it*
elle	la	lui	*(to) her/it*
nous	nous	nous	*(to) us*
vous	vous	vous	*(to) you*
ils	les	leur	*(to) them*
elles	les	leur	*(to) them*

Me, **te**, **le** and **la** become **m'**, **t'** and **l'** before a vowel or unsounded **h**.

D Use of the direct object pronoun

Pourquoi est-ce que tu **me** regardes?	*Why are you looking at **me**?*
Il **la** retrouve une fois par semaine.	*He meets **her** once a week.*
Elle **vous** admire beaucoup.	*She admires **you** very much.*

E Use of the indirect object pronoun

Il **me** dit bonjour chaque matin.	*He says hello **to me** every morning.*
Je **leur** écris deux fois par mois.	*I write **to them** twice a month.*

F In the imperative the indirect object pronouns **me** and **te** change to **moi** and **toi**.

Donnez-les-**moi**.   *Give them to me.*

➤ See verb constructions with objects in Unit 59, negatives in Units 82 and 83.

1 Replace the nouns in the following sentences with the correct direct object pronoun (*le, la, l'* or *les*).

E.g. Paul lit le journal. → Paul *le* lit. *Paul is reading it.*

a Hélène voit Marie. *Hélène sees her.*

b Georges regarde le match. *Georges is watching it.*

c Henri prépare le document. *Henri is preparing it.*

d Pierre aide ses amis. *Pierre helps them.*

e Je connais bien Claire. *I know her well.*

2 Complete the gaps with the correct indirect object pronoun (*me, te, nous* or *vous*). The English translations will help you.

E.g. Il _____ voit dans deux jours. *He's seeing me in two days.* → Il *me* voit dans deux jours.

a Elle _____ répond demain. *She'll answer you tomorrow.* (**tu** form)

b Il _____ sourit beaucoup. *He smiles at you a lot.* (**vous** form)

c Il _____ parle demain. *He's speaking to me tomorrow.*

d Elle _____ donne le livre. *She's giving us the book.*

3 Use the indirect object pronouns *lui* or *leur* to replace the words in bold.

E.g. Il donne le journal **à sa mère**. *He gives the newspaper to his mother.* → Il *lui* donne le journal.

a Je donne les magazines **aux filles**. *I give the magazines to the girls.*

b Il parle souvent **à son frère** au téléphone. *He often speaks to his brother on the telephone.*

c Elle parle **à tous ses collègues** lundi. *She's speaking to all her colleagues on Monday.*

d André téléphone souvent **à sa sœur**. *André often telephones his sister.*

4 Complete the sentences by selecting an appropriate object pronoun from the box, using the English sentences to guide you.

E.g. Il veut _____ garder. *He wants to keep them.* → Il veut *les* garder.

a Hélène rencontre **Yves** au cinéma.

Hélène _____ rencontre au cinéma.

Hélène meets him at the cinema.

l'	le	les	leur

b Jeanne dit au revoir **à ses amis**.

Jeanne _____ dit au revoir. *Jeanne says goodbye to them.*

c Il contrôle **les billets**.

Il _____ contrôle. *He checks them.*

46 UNIT | Object pronouns (2)

The pronoun *y* often means (to) it, (to) them or (to) there. En *replaces* de + noun and translates into English as some, of it or of them.

A **Y** stands for **à** (or another preposition) + noun and generally means *there, to there, it* or *to it*.

| Vont-ils au théâtre? Oui, ils y vont à sept heures. | *Are they going to the theatre? Yes, they're going (there) at 7 o'clock.* |
| Tu connais Biarritz? Oui, j'y ai passé mes vacances. | *Do you know Biarritz? Yes, I spent my holiday there.* |

⚠ Where the English may leave out the word *there* the French never omits **y**.

● In verb constructions with **à** (e.g. **penser à**), **y** can replace **à** + noun.

Le problème? J'y pense beaucoup. *The problem? I think about it a lot.*

But **y** cannot be used to refer to a person. An indirect object pronoun or a preposition with an emphatic pronoun must be used instead.

À Jeanne? Oui, je lui ai répondu. *Jeanne? Yes, I've replied to her.*

B **En** replaces **de** + noun and translates into English in a number of ways. Like **y**, **en** can never be omitted.

| Son article? Il en est très fier. | *His article? He's very proud of it.* |
| Tu connais Paris? Oui, j'en reviens justement. | *Do you know Paris? Yes indeed, I've just come back (from there).* |

● **En** replaces a partitive article + noun.

| Vous voulez du café? Oui, j'en veux bien merci. | *Would you like some coffee? Yes, I would like some please.* |

● It replaces **de** + noun (or a simple noun) in expressions of quantity.

| Elle a trois kilos de tomates. | *She's got three kilos of tomatoes.* |
| J'en ai quatre. | *I've got four (of them).* |

● It is used with verbs and expressions using **de** such as **avoir besoin de** (*to need*), **se souvenir de** (*to remember*), **parler de** (*to talk about*).

Villandry? Je m'en souviens bien. *Villandry? I remember it well.*

But when referring to people **en** is not always used (except in answer to **combien?**).

| Jean et de Christine? Oui, je me souviens bien d'eux. | *Jean and Christine? Yes, I remember them well.* |
| Combien de frères a-t-il? Il en a deux. | *How many brothers has he got? He's got two (of them).* |

➤ See the partitive article in Unit 9, emphatic pronouns in Unit 38, expressions of quantity in Unit 99.

46 UNIT Object pronouns (2) – Exercises

1 Rewrite the following sentences, replacing the words in italics by y.

E.g. Je vais *à Grenoble* tous les ans. *I go there every year.* → J'y vais tous les ans.

a Nous allons *à la gare*. *We are going there.*
b Elle pense *au cadeau*. *She is thinking of it.*
c Il répond *à la lettre*. *He replies to it.*
d Il va souvent *au théâtre*. *He often goes (there).*

2 Use en to replace the words in italics. Then translate your answers.

E.g. Je voudrais six *billets*. *I would like six tickets.* → J'en voudrais six. I would like six (of them).

a Elle prend six bouteilles *de lait*.
b Il achète quatre *journaux*.
c Nous avons plusieurs *livres sur la Révolution*.
d Elle met beaucoup *de brochures* sur le bureau.

3 The answers to the questions below are incomplete. Complete them by adding y or en.

E.g. Il a des cousins? *Has he got any cousins?* Oui, il a plusieurs. → Oui, il *en* a plusieurs. *Yes, he's got several.*

a Vous avez des livres sur la région? *Have you got any books on the area?* Oui, j'ai plusieurs. *Yes, I've got several.*
b Tu vas souvent au théâtre? *Do you often go to the theatre?* Oui, je vais deux fois par mois. *Yes, I go twice a month.*
c Vous avez combien d'amis à Tours? *How many friends have you got in Tours?* J'ai trois. *I've got three.*
d Vous habitez en France depuis longtemps? *Have you lived in France for long?* J'habite depuis trois ans. *I've lived there for three years.*

4 Complete the sentences with either y or an indirect object pronoun.

E.g. Vous venez du bureau? Oui, je _____ viens justement. → Oui. J'*en* viens justement.

a Tu veux parler à Yves? Oui, je veux _____ parler.
b Vous allez au Canada cette année? Oui, nous _____ allons en juin.
c Tu a des nouvelles (*news*) de Marie? Oui, je _____ téléphone chaque jour.
d Jean-Pierre et Hélène, ils habitent encore à Rouen? Oui, ils _____ ont un bel appartement.
e Tu réponds au courrier électronique pour moi? Oui, j' _____ réponds pour toi.

93

47 UNIT Object pronouns (3): position

Object pronoun position varies with the type of verb structure.

A In all tenses, the object pronoun goes before the conjugated verb. In compound tenses this is the auxiliary verb.

Elle **les** aide dans la cuisine.	*She is helping them in the kitchen.*
Elle **lui** téléphonait souvent.	*She used to telephone him frequently.*
Il **l'**a acheté hier.	*He bought it yesterday.*
Elle **leur** avait donné les cadeaux.	*She had given them the presents.*

This position is the same in questions, whichever question form is used.

Le prenez-vous?	*Are you taking it?*
Est-ce qu'il **l'**a acheté hier?	*Did he buy it yesterday?*

B With **aller** + infinitive, and with verbs such as **vouloir** and **pouvoir** + infinitive, the pronoun goes before the verb it relates to.

Je vais **lui** parler demain.	*I'll talk to him tomorrow.*
Tu peux **l'**ouvrir maintenant.	*You can open it now.*

C Where there is more than one pronoun the order is as follows:

	1	2	3	4	5	
SUBJECT	me te se nous vous	le la les	lui leur	y	en	VERB

Il **me le** promet pour demain.	*He's promised it to me for tomorrow.*
Elle **les leur** offre comme cadeau.	*She's giving them to them as a gift.*

D In affirmative imperatives, object pronouns come after the verb and are joined to it with a hyphen. Where there are two or more pronouns the direct object precedes the indirect object. **Me** and **te** become **moi** and **toi**.

Achetez-**le-moi**. *Buy it for me.*   Prends-**en**. *Take some.*

In negative imperatives, object pronouns precede the verb and **moi** and **toi** revert to **me** and **te**. The pronouns appear in the normal order.

Ne **me le** donnez pas.	*Don't give it to me.*
Ne **les lui** donne pas.	*Don't give them to him/her.*

➤ See modal verbs in Units 52 and 53, the infinitive (1) in Unit 57, the perfect tense (4) in Unit 63, asking questios in Units 84–86.

47 UNIT Object pronouns (3): position – *Exercises*

Match the English and French sentences.

E.g. Les as-tu mangés? → *Have you eaten them?*

a Veux-tu l'acheter?
b Le mangez-vous?
c Ils les vendent.
d Donnez-le-lui.
e Il me téléphone chaque jour.
f Veux-tu les acheter?
g Écoutez-le.
h Elles le vendent.

1 *They sell them.*
2 *He telephones me every day.*
3 *They sell it.*
4 *Do you eat it?*
5 *Listen to him.*
6 *Do you want to buy it?*
7 *Do you want to buy them?*
8 *Give it to him.*

Put the pronoun into the sentence in the correct place.

E.g. Veux-tu manger? *le* → Veux-tu *le* manger?

a Il achète. *les*
b Pouvez-vous ouvrir? *le*
c Mangez-vous? *les*
d Prends. *la*

e Ne fermez pas. *le*
f Elles aide. *les*
g Je ne veux pas boire. *le*
h Ils ne cherchent pas. *les*

Complete the imperative statements with the appropriate pronoun.

E.g. Fermez- *them* → Fermez-les.

a Prends- *it*
b Donnez- *it to me*
c Écoutez- *me*

d Achète- *it*
e Ouvre- *them*
f Donne- *it to him*

Fill in the gaps in the following sentences by selecting appropriate object pronouns from the box.

E.g. Henri donne *le cadeau* à *son ami.* → Henri *le lui* donne. *Henri gives it to him.*

la	le	les	lui	leur

a Jean-Luc raconte **l'histoire à son fils.**
Jean-Luc _____ raconte. *Jean-Luc tells it to him.*
b Elle donne **les journaux à son patron.**
Elle _____ donne. *She gives them to him.*
c Marc demande **les documents à ses collègues.**
Marc _____ demande. *He asks them for them.*
d Alice donne **le thé à son amie.**
Alice _____ donne. *She gives it to her.*

95

48 UNIT | Irregular verbs: *avoir*

> Avoir (to have) is an irregular verb. Its pattern is unlike that of any other verb.

A The present tense of **avoir** *to have* is formed as follows.

AVOIR *to have*	
j'ai *I have*	nous avons *we have*
tu as *you have*	vous avez *you have*
il a *he/it has*	ils ont *they have*
elle a *she/it has*	elles ont *they have*

B In many cases **avoir** is used in French in much the same way as the verb *to have* is used in English.

J'ai deux enfants.	*I have two children.*
Tu as des passe-temps?	*Do you have any hobbies?*
Elle a un frère.	*She has a brother.*
Vous avez des sœurs?	*Do you have any sisters?*
Ils ont un nouveau patron.	*They've got a new boss.*

C There are some expressions in French that use **avoir** when in English you would use the verb *to be*. This is because the French expressions use a noun, not an adjective.

Quel âge avez-vous?	*How old are you?*
J'ai 24 ans.	*I'm 24.*

Similarly:

avoir chaud	*to be hot*	j'ai chaud	*I'm hot*
avoir froid	*to be cold*	j'ai froid	*I'm cold*
avoir raison	*to be right*	j'ai raison	*I'm right*
avoir tort	*to be wrong*	j'ai tort	*I'm wrong*
avoir faim	*to be hungry*	j'ai faim	*I'm hungry*
avoir soif	*to be thirsty*	j'ai soif	*I'm thirsty*
avoir peur	*to be afraid*	j'ai peur	*I'm afraid*
avoir de la chance	*to be lucky*	j'ai de la chance	*I'm lucky*
avoir sommeil	*to be tired/sleepy*	j'ai sommeil	*I'm tired/sleepy*
avoir honte	*to be ashamed*	j'ai honte	*I'm ashamed*

➤ See irregular verbs: être in Unit 49, the perfect tense in Unit 60 and other compound tenses in Units 66, 69 and 71.

Fill in the missing parts of the verb *avoir* in the following conversations.

E.g. Vous _____ la lettre? *Have you got the letter?* → Vous *avez* la lettre?

a Vous _____ des enfants? *Have you got any children?*
   Oui, j'en _____ trois. *Yes, I've got three.*
b Vous _____ une voiture? *Have you got a car?*
   Oui, on _____ une Renault. *Yes we've got a Renault.*
c Les enfants, _____ -ils un animal familier? *Have the children got a pet?*
   Ils _____ un lapin. *Yes, they've got a rabbit.*

Complete the sentences with the appropriate personal subject pronouns.

E.g. _____ a mal à la gorge. → *Elle/Il* a mal à la gorge.

a _____ ai de la chance.
b _____ avez des billets?
c _____ a les cheveux longs.
d _____ ont une Peugeot rouge.
e _____ a toujours raison.
f _____ avons une nouvelle secrétaire.

Use words from both boxes to translate the sentences shown below.

E.g. Il a + faim. *He's hungry.*

Tu as	Il a	Nous avons	J'ai	Elle a	Ils ont	Vous avez	Elles ont

peur	faim	tort	de la chance	une maison secondaire
	trois filles	un rendez-vous	une nouvelle voiture	

a *You're wrong.*
b *He's afraid.*
c *You've got a new car.*
d *I'm hungry.*
e *They're lucky.*
f *She's got an appointment.*
g *They've got three daughters.*
h *We've got a second home.*

49 Unit : Irregular verbs: être

Être (to be) is an irregular verb. Its pattern is unlike that of any other verb.

A The present tense of **être** *to be* is formed as follows.

ÊTRE *to be*	
je suis *I am*	nous sommes *we are*
tu es *you are*	vous êtes *you are*
il est *he/it is*	ils sont *they are*
elle est *she/it is*	elles sont *they are*

B In many cases **être** is used in French in much the same way as the verb *to be* is used in English.

Je suis marié(e).	*I'm married.*
Il est célibataire.	*He's single.*
Vous êtes occupé(e)?	*Are you busy?*
Elles sont canadiennes.	*They're Canadian.*
Ils sont en France.	*They're in France.*

⚠ **Être** is not used for saying your age, nor for a number of expressions in which *to be* is used in English. Many use **avoir** instead.

J'ai cinq ans.	*I'm five years old.*

There is a list of these expressions in Unit 48.

C **Être** is used to say what job someone does. The noun is then used without any article (unless there's an adjective or other qualifier).

Elle est ingénieur.	*She's an engineer.*
Vous êtes comptable?	*Are you an accountant?*
C'est un bon médecin.	*He's a good doctor.*
C'est une professeur expérimentéee.	*She's an experienced teacher.*

D In English, the continuous present tense uses the verb *to be* plus another verb ending in *-ing*, for example *He is washing the car* (*is* from *to be*, plus *washing*). In French only one verb is used to express this: **Il lave la voiture**.

➤ See agreement of adjectives in Units 17 and 18, avoir in Unit 48, the perfect tense (2) in Unit 61 and other compound tenses in Units 66, 69 and 71.

49 UNIT

Irregular verbs: être – Exercises

1 Complete the sentences with the appropriate personal subject pronouns.

E.g. _____ êtes anglais? *Vous* êtes anglais?

a _____ suis très heureux!

b _____ sont au théâtre.

c _____ sommes allemands.

d _____ est fou!

e _____ es très gentil.

f _____ sont dans la salle à manger.

2 Use words from both columns to translate the sentences shown below.

E.g. **Vous êtes + en retard.** *You're late.*

a Il est
b Vous êtes
c Nous sommes
d Elles sont
e Tu es
f Ils sont
g Elle est
h Je suis

i italiennes.
j très fatigués.
k avocat.
l médecin.
m en vacances.
n prêt?
o très occupé.
p en retard.

1 *They're Italian.*
2 *She's a lawyer.*
3 *We're very tired.*
4 *He's a doctor.*

5 *I'm very busy.*
6 *Are you ready?*
7 *They're on holiday.*
8 *You're late.*

3 *Être* or *avoir*? Translate the following into English.

a *He's 10.*
b *I'm an engineer.*
c *I'm hungry.*
d *They're Spanish.*

e *You're right.*
f *She's happy.*
g *Are you thirsty?*
h *She's pretty.*

50 Unit: Irregular verbs: *aller* and *faire*

Aller *(to go)* and faire *(to make or do)* are two common irregular verbs.

ALLER *to go* (present tense)	
je vais	nous allons
tu vas	vous allez
il/elle va	ils/elles vont

FAIRE *to make/to do* (present tense)	
je fais	nous faisons
tu fais	vous faites
il/elle fait	ils/elles font

A • **Aller** means *to go*.

Ils vont à la piscine.	*They are going to the swimming pool.*

• **Aller** can also be used to say how people are.

Comment allez-vous? *How are you?*	Je vais bien/mieux. *I'm well/better.*
Comment ça va? *How are things?*	Ça va bien/mal. *They're fine/not good.*

• **Aller** can also be used to say what someone is going to do, usually in the near future. In this case it is always followed by an infinitive.

Elles vont jouer au tennis.	*They're going to play tennis.*
Il va se lever.	*He's going to get up.*

B • **Faire** means *to make* or *to do*.

Elle fait un gâteau.	*She's making a cake.*
Ils font toujours leurs devoirs.	*They always do their homework.*

• **Faire** is also used in impersonal constructions to talk about the weather.

Il fait beau. *It's fine.*	Il fait du brouillard. *It's foggy.*
Il fait chaud. *It's hot.*	Il fait du vent. *It's windy.*
Il fait du soleil. *It's sunny.*	Il fait froid. *It's cold.*

• It is used for sports in the combination **faire + du/de l'/de la** + noun.

Elle fait de la natation.	*She's swimming/she swims.*

Also: **faire du football** *to play football*, **faire du ski** *to ski*, **faire du vélo** *to go cycling*, **faire de la voile** *to sail*, etc.

• **Faire** also describes other activities, in the combination **faire** + noun.

Il fait la lessive.	*He's doing the washing.*

Also: **faire la vaisselle** *to do the washing-up*, **faire la cuisine** *to cook*, etc.

• And it is used with money or measurements.

Ça fait 15 F.	*That's 15 francs (comes to 15 francs).*
La pièce fait 3 mètres sur 2.	*The room measures 3 metres by 2.*

➤ See the future tense in Unit 68, dimensions in Unit 90.

50 Irregular verbs: *aller* and *faire* – *Exercises*

1 Using *aller* and an infinitive, complete the list on the right to say what is going to happen tomorrow.

E.g. Aujourd'hui, je regarde la télévision. Demain, je vais regarder la télévision.

AUJOURD'HUI	DEMAIN
a Elle range son bureau.	_____
b Ils jouent aux boules.	_____
c Tu prends un café.	_____
d Nous écoutons la radio.	_____
e Il mange à la cantine.	_____
f J'écris une lettre au client.	_____
g Elles choisissent un cadeau.	_____
h Il achète un ordinateur.	_____
i Il fait beau.	_____

2 Using *aller* or *faire* say what the following people are doing.

E.g. Elles font du vélo.

3 Complete the following by inserting the correct form of either *aller* or *faire*.

E.g. Hélène _____ à la piscine. → Hélène *va* à la piscine.

a Elles _____ au cinéma.
b Je _____ la cuisine ce soir.
c Que _____ -tu faire demain?
d Où _____ -tu?

51 UNIT Irregular verbs: *mettre* and *prendre*

Mettre *(to put)* and prendre *(to take)* are both irregular verbs.

METTRE *to put* (present tense)	
je mets	nous mettons
tu mets	vous mettez
il/elle met	ils/elles mettent

PRENDRE *to take* (present tense)	
je prends	nous prenons
tu prends	vous prenez
il/elle prend	ils/elles prennent

Compounds of these verbs follow the same pattern (e.g. **promettre** *to promise*, **comprendre** *to understand*.)

A **Mettre** is used in the following ways:

- to mean *to put*
  Il met les livres à l'étagère.   *He puts the books on the shelf.*

- to mean *to put on* (clothes, etc.)
  Elle met ses lunettes/son manteau.   *She puts on her glasses/her coat.*

- to mean *to switch on*
  Il met la radio.   *He switches on the radio.*

- with an expression of time, to indicate time spent
  Je mets une heure à faire mes   *I take/It takes me an hour to do my*
    courses.   *shopping.*

- when reflexive, it means *to begin, to start*
  Ils se mettent à marcher très tôt.   *They start to walk very early.*

B **Prendre** is used in the following ways:

- to mean *to take*, and also *to have/to take* (food, drink or when shopping, etc.)
  Elle prend son sac.   *She takes her bag with her.*
  Je prends un café.   *I'll have a coffee.*
  Il prend ses médicaments.   *He takes his medicine.*
  Je prends un kilo de pommes.   *I'll have/take a kilo of apples.*

- to mean *to catch, to take, to get* (transport) and *to take/to have* (a shower or bath)
  Il prend le train à 10 heures.   *He's catching the train at 10 o'clock.*
  Il prend une douche.   *He's having a shower.*

- to mean *to take/to last* with expressions of time (when used impersonally)
  Ça prend une heure.   *It takes an hour.*

BUT
    Je mets une heure à le faire. *I take an hour to do it.* (see **mettre** above)

1 **Match the following French and English sentences. The verbs are all compounds of *mettre* and *prendre* which conjugate in the same way as the main verbs.**

E.g. Il admet qu'il est en retard. → *He admits he's late.*

a Je comprends l'allemand.

b Il apprend l'espagnol.

c Elle permet à Michèle de venir avec nous.

d Il surprend Christine avec des fleurs.

e Je promets de vous donner les papiers.

1 *I promise to give you the papers.*

2 *She allows Michèle to come with us.*

3 *He surprises Christine with flowers.*

4 *I understand German.*

5 *He's learning Spanish.*

2 **Match the questions with their answers.**

E.g. Vous promettez de venir? → Oui, je vous le promets.

a À quelle heure prenez-vous le petit déjeuner?

b Vous apprenez le russe?

c Tu prends du sucre dans ton café?

d Combien de poires est-ce que vous prenez?

e Vous me permettez de venir avec vous?

1 Non, je prends seulement du lait.

2 Un kilo, s'il vous plaît.

3 Oui, bien sûr!

4 Je prends le petit déjeuner à huit heures.

5 Non, j'apprends le français et l'allemand.

3 **Insert the appropriate form of the verb in brackets.**

E.g. Il _____ le chinois. (apprendre) → Il *apprend* le chinois.

a Vous _____ votre manteau? (mettre)

b Tu _____ toujours ton amie avec de beaux cadeaux. (surprendre)

c Je _____ bien le problème. (comprendre)

d Vous _____ le train à quelle heure? (prendre)

e Il _____ de leur téléphoner demain. (promettre)

4 **Translate the following into French.**

a *Are you learning English?*

b *I'm going to have a cup of tea.*

c *She's having a shower.*

d *He promises a good dinner.*

e *I'm going to put my coat on.*

52 Unit Irregular verbs: *pouvoir* and *vouloir*

Two common irregular verbs are pouvoir and vouloir. They are usually followed by an infinitive and are known as modal verbs.

POUVOIR *to be able to* (present tense)	
je peux	nous pouvons
tu peux	vous pouvez
il/elle peut	ils/elles peuvent

VOULOIR *to wish, to want* (present tense)	
je veux	nous voulons
tu veux	vous voulez
il/elle veut	ils/elles veulent

A **Pouvoir** is mainly used with the infinitive of another verb. It indicates:

● ability

Je ne peux pas me lever.   *I can't get up.*

● permission

Vous pouvez partir si vous voulez.   *You can/may go if you like.*
Je peux regarder le film avec vous?   *Can I watch the film with you?*

● possibility

Il peut avoir dix ans.   *He could be ten years old.*

⚠ When translating verbs of perception or sensation (*to hear, to see, to understand,* etc.) **pouvoir** is not used in French and the verb of sensation stands alone.

J'entends les voisins.   *I can hear the neighbours.*
Je ne vois pas très bien.   *I can't see very well.*

B **Vouloir** is used to indicate:

● a desire or wish (followed by an infinitive or a noun)

Je veux acheter un pullover.   *I want to buy a pullover.*
Tu veux un verre de vin?   *Do you want a glass of wine?*

● an intention or willingness

Je veux rentrer à six heures.   *I want (intend) to go home at six.*

● a wish (in this case it is sometimes used in the conditional and can be used with another verb or a noun).

Je voudrais une omelette.   *I'd like an omelette.*
Il voudrait vous accompagner.   *He'd like to go with you.*
Je voudrais bien y aller.   *I'd really like to go.*

● a polite request

Voulez-vous attendre un moment?   *Please wait a moment.*

➤ See irregular verbs: devoir and savoir in Unit 53, the conditional in Unit 70.

52 Unit Irregular verbs: *pouvoir* and *vouloir* – Exercises

1 Match the following English and French sentences.

E.g. **Ils peuvent venir s'ils veulent.** → *They can come if they like.*

a Je veux un journal.
b Je peux sortir avec lui.
c J'en voudrais un kilo.
d Vous pouvez prendre l'autobus.
e Je peux aller au cinéma?
f Tu veux aller au cinéma?
g Je vois le port.
h Il peut manger maintenant.

1 *Can I go to the cinema?*
2 *I can see the port.*
3 *Do you want to go to the cinema?*
4 *I want a newspaper.*
5 *He can eat now.*
6 *I'd like a kilo.*
7 *You can take the bus.*
8 *I can go out with him.*

2 Make sentences from the columns to match the English ones.

E.g. **Je veux + aller + en France.** *I want to go to France.*

Est-ce que tu peux	aller	la fenêtre?
Je voudrais	fermer	ce soir?
Veux-tu	sortir	une tasse de thé?
Je peux	prendre	une veste.
Je veux	acheter	la porte?
Vous voulez	ouvrir	en France.
Pouvez-vous	faire	du ski.
Elle veut		

a *Would you like to have a cup of tea?*
b *Can you open the door?*
c *Do you want to go out this evening?*
d *I want to buy a jacket.*
e *She wants to go to France.*
f *Can I shut the window?*
g *I would like to go skiing.*

3 Translate the following into French.

a *She wants to go to the bank.*
b *You can eat now.*
c *He wants to buy a bike.*
d *I would like a kilo of apples.*
e *We can go in now.*

53 UNIT Irregular verbs: *devoir* and *savoir*

Devoir and savoir are irregular verbs. They can be followed by an infinitive and, in this case, are known as modal verbs.

DEVOIR *to have to (must)* (present tense)	
je dois	nous devons
tu dois	vous devez
il/elle doit	ils/elles doivent

SAVOIR *to know* (present tense)	
je sais	nous savons
tu sais	vous savez
il/elle sait	ils/elles savent

A **Devoir** is used to indicate
- an obligation or necessity (translating *must, have to*)
Il doit prendre le train de dix heures.	*He has to catch the ten o'clock train.*
Vous devez aller la voir.	*You must go and see her.*
Tu dois attendre une heure.	*You('ll) have to wait an hour.*
- a probability or supposition
  | Elle doit être en retard. | *She must be late.* |
- an intention (meaning *meant to/supposed to*)
  | Le car doit partir à onze heures. | *The coach should/is meant to/is supposed to leave at eleven o'clock.* |
- *should* or *ought to*, when used in the conditional
  | Vous devriez partir bientôt. | *You should leave soon.* |

⚠ **Devoir** also means *to owe* (usually used with a noun).
| Elle lui doit 200 euros. | *She owes him 200 euros.* |

B **Savoir** means
- *to be able to (know how to)* when referring to skills
  | Elle sait nager. | *She can (knows how to) swim.* |

⚠ **Pouvoir** is used for permission or ability in specific circumstances.
| Il peut nager ici/aujourd'hui. | *He can swim here/today.* |

- *to know* when talking about facts or information
  | Il est déjà parti. Oui, je le sais. | *He's already left. Yes, I know.* |
  | Je sais qu'il va arriver à 7 heures. | *I know that he's arriving at 7 o'clock.* |

⚠ **Connaître** *to know, to be acquainted with* must be used if you are talking about knowing people or places.
| Je connais la ville de Nancy. | *I know the town of Nancy.* |

➤ See pouvoir and vouloir in Unit 52, the conditional in Unit 70.

1 Match the following French and English sentences.

E.g. Ils lui doivent 50 F. → *The owe her 50 francs.*

a Il doit rentrer à six heures.
b Elle sait danser.
c Il doit être en France.
d Il sait que vous êtes ici.
e Elle sait jouer au golf.
f Il doit sortir après le repas.
g Elle doit aller voir son ami.
h Nous leur devons 100 F.

1 *He knows that you are here.*
2 *We owe them 100 francs.*
3 *She can dance.*
4 *She knows how to play golf.*
5 *He has to go out after the meal.*
6 *He has to go home at six o'clock.*
7 *He must be in France.*
8 *She has to go and see her friend.*

2 Make sentences that correspond to the English sentences given below.

E.g. Elle doit + faire + la cuisine. *She must do the cooking.*

Dois-je	aller	avant dix heures?
Elle sait	faire	la cuisine.
Elle doit	rentrer	à Rouen.
Savez-vous	finir	bientôt.
Nous devons		de la voile.
Sait-il		du ski?
Doivent-ils		

a *Do I have to come home before ten o'clock?*
b *She knows how to cook.*
c *We have to finish soon.*
d *Do you know how to ski?*
c *She has to go to Rouen.*
f *Does he know how to sail?*

3 Translate the following into French.

a *I must go to Paris.*
b *He must be in the living room.*
c *She must ring Rouen.*
d *We know how to ski.*
e *They must promise.*
f *I know Saumur well.*

4 *Pouvoir* or *savoir*? Insert the correct part of the appropriate verb.

E.g. Je _____ qu'il joue bien du piano. → Je *sais* qu'il joue bien du piano.

a Vous _____ venir avec nous si vous voulez.
b Ils ont de l'argent, donc ils _____ sortir ce soir.
c _____-vous faire du ski?
d Elle _____ parler français.
e Si tu es libre vendredi, tu _____ peut-être aller au théâtre avec moi?

54 UNIT | Verbs with more than one subject

There are rules that govern the form of the verb when it has more than one subject (My friend and I are...).

A Using the **nous** (first-person plural) form of the verb

The **nous** form of the verb is appropriate when the two or more people who make up the subject of the verb include you.

Ma sœur et moi (= nous) **travaillons** ensemble.
My sister and I work together.

Mes amis et moi (= nous) **sortons** aujourd'hui.
My friends and I are going out today.

In such cases the third-person singular subject pronoun **on** is often used to sum up two subjects, and means *we*.

Julie et moi, on **part** ensemble.
Julie and I are going away together.

B Using the **vous** (second-person plural) form of the verb

The **vous** form of the verb is used when the two or more people who make up the subject of the verb include the person you are talking to (but do not include you). This applies whether you are on **tu** or **vous** terms with the person you are speaking to.

Vous et vos amis (= vous) **pouvez** venir avec nous.
You and your friends can come with us.

Louise et toi (= vous) **êtes** arrivés samedi?
Did you and Louise arrive on Saturday?

C Using the **ils/elles** (third-person plural) form of the verb

The **ils/elles** form is the appropriate choice when the two or more people who make up the subject of the verb do not include either you or the person you are talking to.

M et Mme Durand (= ils) **regardent** un film.
M and Mme Durand are watching a film.

Pierre et ses amis (= ils) **sont** allés à la gare.
Pierre and his friends have gone to the station.

Mme Grand et Mlle Duplessis (= elles) **travaillent** ensemble.
Mme Grand and Mlle Duplessis work together.

➤ See subject pronouns in Unit 36, the subject pronoun on in Unit 37, emphatic pronouns in Unit 38.

1 **Join the two halves of the French sentences to match the English sentences.**

E.g. Jean-Pierre et moi + partons en vacances ensemble. *Jean-Pierre and I are going on holiday together.*

a Mon frère et moi
b Ta sœur et toi
c Sylvie et toi
d André et moi
e Les voisins et notre fils
f Votre cousin et ma secrétaire

g allons en Afrique cette année.
h allons à la piscine.
i sont amis.
j vont faire du vélo aujourd'hui.
k pouvez venir jouer au tennis.
l êtes toujours en retard.

1 *Your cousin and my secretary are friends.*
2 *You and your sister can come and play tennis.*
3 *The neighbours and our son are going out on their bikes today.*
4 *André and I are going to Africa this year.*
5 *My brother and I are going to the swimming pool.*
6 *You and Sylvie are always late.*

2 **Complete the gaps with the *nous* or the *ils/elles* form of the verb given in brackets.**

E.g. Jean et Luc _____ au football. (jouer) Jean et Luc *jouent* au football.

a M et Mme Leclerc _____ acheter une nouvelle voiture. (vouloir) *M and Mme Leclerc want to buy a new car.*
b Mon collègue et moi _____ prendre le train. (devoir) *My colleague and I must catch the train.*
c Pierre et moi _____ toujours le dimanche après-midi. (se promener) *Pierre and I always go for a walk on Sunday afternoon.*
d Mon frère et ses amis _____ aller à Paris. (vouloir) *My brother and his friends want to go to Paris.*

3 **Choose the correct form of the verb to complete the following sentences.**

E.g. Mon frère et mon ami fait/faites/font de la voile. *My brother and my friend go sailing.* → Mon frère et mon ami *font* de la voile.

a Votre femme et vous voulez/voudrait/veulent dîner avec nous vendredi? *Do you and your wife want to come for dinner with us on Friday?*
b Mon père et moi vont/allons/allez au match tous les samedis. *My father and I go to the match every Saturday.*
c Où est-ce que vous et André va/allons/allez manger ce soir? *Where are you and André going to eat this evening?*

55 UNIT | The present participle

In English, the present participle is the part of the verb that ends in -ing, as in the sentence She left the room singing.

A The French present participle is formed by taking the **nous** form of the present tense, removing the **-ons** and adding **-ant**.

(nous prenons) pren + ant → **prenant** *taking*

B The spelling change to the stem of verbs ending in **-ger** and **-cer** is maintained.

(nous mangeons) **mangeant**   (nous commençons) **commençant**

C There are three irregular present participles.

(avoir) **ayant** *having*   (être) **étant** *being*   (savoir) **sachant** *knowing*

D The present participle is used alone to describe circumstances, a situation or a sequence.

Étant malade, je ne suis pas allé.   *Being ill I didn't go.*

Il est parti, prenant avec lui tout ce   *He left, taking all he needed with him.*
dont il avait besoin.

E It is used with **en** to convey
- the idea of simultaneity (in English *while, whilst, on, in, when ... -ing*):

En montant dans le bus, j'ai laissé   *(While) getting on the bus, I dropped*
tomber mon sac.   *my bag.*

The fact of two things happening together can be reinforced by using **tout en**:

Tout en écrivant, il m'a répondu.   *He answered me whilst still writing.*

- the manner or method of doing something (in English *by -ing*):

Je me suis occupé en lisant.   *I kept myself busy by reading.*

F The French present participle is used to translate some English verbs of action.

Elle est entrée en courant.   *She ran in (came running in).*

G The present participle can be used as an adjective, and then agrees in number and gender with the noun it refers to. It can also be used as a noun, and as such also shows number and gender.

Elle est amusante. *She's amusing.*   Ils sont amusants. *They're amusing.*

un passant *passer-by (male)*   une passante *passer-by (female)*

⚠ The English *-ing* is sometimes rendered differently in French:

Nous aimons faire du vélo.   *We like cycling.*

Il est parti sans dire au revoir.   *He left without saying goodbye.*

➤ See the present tense in Units 31–35 and 48–51, the infinitive in Units 57 and 58, the perfect infinitive in Unit 73.

55 UNIT The present participle – Exercises

1 **Form the appropriate present participle from the verb indicated.**

E.g. **Il entre dans la pièce en *parlant* à son amie. (parler)**

a Jeanne s'amuse en _____ . (lire)

b Sylvie est sortie de la banque en _____ . (courir)

c En _____ son manteau, il est sorti du bureau. (mettre)

d En _____ la première rue à gauche, vous arrivez à l'école. (prendre)

e Il mange des chips en _____ la télévision. (regarder)

f En _____ son ami, elle se met à courir. (voir)

2 **Rewrite the following sentences by substituting a present participle clause for the second clause.**

E.g. **Quand il mange, il regarde la télévision. → Il mange en regardant la télévision.**

a Quand elle se lève, elle chante.

b Pendant qu'elle attend le train, elle lit.

c Pendant qu'il travaille dans le jardin, il siffle.

d Quand elle prépare le repas, elle boit du vin.

e Pendant qu'elle fait le ménage, elle écoute la radio.

f Quand elle travaille, elle mange des bonbons.

3 **Write a sentence using the language in the box to show what the following people are doing.**

E.g. **Il lit un livre en mangeant.**

| écouter   faire le repassage   se doucher   manger   chanter   regarder la télé |

111

56 UNIT The imperative

The imperative is used to give instructions and orders, to make requests or to offer suggestions.

A In French there are three forms of the imperative: the **tu**, the **nous** and the **vous** forms.

- The **tu** form comes from the **tu** part of the present tense, with **tu** omitted.
  Tu prends un taxi. *You take a taxi.* → Prends un taxi. *Take a taxi.*

The exceptions to this rule are all **-er** verbs, including **aller**. For these, you remove the **-s** from the **tu** part of the present tense:
  Oui, chante. *Yes, sing.*   Va chez le médecin. *Go to the doctor's.*

⚠ When the imperative is followed by the pronouns **y** and **en**, this **-s** is retained for reasons of pronunciation.
  Vas-y! *Go on!*   Manges-en. *Eat some.*

- The **nous** form is the **nous** part of the present tense, with **nous** omitted.
  Regardons un film.   *Let's watch a film.*

- The **vous** form is the **vous** part of the present tense, with **vous** omitted.
  Achetez du pain.   *Buy some bread.*

B The imperative forms of **avoir**, **être** and **savoir** are irregular.

	ÊTRE	AVOIR	SAVOIR
(tu)	sois	aie	sache
(nous)	soyons	ayons	sachons
(vous)	soyez	ayez	sachez

  Sois gentille avec ta sœur.   *Be nice to your sister.*
  Ayez de la patience.   *Be patient.*

C In the negative, **ne ... pas** enclose the imperative and any object pronouns.
  Ne riez pas! *Don't laugh!*   Ne l'ouvrez pas. *Don't open it.*

D Reflexive verbs
- In the affirmative the reflexive pronoun is placed after the verb and joined to it by a hyphen and **te** is replaced by **toi**: **Tais-toi!** *Be quiet!* **Dépêchez-vous!** *Hurry up!*
- However in the negative the pronoun reverts to its normal form and position: **Ne te dépêche pas**. *Don't hurry.*

➤ See position of object pronouns in Unit 47, avoir in Unit 48, être in Unit 49, savoir in Unit 53, negatives in Units 82 and 83.

56 The imperative – Exercises

1 Match the following French sentences with the English ones.

E.g. **Ouvre la porte.** → *Open the door.*

a Essayez le poulet.	**1** *Go and do your homework.*
b Attends-moi ici.	**2** *Look at that.*
c Prenons un train.	**3** *Come here.*
d Ne le lui envoyez pas.	**4** *Give it to her.*
e Regardez ça.	**5** *Let's take a train.*
f Va faire tes devoirs.	**6** *Try the chicken.*
g Viens ici.	**7** *Wait a moment.*
h Attendez un instant.	**8** *Wait for me here.*
i Donnez-le-lui.	**9** *Get up.*
j Levez-vous.	**10** *Don't send it to him.*

2 Form the appropriate imperative of the verbs given in brackets.

E.g. **(Aller) au cinéma. (nous)** *Let's go to the cinema.* → **Allons au cinéma.**

a (Prendre) un café. (tu) *Have a coffee.*

b (Acheter) des cartes postales. (vous) *Buy some postcards.*

c (Jouer) au football. (nous) *Let's play football.*

d (Donner)-moi ce journal. (tu) *Give me that newspaper.*

e (Être) raisonnables! (vous) *Be reasonable!*

f (Rentrer) à l'hôtel. (nous) *Let's go back to the hotel.*

g (Aller) visiter le musée. (tu) *Go and see the museum.*

h (Mettre) un manteau. (tu). *Put a coat on.*

3 Complete the following instructions, using both *tu* and *vous*:

E.g. **(Fermer) la porte.** → **Ferme la porte. Fermez la porte.**

a (Aller) aux magasins. *Go to the shops.*

b N'(avoir) pas peur. *Don't be afraid.*

c (Mettre) du sucre dans le café. *Put some sugar in the coffee.*

d (Prendre) cette rue-là. *Take that road.*

e Ne (pousser) pas. *Don't push.*

f (Penser) à prendre ton/votre passeport. *Don't forget your passport.*

g (Choisir) un cadeau pour ton/votre ami. *Choose a present for your friend.*

h (Acheter) du vin au supermarché. *Buy some wine at the supermarket.*

4 Translate the following into French, again using both *tu* and *vous*.

a *Repeat it.*

b *Don't shut it.*

c *Give me a newspaper.*

d *Reserve me two places, please.*

e *Buy them, please.*

f *Be patient.*

113

57 | UNIT | The infinitive (1)

Infinitives are often used after another verb. They can be the subject of a clause.

Infinitives are frequently used after a finite verb. In such cases any negative is formed by putting **ne … pas** either side of the first verb (or its auxiliary), or both before the infinitive if this is being negated. An infinitive can appear:

A after verbs expressing liking and disliking, e.g. **aimer** *to like, to love,* **adorer** *to adore,* **détester** *to detest, to hate* and **préférer** *to prefer:*

Je n'aime pas chanter.	*I don't like singing.*
Nous préférons aller au théâtre.	*We prefer to go to the theatre.*

B after verbs expressing wishing and willing, e.g. **désirer** *to desire,* **espérer** *to hope* and **souhaiter** *to wish:*

Elle souhaite visiter le château.	*She wants to visit the castle.*
J'espère ne pas y aller.	*I hope not to go.*

C after verbs expressing perception, e.g. **écouter** *to listen to,* **entendre** *to hear,* **regarder** *to watch,* **sentir** *to feel, to smell,* **voir** *to see* and **sembler** *to appear:*

Je le vois arriver chaque matin.	*I see him arrive every morning.*

D after verbs expressing motion, e.g. **aller** *to go,* **entrer** *to enter,* **descendre** *to do down, to descend,* **monter** *to go up, to ascend,* **rentrer** *to return, to go home,* **sortir** *to go out,* **venir** *to come:*

Venez prendre un café avec moi.	*Come and have a coffee with me.*
Il rentre faire ses devoirs.	*He's going home to do his homework.*

E after the modal verbs **devoir** *to have to,* **pouvoir** *to be able to,* **savoir** *to know how to,* **vouloir** *to want to:*

Elle ne sait pas nager.	*She can't swim.*
Vous pouvez commencer.	*You can begin.*

F after the verbs **falloir** *to be necessary,* **laisser** *to let, to permit* and **faire** *to do, to make:*

Il faut payer.	*We must pay.*
Je laisse Pierre regarder le film.	*I'm letting Pierre watch the film.*
Je me suis fait couper les cheveux.	*I had my hair cut.*

G The infinitive can be used as the subject of a clause.

Décider n'est pas toujours facile.	*Deciding is not always easy.*

➤ See position of object pronouns in Unit 47, modal verbs in Units 52 and 53, the future tense (aller + infinitive) in Unit 68, using the subjunctive (il faut/il vaut) in Unit 78, the negative in Unit 82.

1 Match the questions with the appropriate answers.

E.g. À quelle heure veut-il partir? Il veut partir à six heures.

a Est-ce qu'il sait jouer du piano?

b Vous préférez aller au cinéma?

c Tu aimes lire?

d Vous espérez aller à l'université?

e Ils viennent prendre un café avec nous?

f Yvette veut rester chez ses amis?

g Tu peux sortir avec moi samedi soir?

h Vous voulez acheter cette robe?

1 Oui, mais j'aime aussi écouter la radio.

2 Oui, où est-qu'on va?

3 Oui, ils vont arriver vers onze heures.

4 Non, je veux acheter ce pullover.

5 Non, mais il sait jouer du violon.

6 Oui, je veux devenir médecin.

7 Non, elle préfère rentrer ce soir.

8 Non, je préfère dîner avec des amis.

2 Choose verbs from the box to complete the following sentences.

E.g. Je veux _____ quelque chose. *I want to eat something.* → **Je veux manger quelque chose.**

manger	acheter	sortir	lire	regarder	rentrer	m'asseoir	te lever

a Je voudrais _____ avec mes amis. *I would like to go out with my friends.*

b Quand est-ce que tu dois _____? *When do you have to go home?*

c Voulez-vous _____ maintenant ou plus tard? *Do you want to eat now or later?*

d Je peux _____ à côté des enfants? *Can I sit down next to the children?*

e Faut-il _____ un billet? *Do you have to buy a ticket?*

f Elle ne veut pas _____ le journal, elle préfère _____ la télévision. *She doesn't want to read the paper, she prefers to watch the television.*

g Tu préfères _____ à quelle heure? *What time do you prefer to get up?*

3 How would you say that you...

E.g. *... wish to go on holiday in June?* → **Je souhaite aller en vacances en juin.**

a *... like swimming?*

b *... prefer reading?*

c *... must pay?*

d *... want to go to bed?*

e *... love buying presents?*

f *... can swim?*

g *... can come?*

h *... hope to arrive at four o'clock?*

58 The infinitive (2)

A Infinitives are used after simple and complex prepositions and after interrogatives (e.g. **après**, **par**, **pour**, **sans**, **avant de**, **au lieu de**; **comment**, **quand**, **que**, **où**, **combien**, etc.)

Il a commencé par ouvrir la lettre.	*He began by opening the letter.*
Pour aller à la gare, s'il vous plaît?	*How do I get to the station, please?*
Il part sans dire au revoir.	*He's leaving without saying goodbye.*
Avant de partir elle leur a téléphoné.	*Before leaving she telephoned them.*
Comment savoir qu'il était là?	*How were we to know he was here?*
Que faire dans ces circonstances?	*What's to be done in the circumstances?*

- also after a verb + **à** (e.g. **aider à** *to help*, **apprendre à** *to learn to*, **commencer à** *to start*, **se décider à** *to decide*, **hésiter à** *to hesitate*, **inviter à** *to invite*)

Elle a réussi à préparer le repas.	*She managed to get the meal ready.*
Il hésite à acheter la voiture.	*He's hesitating about buying the car.*

- and after a verb + **de** (e.g. **cesser de** *to stop, to cease*, **décider de** *to decide*, **conseiller de** *to advise*, **essayer de** *to try*, **finir de** *to finish*, **oublier de** *to forget*)

A-t-il cessé de pleuvoir?	*Has it stopped raining?*
J'ai essayé de trouver le numéro.	*I've tried to find the number.*

B Infinitives are used after an adjective + **à** (e.g. **facile à** *easy to*, **(im)possible à** *(im)possible to*, **intéressant à** *interesting to*, **prêt à** *ready to*)

Vous êtes tous prêts à partir?	*Are you all ready to leave?*
Ce plat est très facile à cuisiner.	*This dish is very easy to cook.*

- and after an adjective + **de** (e.g. **capable de** *capable of*, **certain de** *certain to*, **content de** *happy to*, **désolé de** *sad/unhappy to*, **heureux de** *happy to*, **sûr de** *sure to*, **surpris de** *surprised to*, **triste de** *sad to*).

Elle est certaine de gagner.	*She is certain to win.*

C Infinitives are also used after a noun, pronoun, or adverb + **à/de**.

Quel plaisir de vous revoir!	*What a pleasure to see you again!*
J'ai un nouveau bureau à visiter.	*I've got a new office to look at.*
Je n'ai rien à vous dire.	*I've got nothing to say to you.*
Il y a trop à faire.	*There's too much to do.*

➤ See prepositions in Units 10–15, the present participle in Unit 55, verb constructions with objects in Unit 59.

58 The infinitive (2) – Exercises

1 **Complete the following sentences with à or de.**

E.g. J'apprends _____ parler français. J'apprends *à* parler français.

a Il a réussi _____ comprendre.

b Elle se décide _____ regarder la télévision.

c Nous avons décidé _____ aller en vacances à Noël.

d J'ai oublié _____ téléphoner à ma mère.

e Il a continué _____ travailler jusqu'à minuit.

f Vous êtes capable _____ réussir.

g Elle a enfin cessé _____ parler!

h Elles essayent _____ choisir un cadeau pour elle.

i Je voudrais apprendre _____ nager.

j Il a trop _____ faire.

2 **Make sentences from the following using the English sentences as a guide.**

E.g. Il est facile + d' + oublier un visage. *It's easy to forget a face.*

Elles continuent	à	lire le journal.
Il oublie toujours		acheter du lait.
Il commence		partir en vacances.
Ils essayent	de (d')	bavarder.
Nous allons essayer		rester à la maison.
Elle hésite		nous accompagner.
Ils sont contents		revenir bientôt.

a *They continue to chat.*

b *He always forgets to buy milk.*

c *He is starting to read the paper.*

d *They are trying to come with us.*

e *We'll try to come back soon.*

f *She's hesitating about going on holiday.*

g *They are happy to stay at home.*

3 **Translate the following into French.**

a *She forgets to buy the newspaper.*

b *He is capable of understanding.*

c *He wants to learn to ski.*

d *She continues to try.*

e *He's leaving without paying.*

f *She's ready to go.*

59 UNIT Verb constructions with objects

Some French verb constructions require direct objects or indirect objects, while in English the pattern can be different.

A Some verbs take a direct object in French but in English have a preposition after them.

J'attends Pierre en bas.	*I'll wait for Pierre downstairs.*
J'ai payé le repas.	*I've paid for the meal.*

attendre *to wait for*   **chercher** *to look for*   **demander** *to ask for*
écouter *to listen to*   **regarder** *to look at*   **payer** *to pay for*

B Some verbs take an indirect object with **de** in French, but a direct object in English.

Je me souviens bien de Cannes.   *I remember Cannes well.*

avoir besoin de *to need*   **(se) changer de** *to change*   **jouer de** *to play*
(an instrument)   **manquer de** *to lack, to miss*   **se souvenir de** *to remember*

C Some verbs take an indirect object with **à** in French, but a direct object in English.

Je vais répondre à Daniel bientôt.   *I'll answer Daniel soon.*

jouer à *to play (a sport)*   **(dés)obéir à** *to (dis)obey*   **répondre à** *to answer*
ressembler à *to look like*   **téléphoner à** *to telephone*

D Some verbs take two objects: a direct and an indirect object.

Il donne un vélo à son fils.	*He gives his son a bike/a bike to his son.*

donner quelque chose à quelqu'un   *to give something to someone*
vendre quelque chose à quelqu'un   *to sell something to someone*
prêter quelque chose à quelqu'un   *to lend something to someone*

This group includes verbs expressing *taking away* with **à**: **acheter/ demander/emprunter/prendre/voler quelque chose à quelqu'un.**

Il m'a emprunté un stylo.   *He borrowed a pen from me.*

E The English construction *to ask someone to do something* is translated into French in two principal ways:

- verb + direct object + **à** + infinitive

Elle a encouragé Paul à participer.	*She encouraged Paul to participate.*
Il l'a invitée à manger.	*He invited her to eat.*

- verb + indirect object + **de** + infinitive

Pierre a demandé à Anne de venir.	*Pierre asked Anne to come.*
Je leur ai dit de ne pas venir demain.	*I told them not to come tomorrow.*
Elle m'a conseillé de rester.	*She advised me to stay.*

➤ See the prepositions de and à in Units 13 and 14, the infinitive in Units 57 and 58, negatives in Unit 82, list of verbs with à/de (page 200)

1 **Make sentences from the following using the English as a guide.**

E.g. J' + aide + nos amis à laver la voiture. *I am helping our friends to wash the car.*

Philippe	aident	nos amis à déjeuner avec nous.
Nous	oblige	mon fils à faire ses devoirs.
J'	aide	leur père à laver la voiture.
Marie	encourage	son frère à prendre une décision.
Ils	allons inviter	son ami à écrire la lettre.

a *Philippe helps his friend to write the letter.*
b *We are going to invite our friends to have lunch with us.*
c *I encourage my son to do his homework.*
d *Marie is forcing her brother to make a decision.*
e *They help their father to wash the car.*

2 **Fill the gaps with** *à* **or** *de* **as appropriate.**

E.g. **Elle propose _____ Danielle _____ manger en ville.** *She suggests to Danielle that they eat in town.* → **Elle propose** *à* **Danielle** *de* **manger en ville.**

a Jean-Yves a demandé _____ son père _____ lui prêter de l'argent. *Jean-Yves asked his father to lend him some money.*
b Il a conseillé _____ sa fille _____ rester à la maison. *He advised his daughter to stay at home.*
c Ses parents n'ont pas obligé André _____ aller à l'université. *His parents did not force André to go to university.*
d Il a défendu _____ son fils _____ sortir ce soir-là. *He forbade his son to go out that evening.*
e Elle m'a invité _____ venir. *She invited me to come.*
f Le médecin lui a dit _____ rester au lit. *The doctor told him to stay in bed.*
g J'ai permis _____ ma fille _____ passer le weekend chez son amie. *I allowed my daughter to spend the weekend at her friend's house.*

3 **Translate the following into French.**

a *I'm waiting for Jean.*
b *Listen to the radio.*
c *Do you want to play tennis?*
d *Marc is helping his sister to write.*
e *I'm looking for the map.*

60 UNIT The perfect tense (1)

The perfect is a compound tense required when you want to refer to a completed action in the past: I went, he has bought.

A This tense has two parts and is formed from:

- the present tense of the verb **avoir** or, for a small number of verbs, **être**; this is called the auxiliary verb;
- the past participle of another verb, normally formed from the stem of the verb + **-é** for **-er** verbs (**manger → mangé**); **-i** for **-ir** verbs (**finir → fini**); **-u** for **-re** verbs (**vendre → vendu**).

ACHETER (+ AVOIR)		ALLER (+ ÊTRE)	
j'ai acheté	*I bought/have bought*	je suis allé(e)	*I went/have been*
tu as acheté	*you bought/have bought*	tu es allé(e)	*you went/have been*
il a acheté	*he bought/has bought*	il est allé	*he went/has been*
elle a acheté	*she bought/has bought*	elle est allée	*she went/has been*
nous avons acheté	*we bought/have bought*	nous sommes allé(e)s	*you went/have been*
vous avez acheté	*you bought/have bought*	vous êtes allé(e)(s)(es)	*you went/have been*
ils ont acheté	*they bought/have bought*	ils sont allés	*they went/have been*
elles ont acheté	*they bought/have bought*	elles sont allées	*they went/have been*

B Irregular past participles

Some past participles are irregular. A few examples are given here.

avoir → eu	faire → fait	savoir → su
devoir → dû	mettre → mis	venir → venu
être → été	pouvoir → pu	vouloir → voulu
dire → dit	prendre → pris	

C Examples:

J'ai trouvé un billet de vingt francs.   *I found/have found a twenty franc note.*

Elles ont vendu leur maison.   *They sold/have sold their house.*

A-t-il acheté la voiture?   *Did he buy/has he bought the car?*

Nous n'avons pas encore mangé.   *We haven't eaten yet.*

➤ See avoir in Unit 48, être in Unit 49, use of the perfect and imperfect tenses in Unit 65, the perfect infinitive in Unit 73, the negative (2) in Unit 83, asking questions (1) in Unit 84.

1 **Select the correct form of the verb in the following sentences.**

E.g. **Elles est/ont fini le voyage.** → **Elles *ont* fini le voyage.**

a Il est/sont allé au match.

b J'ai/as acheté un costume.

c Nous ont/avons perdu notre chat.

d As/a-tu fini le journal?

e Elles a/sont allées en ville.

f Vous avez/avons préparé les sandwichs?

2 **Complete the following sentences, putting the verb in brackets into the perfect tense.**

E.g. **Ce matin il _____ les courses. (faire)** → **Ce matin il *a fait* les courses.**

a Ce matin il _____ la radio. (écouter)

b Ce matin à dix heures elle _____ l'autobus. (prendre)

c Hier elles _____ dans le jardin. (travailler)

d Avant le déjeuner j'_____ la fiche. (remplir)

3 **Insert the appropriate past participles from the box into the postcard. The first one has been done for you.**

Nous nous amusons bien ici à Paris!

Ce matin, nous avons (a) visité le musée du Louvre et j'ai (b)...un déjeuner superbe! J'ai beaucoup (c)...la Joconde. Cet après-midi, nous avons (d)...des cadeaux et des souvenirs, et tu ne vas pas le croire - j'ai (e)...Jacques et Valérie dans une librairie!

À très bientôt,

Hélène

| acheté | ~~visité~~ | rencontré | mangé | aimé |

61 UNIT The perfect tense (2): with *être*

The perfect tense is used when referring to a completed action in the past. Some verbs take être as their auxiliary.

A There are fourteen verbs (plus their compounds and all the reflexive verbs) that use **être** to form the perfect tense. They include regular and irregular verbs. Most indicate motion or a change of state, and to some extent they form pairs.

Infinitive	Past participle
aller *to go*	allé
venir *to come*	venu
arriver *to arrive*	arrivé
partir *to leave*	parti
rester *to stay*	resté
entrer *to go in*	entré
sortir *to go out*	sorti

Infinitive	Past participle
descendre *to go down*	descendu
monter *to go up*	monté
tomber *to fall*	tombé
mourir *to die*	mort
naître *to be born*	né
retourner *to return*	retourné
rentrer *to come/go home*	rentré

B The past participle of these verbs agrees in number and gender with the subject of the verb.

Elle est sortie avec ses amies.   *She's gone out with her friends.*

VENIR *to come*	
je suis venu(e)	nous sommes venu(e)s
tu es venu(e)	vous êtes venu(e)(s)(es)
il/elle est venu(e)	ils/elles sont venu(e)s

⚠ With **on** agreement is optional: **On est allé(e)(s)(es).** *We went.*

C Some of the above verbs can be used transitively, that is with an object. When this is the case they are conjugated with **avoir**.

	with **être**	with **avoir**
descendre	Je suis descendu(e).	J'ai descendu l'escalier.
	I went downstairs.	*I went down the stairs.*
monter	Je suis monté(e).	J'ai monté ma valise dans ma chambre.
	I went up(stairs).	*I took my case up to my room.*
retourner	Je suis retourné(e) à la gare.	J'ai retourné le tableau.
	I went back to the station.	*I turned the painting over.*
sortir	Je suis sorti(e) hier soir.	J'ai sorti l'argent de ma poche.
	I went out last night.	*I took the money from my pocket.*
rentrer	Je suis rentré(e) à minuit.	J'ai rentré la voiture.
	I came home at midnight.	*I have put the car away.*

➤ See être in Unit 49, the perfect tense of reflexive verbs in Unit 62, use of the perfect and imperfect tenses in Unit 65, the perfect infinitive in Unit 73, negatives (2) in Unit 83, asking questions (1) in Unit 84.

Choose the correct auxiliary verb.

E.g. **Elle est/a rentrée vers minuit.** → **Elle *est* rentrée vers minuit.**

a J'ai/je suis descendu de la montagne très vite.

b Elle a/est montée dans sa chambre.

c Il a/est sorti la valise de la voiture.

d Nous sommes/avons rentré le vélo dans le garage.

e J'ai/suis monté l'escalier.

Complete the sentences with the appropriate part of the verb *être*.

E.g. **Je _____ allée en ville ce matin.** → **Je *suis* allée en ville ce matin.**

a Nous _____ arrivés vers dix heures.

b Jean et Claude _____ sortis hier soir.

c Ma mère _____ née en 1928.

d Ta sœur n' _____ pas venue avec toi?

e Je _____ tombé à cause de la neige.

f Vous _____ arrivé trop tard. Il _____ déjà parti.

Use the correct form of the past participle in the following sentences.

E.g. **Jules est _____ très tard. (descendre) Jules est *descendu* très tard.**

a Sophie est malade, donc elle est _____ chez elle. (rester)

b Mes parents sont _____ en vacances hier matin. (partir)

c Je me demande si Pierre est _____ en Écosse? (arriver)

d Vous êtes _____ quand? (sortir)

e Agnès et moi sommes _____ au cinéma lundi soir. (aller)

Translate the following sentences into French.

a *She came out of the station.*

b *They came out of the cinema.*

c *She fell off the bike.*

d *He went into the bank.*

e *She was born on 4 January.*

62 UNIT The perfect tense (3): reflexive verbs

There are important points to remember concerning past participle agreement when reflexive verbs are used in the perfect tense.

A All reflexive verbs use **être** rather than **avoir** to form the perfect tense. As with all other verbs that use **être**, the past participle must agree with the subject of the verb.

SE LEVER (to get up, to stand up)	
je me suis levé(e)	nous nous sommes levé(e)s
tu t'es levé(e)	vous vous êtes levé(e)(s)(es)
il s'est levé	ils se sont levés
elle s'est levée	elles se sont levées

Je me suis réveillé. (*m*)	*I woke up.*
Il s'est douché.	*He had a shower.*
Elle s'est lavée.	*She washed/had a wash.*
Nous nous sommes promenés. (*mpl*)	*We went for a walk.*
Elles se sont recontrées.	*They met each other.*

B The past participle does not change its ending, however, where the reflexive pronoun is actually the *indirect* object of the verb. This happens:

- in phrases involving doing something for yourself or to yourself;
  Elle s'est brossé les cheveux.   *She brushed her hair.*
  (the direct object here is **les cheveux**)

- when the reflexive pronoun means *to/at each other.*
  Ils se sont envoyé des   *They sent e-mails to each other.*
    courriers électroniques.
  Elles se sont téléphoné.   *They telephoned each other.*

C The question form with inversion is as follows:
  S'est-elle assise?   *Has she sat down?/Did she sit down?*

D The negative (e.g. **ne … pas**) encloses both the reflexive pronoun and the verb. In an inverted question it goes round the reflexive pronoun, the verb and the subject pronoun.

Je ne me suis pas couché(e).	*I didn't go to bed.*
Elle ne s'est pas habillée.	*She didn't get dressed.*
Ne s'est-elle pas encore levée?	*Hasn't she got up yet?*

➤ *See reflexive verbs in Unit 35, negatives in Units 82 and 83, asking questions in Units 84–85.*

1 Change the following present tense sentences into the perfect tense. The basic past participles to use are in the box.

E.g. Il se lève. → Il s'est levé.

a Tu te reposes.

b Ils s'arrêtent.

c Nous nous asseyons.

d Vous vous dépêchez.

e Elle s'ennuie.

f Je me lave.

g Elles se promènent.

assis	arrêté
lavé	dépêché
reposé	ennuyé
promené	

2 Rewrite the following jumbled sentences correctly.

E.g. sont réveillés se ils. *They woke up.* → Ils se sont réveillés.

a il en s'est route mis *He set off.*

b s'est devant l'autobus la arrêté banque *The bus stopped in front of the bank.*

c approchée s'est elle lui de *She approached him.*

d nous tard couchés hier nous sommes soir *We went to bed late last night.*

e je reposée le me jardin suis dans *I had a rest in the garden.*

f promenés vous dans vous le êtes parc *You had a walk in the park.*

g avant rasé sortir tu de t'es *You shaved before going out.*

h ils de heure se levés bonne matin sont ce *They got up early this morning.*

3 Change the following statements into questions, using the inverted form.

E.g. Ils se sont levés. → Se sont-ils levés?

a Il s'est rasé ce matin.

b Elle s'est couchée tard.

c Elles se sont rencontrées en France.

4 Answer the following questions in the negative.

E.g. Vous vous êtes réveillé(e) de bonne heure? → Non. Je ne me suis pas réveillé(e) de bonne heure.

a Elle s'est habillée?

b Vous vous êtes couché(e) tard hier soir?

c Ils se sont reposés hier?

d Elle s'est coupé au doigt? (*cut her finger*)

63 UNIT The perfect tense (4): preceding direct objects

When a direct object pronoun precedes a verb in the perfect tense, the past participle must agree in gender and number.

A The past participle agrees with any preceding direct object in number and gender. This is called agreement of the past participle, and occurs with all compound tenses in a number of constructions.

B In the perfect tense the direct and indirect object pronouns are placed immediately before **avoir**. The past participle must agree with any *direct* object pronoun (but not with indirect object pronouns or the pronoun **en**).

Ce livre, tu **l'**as acheté?	*That book – did you buy it?*
Ces journaux, vous **les** avez lus?	*These papers – have you read them?*
Marie-Pierre était là, vous **lui** avez parlé?	*Marie-Pierre was here, did you speak to her?*
J'**en** ai acheté. (des disquettes, *fpl*)	*I've bought some. (floppy disks)*

The following table shows all forms of past participle agreement.

Masculine singular	Le livre? → Oui. Je l'ai acheté.	*I bought it.*
Feminine singular	La voiture? → Oui. Je l'ai acheté**e**.	*I bought it.*
Masculine plural	Les journaux? → Oui. Je les ai acheté**s**.	*I bought them.*
Feminine plural	Les oranges? → Oui. Je les ai acheté**es**.	*I bought them.*

C This rule also applies in questions, including those that begin with **quel** (**quels/quelle/quelles**), **combien de** and (**lequel** (**lesquels/laquelle/lesquelles**).

Quelle voiture as-tu vu**e**?	*Which car did you see?*
Quels journaux as-tu acheté**s**?	*Which newspapers did you buy?*
Combien de livres a-t-elle acheté**s**?	*How many books did she buy?*
Laquelle as-tu acheté**e**?	*Which one did you buy?*
Lesquels avez-vous vu**s**?	*Which ones did you see?*

D Agreement also occurs when the relative pronoun **que** meaning *who(m)*, *that* or *which* comes before a verb in the perfect tense.

Les articles que tu as écri**ts** sont très intéressants.	*The articles (that) you wrote are very interesting.*
Les disquettes que j'ai acheté**es** sont sur mon bureau.	*The floppy disks I bought are on my desk.*

► See relative pronouns (1) in Unit 41, object pronouns in Units 45–47, asking questions (2) and (3) in Units 85 and 86.

1 **Insert an appropriate past participle from amongst those in the box into the gaps in the following sentences.**

E.g. Regarde mes chaussures. Je les ai _____ ce matin. →
Regarde mes chaussures. Je les ai *achetées* ce matin.

vu	choisie	achetée	choisi	laissés	laissé	achetés
mis	faite	visités	vue	achetées	mises	fait	visité

a Tu as perdu tes crayons? Non, je les ai _____ chez moi.

b Ces fleurs? Je les ai _____ au marché.

c Le film français? Je l'ai _____ hier soir.

d Les chaussettes? Il les a _____ dans la valise.

e Voilà le musée que nous avons _____ la semaine dernière.

f Voici la voiture que j'ai _____ hier.

g C'est le gâteau qu'il a _____ .

2 **Make the following past participles agree where necessary.**

E.g. La brochure? Je l'ai (laissé) au bureau. →
La brochure? Je l'ai *laissée* au bureau.

a Les documents? Je les ai (donné) à Christine.

b Les articles? Je les ai (lu).

c Mes amies? Je les ai (rencontré) en ville.

d Mon travail? Je l'ai (fini) ce matin.

e Hélène? Je lui ai (parlé) hier soir.

f Ça, c'est la clé qu'il a (perdu).

3 **Following the example, write sentences using the verbs in brackets.**

E.g. la chemise (laver) → Je l'ai lavée hier.

a le musée (visiter)

b les lettres (envoyer)

c la jupe (acheter)

d les stylos (perdre)

e l'ouvre-boîte (*nm*) (utiliser)

f le tire-bouchon (trouver)

g les chemises (laver)

h les radios (*nf*) (réparer)

3 **Complete the following sentences using the verb in brackets.**

E.g. Où sont les documents que Maurice a (préparer)? →
Où sont les documents que Maurice a *préparés*?

a Combien de disquettes avez-vous (acheter)?

b Quel ordinateur a-t-il (utiliser)?

c Lesquels as-tu (laver)?

d Où est la lettre que j'ai (recevoir)?

64 UNIT The imperfect tense

The imperfect tense is used in description and to refer to repeated actions in the past.

A The imperfect tense is formed from the **nous** form of the present tense. You remove the **-ons** ending, then add the appropriate imperfect tense ending.

aller *to go* → nous all**ons** → all-

The pronunciation is the same for **-ais**, **-ait** and **-aient**.

ALLER *to go*	
j'all**ais**	nous all**ions**
tu all**ais**	vous all**iez**
il/elle all**ait**	ils/elles all**aient**

The spelling change that affects **-er** verbs with stems ending in **-g** or **-c** in the present tense also applies in the imperfect in all persons except the **nous** and **vous** forms, e.g. **je mangeais** *I was eating*, **il lançait** *he threw*.

Être is irregular in the imperfect.

ÊTRE *to be*	
j'étais	nous étions
tu étais	vous étiez
il/elle était	ils/elles étaient

The imperfect tense has several meanings in French. It can be used:

B • to describe regular or repeated actions in the past, in the sense of *used to*
  Tous les samedis Claudine   *Every Saturday Claudine met/*
    retrouvait son amie.   *used to meet/would meet her friend.*

• to describe a continuous action in the past
  Elles regardaient la télévision.   *They were watching television.*
  Il lisait le journal.   *He was reading the paper.*

• to describe conditions, circumstances or a state of mind, possibly when something else occurred
  Il pleuvait quand je suis arrivé.   *It was raining when I arrived.*

A The following English pluperfects are translated by the imperfect in French, using **depuis** and **venir de**.
  J'y travaillais depuis trois ans.   *I had worked there for three years.*
  Je venais d'arriver.   *I had just arrived.*

➤ See present tense: -er verbs with changes in the stem in Unit 32, past tenses: perfect or imperfect? in Unit 65, pluperfect in Unit 66, depuis, il y a, venir de in Unit 93.

64 UNIT : The imperfect tense – Exercises

1 Match the following to make sentences, using the English sentences below as a guide.

E.g. Quand il était au Canada + il faisait de la voile.
When he was in Canada he used to sail.

a Quand j'étais jeune
b Quand je travaillais le soir
c Quand j'étais riche
d Quand nous étions en vacances
e Quand j'habitais en France
f Quand il pleuvait
g Quand nous étions à l'école

h nous travaillions peu.
i je sortais tous les soirs.
j je parlais couramment le français.
k j'écoutais de la musique.
l je restais à la maison.
m nous faisions du ski.
n j'achetais tous les jours des vêtements.

1 *When I was young I used to go out every evening.*
2 *When I lived in France I used to speak French fluently.*
3 *When we were on holiday we skied.*
4 *When I worked in the evenings I would listen to music.*
5 *When it rained I would stay at home.*
6 *When I was rich I used to buy clothes every day.*
7 *When we were at school we didn't do much work.*

2 Rewrite the following sentences in the imperfect tense.

E.g. Je mange une orange tous les jours. → Je mangeais une orange tous les jours.

a Ils prennent souvent le train.
b D'habitude, vous finissez votre travail avant de sortir.
c De temps en temps, je joue au tennis.
d Je me couche généralement vers minuit.
e Je travaille à l'hôpital.
f Elles rentrent à six heures à la maison.

3 Correct the information under each of the following pictures.

E.g. Elle faisait la cuisine. → Non. Elle écrivait une lettre.

Il jouait au golf.

Elles travaillaient à l'ordinateur.

Elle lisait un livre.

65 UNIT | Past tenses: perfect or imperfect?

Although the perfect and the imperfect are both past tenses they have different functions, and these can differ from English usage.

A You will need to use both the perfect and imperfect tenses when referring to what happened in the past. The perfect is generally used to express single actions or events. The imperfect expresses (a) regular or repeated action, (b) a continuous action and (c) what was happening or conditions, circumstances, a state of mind (perhaps when something else occurred). These examples show their contrasting use.

- regular or repeated action (imperfect), one-off action or event (perfect)

  Paul allait souvent en France.   *Paul often used to go to France.*
                                        (repeated action)

  Moi, j'y suis allé une fois.   *I myself only went once.*
                                        (single action)

- continuous action (imperfect)

  Jean regardait la télévision.   *Jean was watching television.*
  Je travaillais à l'ordinateur.   *I was working on the computer.*

- what was happening (imperfect) when something else occurred (perfect)

  Elisabeth faisait le ménage   *Elisabeth was doing the housework*
    quand le téléphone a sonné.   *when the telephone rang.*
  Claudine regardait un film à la   *Claudine was watching a film on*
    télévision quand Bernard a   *television when Bernard*
    frappé à la porte.   *knocked at the door.*
  Il neigeait quand nous sommes partis. *It was snowing when we left.*
  J'ai mis un pullover parce   *I put on a sweater because*
    que j'avais froid.   *I was cold.*
  Je suis allé voir le médecin parce   *I went to see the doctor because*
    que j'étais malade.   *I was ill.*

B If two events occurred at the same time, or two actions were taking place simultaneously, the same tense is used for both verbs.

  Jean est arrivé et Pierre est parti.   *Jean arrived and Pierre left.*
  Michel nageait pendant que sa   *Michel was swimming while his*
    sœur se reposait sur la plage.   *sister relaxed on the beach.*

 ➤ *See the perfect tense in Units 60–63, the imperfect tense in Unit 64.*

65 Past tenses: perfect or imperfect? – *Exercises*

1 Put the verb in brackets into the perfect or imperfect tense. The time expression (*ce matin*, etc.) will help you.

E.g. Il _____ un café très souvent avec nous. (prendre) Il *a pris* un café avec nous ce matin.

Il _____ un café très souvent avec nous. (prendre) → Il *prenait* un café très souvent avec nous.

a Sylvie _____ me voir hier soir (*yesterday evening*). (venir)

Sylvie _____ me voir tous les soirs (*every evening*). (venir)

b Samedi dernier (*last Saturday*), ils _____ au football. (jouer)

Ils _____ au football tous les samedis (*every Saturday*). (jouer)

c Il _____ au cinéma lundi soir (*on Monday evening*). (aller)

Il _____ souvent au cinéma. (aller)

d Elle _____ Henri l'autre jour. (voir)

Elle _____ Henri tous les jours (*every day*). (voir)

e Il _____ une voiture l'année dernière (*last year*). (acheter)

Il _____ une voiture tous les deux ans (*every other year*). (acheter)

f Cette année (*this year*) on _____ du ski en Suisse. (faire)

Chaque année (*every year*) on _____ du ski en Suisse. (faire)

2 Complete the following sentences with the appropriate form of the perfect or imperfect tense of the verbs shown.

E.g. Il _____ quand son fils _____ . (dormir, appeler) →

Il *dormait* quand son fils *a appelé*.

a Hier je _____ quand ma mère _____ . (travailler, arriver)

b Je _____ quand le téléphone _____ . (lire, sonner)

c Elle _____ la radio quand quelqu'un _____ à la porte. (écouter, frapper)

d Pendant que nous _____ des courses (*shopping*), j'_____ mon porte-monnaie. (faire, perdre)

3 Rewrite the following passage using the perfect and imperfect tenses instead of the present.

C'est le 22 août, et il fait très chaud. Je me promène quand je rencontre mon amie Catherine. Nous décidons de prendre un café ensemble. Pendant que nous buvons un café, nous voyons un petit accident au coin de la rue. Deux voitures se heurtent l'une contre l'autre et les deux hommes qui conduisent commencent à se disputer.

131

66 UNIT | The pluperfect tense

The pluperfect is a compound tense conjugated with avoir and être and is used to say what had happened.

The pluperfect tense is formed using the imperfect tense of **avoir** or **être** and a past participle.

A All verbs that take **avoir** in the perfect tense do so in the pluperfect tense.

TRAVAILLER *to work*	
j'avais travaillé	nous avions travaillé
tu avais travaillé	vous aviez travaillé
il/elle avait travaillé	ils/elles avaient travaillé

Elle avait travaillé toute la journée.
She had worked all day.

The rules for the agreement of the past participle with any preceding direct object are the same as for the perfect tense.

B All verbs that take **être** in the perfect tense also do so in the pluperfect tense. The rules for past participle agreement with the subject are also the same.

SORTIR *to go out*	
j'étais sorti(e)	nous étions sorti(e)s
tu étais sorti(e)	vous étiez sorti(e)(s)(es)
il/elle était sorti(e)	ils/elles étaient sorti(e)s

Elle était sortie avant lui.   *She had gone out before him.*

C Reflexive verbs, as in the perfect tense, also take **être** in the pluperfect tense, and the reflexive pronoun changes according to the subject of the verb.

Je m'étais déjà couché   *I had already gone to bed*
quand tu as téléphoné.   *when you phoned.*

D The pluperfect tense often occurs with other past tenses, and expresses an earlier event.

Quand nous sommes arrivés au   *When we arrived at the restaurant,*
restaurant, il avait déjà fini son repas.   *he had already finished his meal.*
Je pensais que tu avais acheté   *I thought you had bought*
les livres.   *the books.*
J'avais oublié qu'elle était   *I had forgotten that she was*
végétarienne.   *a vegetarian.*

➤ See the perfect tense in Units 60–63, the imperfect tense in Unit 64, depuis and venir de in Unit 93.

The pluperfect tense – Exercises

1 **Choose a past participle from the box to complete the sentences below.**

E.g. Je lui avais _____ que je ne pouvais pas aller. →
Je lui avais *expliqué* que je ne pouvais pas aller.

parties	reconnu (*recognised*)	levés	mangé	bu
rentré	lu	plu (*rained*)	arrivé	expliqué

a Il avait trop _____ et ne pouvait pas conduire.

b Nous nous étions _____ de bonne heure, parce que le train partait à six heures.

c J'avais déjà _____ le livre quand elle me l'a demandé.

d Elles étaient _____ avant mon arrivée.

e On voyait bien qu'il avait _____ pendant la nuit.

f Elle avait faim parce qu'elle n'avait rien _____ .

g J'avais _____ le problème plusieurs fois, mais il ne comprenait pas.

2 **Insert the correct form of *avoir* or *être* to form the pluperfect in the following sentences.**

E.g. Elle _____ sortie quand vous la cherchiez. →
Elle *était* sortie quand vous la cherchiez.

a Il _____ fini son travail avant de partir.

b Elle _____ partie sans dire au revoir.

c Tu t'_____ couché tôt ce soir-là.

d Ils _____ déjà vu le film au cinéma avant de le louer en vidéo.

e J'_____ trop mangé à midi pour dîner le soir.

f Nous _____ allés voir des amis quand on a eu l'accident.

3 **Now complete the following sentences with the pluperfect tense of the verb given in brackets.**

E.g. Vous _____ _____ et on n'a pas pu vous trouver. (partir) →
Vous *étiez partis* et on n'a pas pu vous trouver.

a J'_____ déjà _____ le dessert quand ils sont arrivés. (préparer)

b Elle _____ _____ à l'heure et voulait prendre le train. (arriver)

c Il _____ _____ son portefeuille en route pour l'aéroport. (perdre)

d Nous nous _____ _____ de bonne heure pour voir le lever du soleil. (se réveiller)

e Elles _____ _____ leurs cartes postales et sont allées à la poste. (écrire)

f Avant de partir j'_____ _____ ma voiture. (laver)

g Je ne savais pas que tu _____ _____ . (arriver)

67 | The past historic tense

The past historic tense is used in written but rarely in spoken French to describe past actions and events.

A Formation

• All **-er** verbs follow the same pattern. Begin by removing the **-er**, then add the appropriate **-a** ending:

Il parla à l'agent de police.
He spoke to the policeman.

PARLER *to speak* (**-a** endings)	
je parl**ai**	nous parl**âmes**
tu parl**as**	vous parl**âtes**
il/elle parl**a**	ils/elles parl**èrent**

• All regular **-ir** verbs, all regular **-re** verbs, and some irregular verbs take the **-i** endings.

Elle vendit sa voiture.
She sold her car.

VENDRE *to sell* (**-i** endings)	
je vend**is**	nous vend**îmes**
tu vend**is**	vous vend**îtes**
il/elle vend**it**	ils/elles vend**irent**

Also **faire (il fit), dire (il dit), mettre (il mit), prendre (il prit), voir (il vit), rire (il rit)** and **s'asseoir (il s'assit)**, etc.

• The **-u** endings are used for irregular **-ir** and **-re** verbs whose past participle ends in **-u**, and for **être** (**voir** and **battre** are exceptions: they follow the pattern illustrated by **vendre** above).

L'agent put arrêter le voleur.

LIRE *to read* (**-u** endings)	
je l**us**	nous l**ûmes**
tu l**us**	vous l**ûtes**
il/elle l**ut**	ils/elles l**urent**

The officer was able to arrest the thief.

Also **avoir (il eut), boire (il but), croire (il crut), devoir (il dut), pouvoir (il put), savoir (il sut)** and **vouloir (il voulut)**, etc.

• **Venir**, **tenir** and their compounds have this pattern in the past historic.

Il vint me voir.
He came to see me.

VENIR *to come*	
je v**ins**	nous v**înmes**
tu v**ins**	vous v**întes**
il/elle v**int**	ils/elles v**inrent**

⚠ When a verb stem ends in **-c** or **-g** this changes to **-ç** or **-g** before an **a**, an **â** or a **u**: **je lançai** *I threw*, **il mangea** *he ate*, **ils reçurent** *they received*.

B The past historic is a narrative tense found in books, newspapers, magazines and official documents to describe completed events in the past. In speech and in less formal writing the perfect tense takes its place.

1 Provide the infinitive for the following verbs in the past historic.

E.g. il prit → **prendre**

a elles vinrent

b nous fûmes

c il put

d ils mirent

e nous nous assîmes

f je lus

g je revins

h il battit

2 Change the verb from the past historic into the perfect tense.

E.g. **Ils furent frappés de panique.** → Ils *ont été* frappés de panique.

a Ils frappèrent à la porte.

b Elle attendit le train.

c Je choisis une chemise bleue.

d Il perdit sa clé.

e Elles achetèrent des fraises.

f Nous allâmes chez nos amis.

g Il finit son travail.

h Ils répondirent à ma question.

3 Rewrite the following paragraph, putting the verbs given in brackets into the past historic tense.

Minuit (sonner) (*struck*). Jean-Luc (entendre) quelque chose. Il (regarder) par la fenêtre et (voir) quelqu'un. Après un moment, on (frapper) à la porte. C'etait Gaston. "Vite, entre", (dire) Jean-Luc. Gaston (prendre) un morceau de papier dans sa poche, puis (lire) le message. Jean-Luc (écouter) attentivement. Ils (se regarder).

68 UNIT The future tense

A The future tense of most regular and many irregular verbs is formed by using the infinitive as the stem, and adding the future tense endings (-**re** verbs drop the final -**e** before adding the endings).

ARRIVER to arrive	
j'arriver**ai**	nous arriver**ons**
tu arriver**as**	vous arriver**ez**
il/elle arriver**a**	ils/elles arriver**ont**

Je vendrai ma voiture.   *I will/am going to sell my car.*

Most -**er** verbs that have a spelling change in the present tense maintain the change in the future tense. This occurs in all persons.

j'ach**è**terai   *I will sell*   j'appe**ll**erai   *I will call*

B Some verbs are irregular in the future tense and do not form their stem from the infinitive, for example:

Infinitive	Future	Infinitive	Future
aller to go	j'irai	mettre to put	je mettrai
avoir to have	j'aurai	pouvoir to be able	je pourrai
devoir to have to	je devrai	savoir to know	je saurai
envoyer to send	j'enverrai	venir to come	je viendrai
être to be	je serai	voir to see	je verrai
faire to make, to do	je ferai	vouloir to want	je voudrai

C Ways of expressing the future in French
- with the future tense:
  L'année prochaine je changerai d'emploi. *Next year I'll change jobs.*

  ⚠ with **quand** the future tense is used in French (present tense in English).
  Quand vous arriverez appelez-moi.   *When you arrive call me.*
- with the simple future tense (**aller** + infinitive), mainly for the immediate future:
  Je vais te le montrer.   *I'll show you it.*
- with the present tense:
  Le spectacle commence à sept heures. *The show starts at seven o'clock.*
  Je pars demain.   *I'm leaving tomorrow.*

➤ **See present tense: regular -er verbs with changes in the stem in Unit 32.**

68 UNIT The future tense – Exercises

1 Complete the sentences by joining the two parts to match the illustrations.

E.g. Quand je serai grande, j'irai + au Canada.

Quand je serai grande...

1 j'habiterai	**a** à Paris.
2 j'aurai	**b** une voiture.
3 je louerai	**c** un appartement.
4 j'achèterai	**d** trois enfants.

2 Say what Andrew will do on holiday, using the future tense of the verbs in brackets.

E.g. (aller) en France → *Il ira* en France.

a (faire) du camping   **d** (acheter) des souvenirs

b (louer) un vélo   **e** (visiter) des endroits intéressants

c (écrire) des cartes postales   **f** (téléphoner) à sa mère

3 Complete the following horoscopes, putting the appropriate verb in the box into the future tense and using each verb only once. The first one has been done for you.

acheter	recevoir (recevr-)	s'amuser	écrire	~~être~~

CAPRICORNE: Vous **serez** en forme, et vous _____ bien cette semaine. Vous _____ un cadeau, et le 30 _____ une journée exceptionnelle. Vous _____ beaucoup de lettres, et vous _____ quelque chose d'important.

oublier	se disputer	aider	sortir	dépenser	avoir

SCORPION: Vous _____ une semaine difficile. Vous _____ beaucoup et vous _____ trop d'argent. Vous _____ avec une amie et vous _____ une date importante. Mais d'autres amis vous _____ .

69 UNIT The future perfect tense

The future perfect is a compound tense conjugated with avoir or être. It is used to say what will have happened.

A The future perfect tense is formed with the future tense of **avoir** or **être** and a past participle.

• All verbs that take **avoir** in the perfect tense do so in the future perfect.

ACHETER *to buy*	
j'aurai acheté	nous aurons acheté
tu auras acheté	vous aurez acheté
il/elle aura acheté	ils/elles auront acheté

Il aura acheté le cadeau
  avant mardi.
*He will have bought the
  present by Tuesday.*

The rules for the agreement of the past participle with any preceding direct object are the same as for the perfect tense.

• All verbs that take **être** in the perfect tense also do so in the future perfect. The rules for past participle agreement with the subject are also the same.

PARTIR *to leave*	
je serai parti(e)	nous serons parti(e)s
tu seras parti(e)	vous serez parti(e)(s)(es)
il/elle sera parti(e)	ils/elles seront parti(e)s

Tu seras parti avant juillet.   *You will have left by July.*

• Reflexive verbs again take **être**, and rules for past participle agreement with the subject also apply as in the perfect.

Je me serai levé(e) tôt.   *I will have got up early.*

B You use the future perfect to talk about a future action which will be completed before another future action.

Ils auront fini quand vous   *They will have finished when/by the*
  arriverez.   *time you arrive.*

• It is used after certain time expressions, such as **quand** *when*, **après que** *after*, **aussitôt que** *as soon as*, **dès que** *as soon as* and **tant que** *as long as*.

Aussitôt qu'il aura fini,   *As soon as he has finished,*
  nous sortirons.   *we will go out.*

⚠ There is a difference in tenses used in English and French. In English we use the perfect tense, whereas in French the future perfect is used.

➤ See the perfect tense in Units 60–63, the future tense in Unit 68.

Match the following sentence halves to make whole sentences.

E.g. **Ils seront + arrivés maintenant. → Ils seront arrivés maintenant.**

a Il sera   f fini mon travail.
b J'aurai   g rentrées de Paris.
c Elles seront   h parti de bonne heure.
d Vous aurez   i resté chez toi.
e Tu seras   j acheté des fleurs.

Complete the following sentences with the future perfect of the verb given in brackets.

E.g. **Il _____ du centre commercial maintenant, j'en suis sûr. (sortir) →**
Il *sera sorti* du centre commercial maintenant, j'en suis sûr.

a Demain à cette heure-ci, nous _____ _____ en France. (arriver)
b Vous _____ déjà _____ avant le film? (manger)
c La prochaine fois qu'on se reverra, tu _____ _____ ton cours. (commencer)
d J'_____ _____ les disques avant le weekend. (acheter)
e Écrivez-moi dès que vous _____ _____ ma lettre. (recevoir)
f Nous sortirons après que vous vous _____ _____ . (se reposer)
g On _____ _____ votre article avant lundi. (lire)
h Quand je te reverrai, tu _____ _____ de tes vacances. (rentrer)
i Vous _____ _____ le travail avant la fin du mois? (finir)

Use the future perfect to answer the following questions.

E.g. **Quand liras-tu le journal? (faire, lits) → Quand j'aurai fait les lits.**

a Quand iront-ils au cinéma? (finir, repas)
b Quand est-ce qu'il reviendra? (faire les courses)
c Quand partiras-tu? (voir, film)
d Quand est-ce qu'elle verra la patronne? (retourner, vacances)
e Quand mangeront-ils? (acheter, vin)
f Quand est-ce qu'elle prendra du congé? (finir, travail)
g Quand se levera-t-elle? (se réveiller)
h Quand est-ce qu'il fera ses devoirs? (lire, livre)

70 UNIT The conditional

A The conditional is formed from the future stem (regular or irregular) of a verb and the imperfect tense endings.

Si j'avais assez d'argent, j'achèterais *If I had enough money, I would buy*
une nouvelle voiture.   *a new car.*

TROUVER *to find*	
je trouver**ais**	nous trouver**ions**
tu trouver**ais**	vous trouver**iez**
il/elle trouver**ait**	ils/elles trouver**aient**

Most **-er** verbs that have a spelling change in the present tense maintain the change in the conditional, in all persons, as they do in the future tense.

j'achèterais *I would sell*   j'appe**ll**erais *I would call*

B Use of the conditional

● The main purpose of the conditional is to say what *would happen*.
  J'achèterais ce livre si j'avais   *I would buy this book if I had*
    assez d'argent.   *enough money.*
  Si j'étais malade, j'irais chez   *If I was ill, I would go to the*
    le médecin.   *doctor's.*

● It is used to make polite statements.
  Je vous serais très reconnaissant   *I would be very grateful if you*
    si vous pouviez venir.   *could come.*
  Je préférerais y aller demain.   *I would prefer to go tomorrow.*

● The conditional of **vouloir** and **pouvoir** is used to make polite requests.
  Je voudrais un café, s'il vous plaît. *I would like a coffee, please.*
  Pourriez-vous m'aider, s'il vous plaît? *Could you help me, please?*

● The conditional of **pouvoir** is used to express possibility.
  Elle pourrait arriver lundi.   *She could (might) arrive on Monday.*

● The conditional of **devoir** is used to say that someone should or ought to do something.
  Tu devrais te reposer.   *You ought to (should) rest.*

➤ See -er verb spelling changes in Unit 32, modal verbs in
Units 52 and 53, the imperfect tense in Unit 64, the future tense
in Unit 68, using si in Unit 72.

70 UNIT The conditional – Exercises

1 Match the following questions and answers.

E.g. Qu'est-ce qu'il ferait s'il pleuvait? Il mettrait un anorak.

a Qu'est-ce qu'il ferait s'il avait faim?

b Qu'est-ce que vous feriez si vous étiez riche?

c Qu'est-ce qu'il ferait s'il était fatigué?

d Qu'est-ce que vous feriez si vous aviez soif?

e Qu'est-ce qu'ils feraient s'ils gagnaient à la Loterie nationale?

f Qu'est-ce que vous feriez si vous aviez plus de temps libre?

g Qu'est-ce qu'elles feraient, si elles étaient libres ce soir?

1 Je boirais quelque chose.

2 Ils feraient le tour de monde.

3 Elles iraient au théâtre.

4 Il mangerait un grand repas.

5 Nous lirions et nous regarderions la télé!

6 J'achèterais une maison en France.

7 Il dormirait.

2 Write out the conditional forms of the verbs indicated.

E.g. Savoir   tu _____ → tu saurais

a avoir   il _____

b devoir   je _____

c prendre   nous _____

d pouvoir   vous _____

e vouloir   tu _____

f finir   elle _____

g être   je _____

h faire   elles _____

i acheter   vous _____

j venir   il _____

k aller   nous _____

l voir   je _____

3 Look at the illustrations and, using the verbs in the box, say what you would do.

E.g. Je me reposerais à la plage.

visiter des musées   envoyer des cartes postales   bien manger

141

71 UNIT | The conditional perfect

The conditional perfect is a compound tense conjugated with avoir or être, and is used to say would what have happened.

A The conditional perfect is formed with the conditional of **avoir** or **être** and a past participle.

FINIR *to finish*	
j'aurais fini	nous aurions fini
tu aurais fini	vous auriez fini
il/elle aurait fini	ils/elles auraient fini

- All verbs that take **avoir** in the perfect do so in the conditional perfect.

Il aurait fini, s'il avait eu le temps.   *He would have finished, if he had had the time.*

The rules for the agreement of the past participle with any preceding direct object are as for the perfect tense.

- All verbs that take **être** in the perfect tense also do so in the conditional perfect. The rules for past participle agreement with the subject are also the same.

ARRIVER *to arrive*	
je serais arrivé(e)	nous serions arrivé(e)s
tu serais arrivé(e)	vous seriez arrivé(e)(s)(es)
il/elle serait arrivé(e)	ils/elles seraient arrivé(e)s

Elle serait arrivée, mais son train   *She would have arrived, but her*
était en retard.   *train was late.*

- Reflexive verbs again take **être**, and rules for the past participle agreement with the subject also apply as in the perfect.

Elle se serait douchée, mais elle   *She would have showered but she*
était trop pressée.   *was in too much of a hurry.*

B The conditional perfect is used to describe what would have happened if something else or circumstances had not prevented it.

Elle serait partie, mais il neigeait.   *She would have left but it was snowing.*

- You use the conditional perfect of modal verbs to describe what you *should have*, *could have* or *would have liked to do*.

J'aurais dû lire l'article.   *I should have read the article.*
J'aurais pu lire l'article.   *I could have read the article.*
J'aurais voulu lire l'article.   *I would have liked to read the article.*

➤ See modal verbs in Units 52 and 53, the perfect tense in Units 60–63, the conditional tense in Unit 70, using si in Unit 72.

The conditional perfect – Exercises

1 Match the sentence halves to make complete sentences.

E.g. Si vous étiez arrivés plus tôt + on aurait pu commencer. → Si vous étiez arrivés plus tôt, on aurait pu commencer.

a Si tu avais regardé la carte,   1 vous ne seriez pas devenu si malade.

b Si nous avions regardé l'horaire,   2 j'aurais acheté quelque chose.

c Si j'avais écouté la météo,   3 j'aurais vu les châteaux.

d Si vous aviez écouté le médecin,   4 nous ne serions pas arrivés en retard.

e Si j'étais allée dans le Val de Loire,   5 nous serions sortis ensemble.

f Si elle avait eu assez d'argent,   6 nous aurions pris l'autoroute.

g Si vous m'aviez donné de l'argent,   7 elle aurait acheté la robe.

h S'il était arrivé à temps,   8 j'aurais su qu'il allait pleuvoir.

2 Put the following into the conditional perfect, using the verb given in brackets and the English sentences as a guide.

E.g. Si Jean-Paul était arrivé, nous _____ manger ensemble. (pouvoir)
If Jean-Paul had arrived we could have eaten together. → Si Jean-Paul était arrivé, nous aurions pu manger ensemble.

a S'il avait eu l'argent, René _____ _____ le TGV. (prendre)
If he had had the money René would have taken the TGV.

b Si elle s'était levée, elle _____ _____ à l'heure. (partir)
If she had got up, she would have left on time.

c Si les documents étaient arrivés, André _____ _____ son travail. (commencer)
If the documents had arrived, André would have started his work.

d Si elle avait su que c'était son anniversaire, Aimée _____ _____ un gâteau. (faire)
If she had known that it was his/her birthday, Aimée would have made a cake.

e S'il avait plu, Michel et Françoise _____ _____ chez eux. (rester)
If it had rained Michel and Françoise would have stayed at home.

3 Respond to the English sentences by using the verb *devoir* with the words in brackets.

E.g. *He got sunstroke.* (porter un chapeau) → Il aurait dû porter un chapeau.

a *She got soaked.* (prendre un parapluie)

b *They ran out of petrol.* (acheter de l'essence)

c *They arrived late.* (partir plus tôt)

d *I got very cold.* (porter un anorak)

72 UNIT | Using *si*

A When you use **si**, the rules concerning tenses are as follows.
- main clause + future tense; **si** clause + present tense

  Je pourrai porter cette robe ce
  soir, si je l'achète.

  *I will be able to wear this dress this
  evening, if I buy it.*
- main clause + conditional; **si** clause + imperfect tense

  J'achèterais une robe en soie, si
  j'avais assez d'argent.

  *I would buy a silk dress, if I had
  enough money.*
- main clause + conditional perfect; **si** clause + pluperfect tense

  J'aurais pu porter la robe ce soir,
  si je l'avais achetée.

  *I would have been able to wear the
  dress this evening, if I had bought it.*

In most cases the **si** clause can also come before the main clause.

Si elle n'est pas trop chère,
j'achèterai cette robe.

*If it is not too expensive I will buy
this dress.*

B **Si** can mean *if* in the sense of *provided that*:

J'achèterai cette robe si elle n'est
pas trop chère.

*I will buy this dress if it is not too
expensive.*

C **Si** + imperfect tense can mean *Suppose...?*, *How about...?* or *What if...?*

Si nous partions maintenant?   *Suppose/What if we left now?*

D *If (only)* can be translated by **si** (**seulement**) + the imperfect or pluperfect
tense.

Si seulement tu pouvais rester!   *If only you could/were able to stay!*

Si (seulement) j'avais su!   *If (only) I had known!*

E **Si** meaning *whether* to introduce an indirect question (i.e. used as a
subordinating conjunction) can be followed by any tense.

Je me demande si elle vient.   *I wonder if/whether she's coming.*

Je me demande s'il est arrivé.   *I wonder if/whether he's arrived.*

⚠ **Si** shortens to **s'** only when followed by **il** and **ils**. **Si on** can become **si l'on**.

On n'entre pas si l'on ne
porte pas de veston.

*They don't let you in if you're
not wearing a jacket.*

➤ See the appropriate units for information on tenses (present,
imperfect, pluperfect, future, conditional, conditional perfect); see
also *si* meaning *yes* in Unit 95, and conjunctions (2) in Unit 81.

Match the sentence halves appropriately and find their English equivalents.

E.g. **Si Claudine vient avec nous + nous passerons chez Maurice.** *If Claudine comes with us we'll call in on Maurice.*

a Si j'avais le temps
b S'il avait fait froid
c Si seulement
d Je ne sais pas
e S'il fait beau

f tu pouvais venir!
g il aurait mis son manteau.
h s'ils réussiront.
i je lirais beaucoup plus de livres.
j nous ferons une promenade.

1 *I don't know if they will succeed.*
2 *If I had the time I would read many more books.*
3 *If it's fine we'll go for a walk.*
4 *If it had been cold he would have put on his coat.*
5 *If only you could come!*

Fill in the gaps with the words from the box.

E.g. **Quand j'***aurai* **de l'argent, je** *sortirai* **avec vous.** *When I have some money I will go out with you.*

pourrais	avais	sors	étais	aurais	verrai

a Si j'_____ en France je _____ parler français tous les jours. *If I were in France I would be able to speak French every day.*
b Si je _____ le weekend je _____ mes amis. *If I go out at the weekend, I will see my friends.*
c Si je n'_____ pas pris mes vacances, j'_____ pu commencer mon nouvel emploi. *If I hadn't taken my holidays I could have started my new job.*

Put each verb in brackets into the correct tense.

E.g. **Si je (passer) une année en France, je (parler) couramment le français.** *If I spend a year in France, I will speak French fluently.* → **Si je** *passe* **une année en France, je** *parlerai* **couramment le français.**

a Si j' (travailler), j' (faire) des progrès.
 If I had worked, I would have made progress.
b Si j' (avoir) beaucoup d'argent j' (acheter) une maison en France.
 If I had a lot of money I would buy a house in France.
c Si je (finir) mon travail, je (pouvoir) sortir plus tard.
 If I finish my work, I will be able to go out later.

73 UNIT The perfect infinitive

The perfect infinitive is used to say after having done... or after having done..., and following certain verbs.

A When a sentence describes two consecutive actions carried out by the same person, you can use **après avoir/être** + past participle. For **avoir** verbs the rules for agreement of the past participle with any preceding direct object are the same as for the perfect tense. All verbs that take **être** in the perfect tense again do so here, and the rules for past participle agreement with the subject are also the same.

- With **avoir** verbs, use **après** + **avoir** + past participle.

  Après avoir fini son travail, elle est rentrée chez elle.

  After finishing her work, she went home.

- With **être** verbs, use **après** + **être** + past participle.

  Après être arrivée à la gare, elle a acheté un billet.

  After arriving at the station, she bought a ticket.

  Après être tombé, il a commencé à pleurer.

  After falling, he began to cry.

- With reflexive verbs the reflexive pronoun appears before **être**, and it must agree in number and gender with the subject of the clauses.

  Après m'être réveillé(e), j'ai pris une tasse de thé.

  After waking up, I had a cup of tea.

  Après s'être levée, elle est partie.

  After getting up, she left.

B The perfect infinitive is also used after certain verbs, mostly expressing attitude or memory, where again the subject of both clauses is the same.

  Elle se souvenait d'avoir bien mangé chez Gaston.

  She remembered eating well at Gaston's.

Other such verbs include: **être content de** *to be happy that*, **remercier de** *to thank for/that*, **regretter de** *to regret that*.

C The present participles of **avoir** (**ayant**) and **être** (**étant**) can also be used in this way with the past participle.

  Ayant fini son travail, elle a quitté le bureau.

  Having finished her work, she left the office.

  Étant venue par le train, elle est arrivée la première.

  Having come by train she arrived first.

➤ See the perfect tense in Units 60–63, the present participle in Unit 55.

73 UNIT The perfect infinitive – Exercises

Insert a suitable *après* construction from the box into the sentences below.

E.g. **Après avoir terminé** le projet, il a pris du congé. *After finishing the project, he took some leave.*

| Après m'être reposé(e)   Après être arrivés   Après être arrivé |
| Après avoir appris   Après s'être dépêché |

a _____ à conduire elle a acheté une voiture. *After learning to drive she bought a car.*

b _____ Jean nous a parlé de ses vacances. *After arriving Jean talked to us about his holidays.*

c _____ un peu j'ai continué à travailler. *After resting a little I continued to work.*

d _____ trop tard, nous avons raté le train. *After arriving too late, we missed the train.*

e _____ il est arrivé à l'heure. *After hurrying he arrived on time.*

Recast the above sentences using *ayant/étant* + past participle.

E.g. **Ayant terminé** le projet, il a pris du congé. *Having finished the project, he took some leave.*

Complete the following sentences by inserting an appropriate *après* construction.

E.g. **Après avoir** mangé, il s'est endormi. *After eating, he fell asleep.*

a _____ arrivée, elle est venue me voir. *After arriving, she came to see me.*

b _____ dit au revoir, il est parti. *After saying goodbye, he left.*

c _____ habillé, il a lu le journal. *After getting dressed, he read the newspaper.*

Combine the following sentences according to the example and using the English sentences to guide you.

E.g. **Il a travaillé. Ensuite, il est sorti.** *After working, he went out.* →
Après avoir travaillé, il est sorti.

a Il a fait le ménage. Ensuite, il a déjeuné avec une amie. *After doing the housework he had lunch with a friend.*

b Il s'est levé. Ensuite, il a préparé son petit déjeuner. *After getting up he prepared his breakfast.*

c Elle est rentrée à la maison. Ensuite, elle a écrit une lettre. *After returning home, she wrote a letter.*

147

74 UNIT The passive

A passive construction is used when the subject of the verb is the person or thing not doing but receiving the action: The present was given.

A The French passive, like the English, is formed with an appropriate tense of the verb **être** *to be*, plus a past participle (which in French must agree with the subject). An active sentence containing a subject, verb and direct object can be changed into a passive sentence.

ACTIVE: Henri a envoyé la lettre. *Henri sent the letter.*

PASSIVE: La lettre a été envoyée par Henri. *The letter was sent by Henri.*

B This table shows the formation and meaning of the passive in several tenses.

Present	La pièce est repeinte chaque année.	*The room is repainted every year.*
Perfect	La pièce a été repeinte.	*The room has been repainted.*
Imperfect	La pièce était repeinte chaque année.	*The room was repainted every year.*
Pluperfect	La pièce avait été repeinte.	*The room had been repainted.*
Future	La pièce sera repeinte.	*The room will be repainted.*
Conditional	La pièce serait repeinte.	*The room would be repainted.*

⚠ In the present and imperfect tenses the past participle can sometimes be purely descriptive and give no indication of a particular action.

La voiture est vendue. *The car's sold.*

La pièce était peinte en bleu. *The room was painted blue.*

C In French the indirect object of a verb cannot become the subject of a passive clause, as it can in English, so another structure has to be used.

On lui a donné des nouvelles. (donner à) *(He was given some news.)*

On m'a parlé du projet. (parler à) *(I was told about the project.)*

D French often avoids the passive, and this can be done in several ways:

- by using **on** + an active verb (as in C above), or another active construction

  On a écrit l'article. *(The article has been written.)*

  Deux infirmières l'ont accompagné. *(He was accompanied by two nurses.)*

- by using a reflexive construction, adding a reflexive pronoun to the verb; this is most common in the **il(s)** and **elle(s)** forms

  Les journaux se vendent ici. *(Newspapers are sold here.)*

  Ce mot ne s'emploie pas. *(This word is not used.)*

➤ See appropriate units for information on tenses, reflexive verbs in Unit 35, the subject pronoun on in Unit 37, verb constructions with objects in Unit 59.

▌ **Fill the gaps using the tense indicated and the verb in brackets.**

E.g. (present) *Je suis invité(e)* à la réunion. (inviter) *I am invited to the reunion.*

Present

a Ils _____ par tout le monde. (aimer) *They are liked by everyone.*

b Le jardin _____ par mon ami. (soigner) *The garden is tended by my friend.*

Perfect

c Le vase _____ . (casser) *The vase has been broken.*

d Tous les sandwichs _____ . (manger) *All the sandwiches have been eaten.*

Imperfect

e Le pont _____ souvent. (repeindre) *The bridge was often repainted.*

f Les malades _____ par deux infirmières. (soigner) *The patients were looked after by two nurses.*

Pluperfect

g Les boissons _____ . (servir) *Drinks had been served.*

h La voiture _____ . (vendre) *The car had been sold.*

Future

i Il _____ par le policier. (interroger) *He will be questioned by the policeman.*

j Le paquet _____ demain. (livrer) *The parcel will be delivered tomorrow.*

Conditional

k Le musée _____ par la municipalité. (fermer) *The museum would be closed by the council.*

l Le déjeuner _____ à midi. (servir) *Lunch would be served at midday.*

▌ **Change the following sentences from passive to active using *on*.**

E.g. **Le gâteau avait été coupé.** *The cake had been cut.* → **On avait coupé le gâteau.**

a Le repassage a été fait. *The ironing has been done.*

b Les clés ont été perdues. *The keys have been lost.*

c Vous serez reconnu. *You will be recognised.*

d La carte postale avait été envoyée. *The postcard had been sent.*

▌ **Complete the following sentences with appropriate verbs from the box using a reflexive construction.**

E.g. **Ils** _____ **au guichet. (vendre) Ils se vendent au guichet.**

a Ça _____ avec un M majuscule. *It's written with a capital M.*

b En français ça _____ 'Bonjour'. *In French you say 'Bonjour'.*

c Ce vin _____ avec le poisson. *This wine is drunk with fish.*

d Les huîtres _____ crues. *Oysters are eaten raw.*

> manger
> dire
> boire
> écrire

The present subjunctive

A The present subjunctive is formed by taking the **ils/elles** form of the present tense, removing the **-ent** and adding the appropriate subjunctive ending.

TROUVER *to find* present: ils **trouv**ent	FINIR *to finish* present: ils **finiss**ent	ATTENDRE *to wait* present: ils **attend**ent
que je trouv**e**	que je finiss**e**	que j'attend**e**
que tu trouv**es**	que tu finiss**es**	que tu attend**es**
qu'il/elle trouv**e**	qu'il/elle finiss**e**	qu'il/elle attend**e**
que nous trouv**ions**	que nous finiss**ions**	que nous attend**ions**
que vous trouv**iez**	que vous finiss**iez**	que vous attend**iez**
qu'ils/elles trouv**ent**	qu'ils/elles finiss**ent**	qu'ils/elles attend**ent**

B **Avoir** and **être** are irregular.

AVOIR *to have*		ÊTRE *to be*	
que j'aie	que nous ayons	que je sois	que nous soyions
que tu aies	que vous ayez	que tu sois	que vous soyez
qu'il/elle ait	qu'ils/elles aient	qu'il/elle soit	qu'ils/elles soient

C The present subjunctive stem of these verbs is irregular.

aller	qu'il **aille** (BUT nous **allions**, vous **alliez**)
faire	qu'il **fasse**
pouvoir	qu'il **puisse** (BUT nous **pouvions**, vous **pouviez**)
savoir	qu'il **sache**
vouloir	qu'il **veuille** (BUT nous **voulions**, vous **vouliez**)

D Some verbs are irregular only in the **nous** and **vous** forms, where they are identical to the imperfect (**qu'il boive** but **nous buvions, vous buviez**). Others include **croire** *to believe* (croie/croyions), **devoir** *to have to* (doive/devions), **mourir** *to die* (meure/mourions), **prendre** *to take* (prenne/prenions), **voir** *to see* (voie/voyions).

⚠ Verbs with spelling changes in the present indicative stem change also in the subjunctive, except those with stems ending in **-g** and **-c** (**manger** *to eat*, **commencer** *to start*) where the change for pronunciation is unnecessary.

➤ *See -er verbs with stem changes in Unit 32, irregular verbs in Units 48–53, when to use the subjunctive in Units 77–79.*

75 The present subjunctive – Exercises

1 Complete the following sentences using words from the box and the English sentences as a guide.

E.g. Il faut que vous _____ en France voir l'usine. *You must go to France to see the factory.* → Il faut que vous alliez en France voir l'usine.

soit	vienne	~~alliez~~	partes	puisse

a Bien que le rapport _____ bon, il est beaucoup trop long. *Although the report is good, it's much too long.*

b Tu connais quelqu'un qui _____ nous aider? *Do you know anyone who could help us?*

c Je ne crois pas qu'elle _____ aujourd'hui. *I don't think she'll come today.*

2 Give the appropriate present subjunctive form of these verbs.

E.g. partir   que je _____ → que je parte

a parler   que tu _____   **d** vendre   que vous _____
b dire   que nous _____   **e** choisir   qu'elle _____
c mettre   qu'ils _____

3 Complete the following sentences by putting the verbs in brackets into the *je* form of the present subjunctive. Each sentence begins with *Il faut que je* (*It is necessary that I/I must*)

E.g. _____ (écrire) des lettres. → Il faut que j'écrive des lettres.
Il faut que je...

a _____ (apprendre) mes verbes. *learn my verbs*
b _____ (aller) en France. *go to France*
c _____ (choisir) une nouvelle voiture. *choose a new car*
d _____ (lire) ce livre. *read this book*
e _____ (être) patient. *be patient*
f _____ (venir) te voir. *come and see you*
g _____ (prendre) des notes. *take notes*

3 Give the *je* and *vous* forms of the present subjunctive of the following verbs.

E.g écrire → que j'écrive   que vous écriviez

a vouloir   **e** boire
b aller   **f** être
c savoir   **g** prendre
d venir

76 The perfect subjunctive

A The perfect subjunctive is formed with the present subjunctive of **avoir** or **être** and a past participle.

TROUVER *to find*	ARRIVER *to arrive*
que j'**aie trouvé**	que je **sois arrivé(e)**
que tu **aies trouvé**	que tu **sois arrivé(e)**
qu'il/elle **ait trouvé**	qu'il/elle **soit arrivé(e)**
que nous **ayons trouvé**	que nous **soyons arrivé(e)s**
que vous **ayez trouvé**	que vous **soyez arrivé(e)(s)(es)**
qu'ils/elles **aient trouvé**	qu'ils/elles **soient arrivé(e)s**

The rules for agreement of the past participle with any preceding direct object are as for the perfect tense. All verbs that take **être** in the perfect tense do so in the perfect subjunctive, and the rules for past participle agreement with the subject are the same as in the perfect tense.

B Reflexive verbs again take **être**, and rules for past participle agreement with the subject apply as in the perfect tense.

SE LEVER *to get up, to stand up*	
que je me **sois levé(e)**	que nous nous **soyons levé(e)s**
que tu te **sois levé(e)**	que vous vous **soyez levé(e)(s)(es)**
qu'il/elle se **soit levé(e)**	qu'ils/elles se **soient levé(e)s**

'Quoique je sois contente qu'elle ait enfin trouvé un passe-temps qui lui plaît, je regrette qu'il soit un peu dangereux'

➤ See the perfect tense in Units 60–63 and when to use the subjunctive in Unit 77–79.

76 The perfect subjunctive – Exercises

1 Give the appropriate perfect subjunctive form of the following verbs, starting with *que*.

E.g. finir   que je _____ → que j'aie fini

a prendre	qu'il _____	**e** pouvoir	que nous _____	
b se dépêcher	qu' ils _____	**f** avoir	que je _____	
c lire	que tu _____	**g** aller	que vous _____	
d savoir	qu'elles _____	**h** faire	qu'elle _____	

2 Translate the following English sentences, using *Je regrette que* (I'm sorry that) or *Je suis content que* (I'm pleased that) plus an item from the box.

E.g. *I'm sorry that they ('people') laughed.* Je suis désolé qu'on ait rit.

elle soit venue	tu sois arrivée	vous ayez perdu votre collier	~~on ait rit~~
il soit arrivé	elle ait fini son travail	tu aies fini ton travail	
il soit venu	je sois arrivé en retard	elle ait perdu son collier	

a *I'm sorry I arrived late.*
b *I'm pleased you've arrived.*
c *I'm pleased that he's come.*
d *I'm sorry you've lost your necklace.*
e *I'm pleased you've finished your work.*

3 Rewrite the following sentences in the perfect subjunctive, beginning each one with *Je suis content que...*

E.g. Nous (aller) au concert. *I'm pleased that we went to the concert.* Je suis contente que nous *soyions allés* au concert.

a Il (gagner) le prix. *I'm pleased that he has won the prize.*
b Elle (apprendre) à conduire. *I'm pleased that she has learned to drive.*
c Tu (se reposer) un peu. *I'm pleased that you've had a bit of a rest.*
d Vous (passer) le weekend chez eux. *I'm pleased that you have spent the weekend at their place.*
e Elles (aller) en vacances. *I'm pleased that they have gone on holiday.*
f Il (partir) à l'heure. *I'm pleased that he left on time.*
g Vous (parler) au curé. *I'm pleased that you have spoken to the priest.*
h Vous (écrire) la lettre. *I'm pleased that you have written the letter.*

77 UNIT | When to use the subjunctive (1)

The subjunctive is used following verbs that express an emotion or an uncertainty. It is usually introduced by que.

A The subjunctive is used with verbs expressing wish, will, preference or desire (e.g. **aimer que** *to like that*, **désirer que** *to desire that*, **préférer que** *to prefer that*, **souhaiter que** *to wish that*, **vouloir que** *to want that*). **Espérer** *to hope* however is followed by the indicative.

Il veut que Guy **aille** au match.	*He wants Guy to go to the match.*
J'espère que tu pourras venir.	*I hope you will be able to come.*

B It is used after verbal phrases expressing pleasure, regret, concern or emotion.

Je suis content que vous puissiez venir.	*I'm pleased you can come.*
Je regrette qu'il soit si fâché.	*I'm sorry he's so angry.*

être heureux que *to be happy that*	avoir peur que … ne *to be afraid that*
être triste que *to be sad that*	avoir crainte que … ne *to fear that*
être fier que *to be proud that*	craindre que … ne *to fear that*
être désolé que *to be sorry that*	être fâché que *to be annoyed that*
être furieux que *to be furious that*	être déçu que *to be disappointed that*
être surpris/étonné que *to be surprised/astonished that*	

⚠ Where shown above, **ne** is inserted before the verb that follows.

C It is used after verbs of doubt, uncertainty or denial, mainly when being used negatively or interrogatively.

Je doute qu'il vienne.	*I doubt he is coming.*
Tu crois qu'il vienne?	*Do you think he'll come?*
Je ne pense pas qu'il vienne.	*I don't think he's coming.*

douter que *to doubt that*	nier que *to deny that*

(ne … pas) croire que *(not) to believe that*
(ne … pas) penser que *(not) to think that*
(ne … pas) être sûr que *(not) to be sure that*

D It's also needed after verbs involving commands or permission, and after **attendre que** *to wait until*.

Il permet que le match ait lieu.	*He's allowing the match to take place.*
Elle attend que le match soit fini.	*She's waiting until the match is over.*

⚠ When both clauses have the same subject, it is usual to use **de** + infinitive rather than **que** + subjunctive.

Elle est heureuse de savoir le résultat. *She's pleased to know the result.*

▶ *See negatives in Units 82 and 83, asking questions in Units 84–86.*

1 **Form the following sentences from the two columns below using the English sentences to guide you.**

E.g. Je doute + qu'elle ait terminé le programme. *I doubt whether she's finished the programme.*

a Je suis content		**h**	que vous partiez.
b Elle est furieuse		**i**	qu'elle n'attende pas.
c Je suis très fière		**j**	que tu reçoives le prix.
d Je suis triste		**k**	qu'il ne soit pas à l'heure.
e Je ne crois pas		**l**	que vous puissiez venir.
f Il craint		**m**	que tu sois malade.
g Il nie		**n**	qu'ils viennent me voir.

1 *He is afraid that she will not wait.*
2 *She is furious that he is not on time.*
3 *I'm pleased that you can come.*
4 *I'm very proud that you are receiving the prize.*
5 *I'm sad that you are leaving.*
6 *I don't believe that you are ill.*
7 *He denies that they're coming to see me.*

2 **Complete the following sentences with the appropriate expression.**

E.g. _____ les journaux ne soient pas arrivés ce matin. *I'm annoyed that the papers haven't come this morning.* → Je suis fâché que les journaux ne soient pas arrivés ce matin.

a _____ elle soit là. *He's very happy that she's there.*
b _____ le projet soit terminé si tôt. *They regret that the project has finished so soon.*
c _____ tu participes au match. *Paul wants you to take part in the match.*

3 **Complete the following sentences with the correct form of the verb in brackets.**

E.g. Il regrette qu'on ne (être) pas avec vous. *He regrets that we're not with you.* → Il regrette qu'on ne soit pas avec vous.

a Je veux qu'elle (écrire) une lettre. *I want her to write a letter.*
b Je doute que tu (arriver) à l'heure. *I doubt you will arrive in time.*
c Elle veut que vous (faire) attention. *She wants you to pay attention.*
d Il nie qu'elle (savoir) la réponse. *He denies that she knows the answer.*
e Vous voulez que je (venir)? *Do you want me to come?*
f Es-tu sûr que tu (vouloir) y aller? *Are you sure you want to go?*

78 UNIT | When to use the subjunctive (2)

A The following conjunctions are followed by a verb in the subjunctive.

avant que … je (**ne**) parte	*before I leave*
bien que je sache la vérité	*although I know the truth*
quoique je sache la vérité	*although I know the truth*
pour que je puisse rester chez moi	*so that/in order that I can stay at home*
afin que je puisse rester chez moi	*so that/in order that I can stay at home*
sans que je sois inquiet	*without my being worried*
à condition que tu y ailles avec moi	*provided that you go with me*
jusqu'à ce qu'elle arrive	*until she arrives*
de peur/crainte que tu **ne** viennes	*for fear that (in case) you don't come*
à moins que tu (**ne**) sois seul	*unless you are alone*

⚠ **Avant que** and **à moins que** can take a **ne** before the verb, and **de peur que** and **de crainte que** usually do so.

B **De sorte/façon/manière que** (*so that*) take the subjunctive when describing an intention, but the indicative when expressing a result.

C The subjunctive is also used with impersonal constructions that express opinion, necessity, possibility, doubt and denial.

Il vaut mieux que tu viennes.	*It's better that you come.*
Il faut que je le voies.	*I must/it is necessary that I see him.*
Il se peut qu'il revienne.	*It is possible that he will come back.*
il est (im)possible que	*it's (im)possible that*
il est peu probable que	*it's unlikely that*
c'est dommage que	*it's a pity that*
il n'est pas évident que	*it's not evident that*
il n'est pas certain/sûr que	*it's not certain/sure that*
il n'est pas vrai que	*it's not true that*
il semble que	*it seems that*

⚠ When some of these expressions are used positively they are followed by the indicative.

Il est vrai que vous avez raison.   *It's true that you are right.*

⚠ Although **il semble que** is followed by the subjunctive, **il *me* semble que** (*it seems to me that*) is followed by the indicative.

1 Choose the correct form of the verb to be used in each sentence.

> *E.g.* Quoique cela *soit*/est étrange, c'est vrai. *Although it's strange, it's true.*

a À condition que ta mère est/soit d'accord, tu peux passer le weekend chez moi. *Provided your mother agrees, you can spend the weekend at my house.*

b Maintenant que je comprends/comprenne la situation, il n'y a plus de problème. *Now that I understand the situation, there is no longer a problem.*

c Pendant que tu prends/prennes ton petit déjeuner, tu peux lire le journal. *While you have your breakfast, you can read the newspaper.*

d Donnez-moi un coup de téléphone pour que je sais/sache que vous êtes bien arrivée. *Give me a call so that I know you've arrived safely.*

2 Put the verbs in brackets into the correct form of the subjunctive.

> *E.g.* J'ai tout préparé de crainte qu'ils n'*aient* pas le temps. *I've prepared it all in case they don't have the time.*

a Bien qu'il (être) riche, il n'est pas généreux. *Although he is rich, he is not generous.*

b Je peux sortir à condition que je leur (dire) où je vais. *I can go out provided that I tell them where I'm going.*

c Je vais travailler ce matin, pour que nous (pouvoir) sortir plus tard. *I'm going to work this morning so that we can go out later.*

d Avant que j'(aller) à Bruxelles, je dois téléphoner au bureau. *Before I go to Brussels, I must telephone the office.*

3 Introduce each of the following sentences using the expression in brackets. They all require the subjunctive.

> *E.g.* Elle écrit la lettre. (Il est essentiel que) → Il est essentiel qu'elle *écrive* la lettre.

a Il fait ses devoirs. (Il est important que)

b Vous travaillez. (Il faut que)

c Il réussit. (Il est impossible que)

d Elle vient. (Il se peut que)

e Il fait des études. (Il est nécessaire que)

f Nous ne prenons pas de vacances. (C'est dommage que)

79 UNIT | When to use the subjunctive (3)

The subjunctive is used in relative clauses after a superlative expression, a negative or an indefinite pronoun, and also certain imperatives.

A The subjunctive is used after a negative or indefinite pronoun + **qui** or **que**. However, if the pronoun is used in a positive sense, the indicative is used.

Je ne sais rien qui puisse vous aider.	*I don't know of anything that could help you.*
Il n'y a rien que je puisse vous dire.	*There is nothing I can tell you.*
Il n'y a personne qui puisse vous aider.	*There's no one who can help you.*
Il y a quelqu'un qui puisse le faire?	*Is there anyone who can do it?*
Je cherche quelqu'un qui sache parler français.	*I am looking for someone who can speak French.* (i.e. I haven't found him/her yet.)

BUT

Je connais quelqu'un qui sait parler français.	*I know someone who can speak French.*
Il y a quelqu'un qui peut le faire.	*There is someone who can do it.*

B The subjunctive occurs after a superlative, and after **dernier** *last*, **premier** *first* and **seul** *only*.

C'est la voiture la plus puissante que j'aie jamais conduite.	*It's the most powerful car I've ever driven.*
C'est le meilleur livre qu'il ait jamais lu.	*It's the best book he has ever read.*
Elle est la seule qui puisse le faire.	*She is the only one who can do it.*

C The subjunctive is used after certain indefinite expressions.

Qui que vous soyez, vous n'avez pas le droit d'entrer.	*Whoever you are, you don't have the right to enter.*

Other examples of such expressions are:

quoi que tu fasses	*whatever you do*
où que tu ailles	*wherever you go*
d'où que vous veniez	*wherever you come from*
à qui que vous parliez	*whoever you talk to*
quelle que soit ton opinion	*whatever your opinion (may be)* (i.e. *whatever* in the sense of *which ever*)

⚠ Quel que is used with a noun and must agree with it in number and gender.

➤ See also superlative adjectives in Unit 26, indefinite adjectives and pronouns in Units 28 and 29, negatives in Units 82 and 83.

1 **Select the correct option to complete the following sentences.**

E.g. Je voudrais parler à quelqu'un qui sait/*sache* son numéro de téléphone. *I'd like to talk to someone who knows his telephone number.*

a Il cherche quelqu'un qui sait/sache la verité. *He is looking for someone who knows the truth.*

b Vous cherchez un médecin qui peut/puisse l'aider? *Are you looking for a doctor who can help her?*

c J'ai trouvé un électricien qui peut/puisse venir. *I've found an electrician who can come.*

d C'est la seule chose qu'il sait/sache faire. *It's the only thing he knows how to do.*

e C'est le meilleur film que j'ai/aie jamais vu. *It's the best film I've ever seen.*

2 **Complete the sentences with the appropriate form of the verb in brackets.**

E.g. D'où qu'il (venir), les conditions de vie ont dû être difficiles. *Wherever he comes from, the living conditions must have been hard.* → D'où qu'il *vienne*, les conditions de vie ont dû être difficiles.

a Quoi que vous (dire), je ne vous crois pas. *Whatever you say, I don't believe you.*

b Où que tu (aller), je t'accompagnerai. *Wherever you go, I'll go with you.*

c Qui qu'il (être), je ne l'aime pas. *Whoever he may be, I don't like him.*

d À qui que tu (parler), tu entends la même chose. *Whoever you talk to, you hear the same thing.*

3 **Complete the following sentences with *quel que* or *quoi que*.**

E.g. _____ soit le résultat du test, je vais vendre la voiture. *Whatever the result of the test, I'll sell the car.* → *Quel que* soit le résultat du test, je vais vendre la voiture.

a _____ soient vos idées, vous devez les discuter. *Whatever your ideas, you must discuss them.*

b _____ vous prépariez, il le mangera! *Whatever you prepare, he will eat it!*

c _____ vous décidiez, je vous aiderai. *Whatever you decide, I'll help you.*

d _____ soit ta décision, il sera d'accord. *Whatever your decision, he will agree.*

80 UNIT | Conjunctions (1)

Conjunctions link items to form longer sentences. They fall into three categories: coordinating, subordinating and correlating conjunctions.

Coordinating conjunctions link sentences, clauses, phrases or words of equal status, e.g. main clause + main clause, subordinate clause + subordinate clause, noun + noun, comparative phrases, etc.

J'ai fini mon travail **puis** j'ai quitté le bureau.	*I finished my work then I left the office.*

A The main coordinating conjunctions are:

ainsi *thus, so, therefore*	ensuite *then*
alors *then, so*	et *and*
au contraire *on the contrary*	mais *but*
aussi *so, therefore*	néanmoins *nevertheless*
car *because*	or *however*
c'est-à-dire *that is to say*	que *than*
c'est pourquoi *that's why*	ou *or*
d'ailleurs *besides*	pourtant *however*
donc *so*	puis *then*
en effet *indeed*	toutefois *however*

B Main clause + main clause

Le train est arrivé **et** je suis monté dedans.	*The train arrived and I got on.*

Donc can be placed either between two main clauses or within the second one.

Il n'était pas content, donc je suis allé le voir/je suis donc allé le voir.	*He wasn't happy, so I went to see him.*

C Subordinate clause + subordinate clause

Cette femme, qui était renommée **mais** qui était mécontente, s'est retirée du monde.	*This woman, who was famous but who was unhappy, withdrew from the world.*

D Noun + noun

Elle est devenue vedette du cinéma **puis** femme politique.	*She became a film star then a politician.*

E Comparative

Elle était plus tolérante **que** lui.	*She was more tolerant than him.*

> ➤ *See comparative of adjectives in Unit 24 and of adverbs in Unit 25.*

80 Conjunctions (1) – Exercises

1 Match the two parts of the French sentences using the English as a guide.

E.g. **J'ai reçu les brochures + et les ai envoyées à Barcelone.**
I received the brochures and sent them to Barcelona.

a J'ai préparé les documents
b Le produit est prêt
c Il a beaucoup organisé
d Elle est sans emploi
e Nous cherchons de nouveaux bureaux
f J'ai vu le client
g Elle ne sera pas là pour la réunion

h néanmoins il reste des choses à faire.
i c'est pourquoi elle veut vendre la voiture.
j pourtant ceux-ci sont trop petits.
k car elle veut partir en vacances.
l donc on peut l'annoncer à la presse.
m mais je ne les ai pas encore photocopiés.
n puis je suis rentré à la maison.

1 *I saw the client then I went home.*
2 *We're looking for new offices, however these are too small.*
3 *She won't be there for the meeting because she wants to go on holiday.*
4 *I've prepared the documents but I haven't photocopied them yet.*
5 *The product's ready so we can announce it to the press.*
6 *She hasn't got a job, that's why she wants to sell the car.*
7 *He's organised a lot, however there are still some things to do.*

2 Complete each sentence using one of the three conjunctions in the box next to each set. Then translate each sentence into English.

E.g. **Tu veux venir _____ tu veux rester chez toi? Tu veux venir *ou* tu veux rester chez toi?** → *Do you want to come or do you want to stay at home?*

a Moi, je l'aime, mais elle _____ ne l'aime pas du tout.
b Il neigeait _____ je n'y suis pas allé.
c Il voulait venir _____ il n'avait pas le temps.

> donc
> mais
> au contraire

d Il a fait la cuisine _____ moi j'ai fait la vaisselle.
e Il l'a réparée, _____ nous avons pu partir.
f Je ne veux pas l'acheter, _____ je n'ai pas assez d'argent`

> d'ailleurs
> puis
> ainsi

g J'ai perdu mon passeport, _____ je ne peux pas partir.
h Tu peux m'accompagner _____ tu peux rester ici.
i On peut aller au Canada, _____ c'est assez coûteux.

> c'est pourquoi
> ou
> pourtant

161

81 UNIT | Conjunctions (2)

> Conjunctions link items to form longer sentences.
> They fall into three categories: coordinating, subordinating and
> correlating conjunctions.

A Subordinating conjunctions link main and subordinate clauses. The subordinate clause adds more information to the content or message of the main clause.

J'ai dit **que** je n'avais pas le temps.	*I said that I didn't have the time.*
Elle l'a félicité **parce qu'**il avait fini.	*She congratulated him because he had finished.*
J'ai rangé sa chambre **pendant qu'**elle jouait en bas.	*I tidied her room while she played downstairs.*
Vous voulez manger **avant qu'**on (**ne**) sorte?	*Do you want to eat before we go out?*

The main subordinating conjunctions are:

à moins que … (ne) *unless*	jusqu'à ce que *until*
afin que *so that*	lorsque *when*
après que *after*	parce que *because*
aussitôt que *as soon as*	pendant que *while*
avant que … (ne) *before*	pour que *so that*
bien que *although*	puisque *since (= because)*
comme *as (= because)*	quand *when*
de crainte que … ne *for fear that*	quoique *although*
de façon/de sorte que *so that*	que *that*
de peur que … ne *for fear that*	si *if, whether*
depuis que *since*	tandis que *while*
dès que *as soon as*	

B Correlating conjunctions link several items together (e.g. to make a double subject or object).

Et les patrons **et** les employés étaient contre la nouvelle loi.	*Both employers and employees were against the new law.*
Vous pouvez **ou** venir **ou** rester.	*You can either come or stay.*

The main correlating conjunctions are:

et … et *both … and*	ou … ou *either … or*
ne … ni … ni *neither … nor*	

> ➤ See when to use the subjunctive (2) in Unit 78,
> negatives in Units 82 and 83.

81 UNIT Conjunctions (2) – Exercises

1 Match the two halves of the French sentences, using the English as a guide.

E.g. Il le fera demain + quand il rentrera chez lui. *He'll do it tomorrow when he goes home.*

a Aussitôt qu'il est arrivé
b Je vais le faire lundi
c Il fumait sans cesse
d Je ne vais ni aller,
e Je vais le faire

f pendant qu'il jouait aux cartes.
g si la patronne me paie avant.
h quand je serai au bureau.
i elle m'a donné un coup de téléphone.
j ni participer au match.

1 *I'll do it on Monday when I'm in the office.*
2 *I'm neither going to nor taking part in the match.*
3 *As soon as he arrived she gave me a call.*
4 *He chain-smoked while he played cards.*
5 *I'll do it if the boss pays me first.*

2 Complete the following sentences using appropriate conjunctions from the box, then translate the sentences into English.

E.g. Je te le donne _____ je t'aime. → Je te le donne *parce que* je t'aime.

comme	depuis que	dès que	quoique	~~parce que~~

a Nous allons commencer la réunion _____ vous arriverez.
b J'ai payé par chèque _____ je n'avais pas d'argent.
c Il est venu _____ il ne se porte pas bien.
d _____ elle travaille ici nos méthodes ont beaucoup changé.

3 Complete the following story with the conjunctions indicated. Look back at Unit 80 if necessary.

(*As*) il faisait mauvais en juillet, nous avons décidé de passer un weekend en France. (*While*) je faisais ma valise, mon mari m'a dit (*that*) il ne trouvait pas son passeport. À mon avis le passeport était (*either*) dans le bureau (*or*) dans le tiroir. (*So*) je lui ai demandé (*whether*) il avait cherché dans le bureau. Pas encore. "Dis-le-moi (*as soon as*) tu le trouveras."

4 Translate the following into French.

a *Both Jean-Pierre and Max played tennis today.*
b *As you see, the brochure is ready.*
c *She told me that she had eaten.*
d *We'll either go to France or to Spain this year.*

82 Unit | Negatives (1)

> There is a range of negatives in French which express
> not, nothing, never, no more, no longer, etc.

A Most negatives in French consist of two words placed on either side of the conjugated verb, enclosing also any reflexive and object pronouns (and any subject pronouns in questions). The most common is **ne ... pas**. Ne becomes **n'** when the next word begins with a vowel.

Je n'y vais pas souvent.   *I don't go there often.*

B The most common negatives are:

Group A	Group B
ne ... guère *hardly*	ne ... aucun(e) *not any, none*
ne ... jamais *never*	ne ... ni ... ni *neither ... nor*
ne ... pas *not*	ne ... personne *nobody*
ne ... plus *no longer*	ne ... que *only*
ne ... rien *nothing*	

⚠ Aucun(e) agrees in number and gender with the noun it relates to.

Elle ne va jamais au théâtre.	*She never goes to the theatre.*
Vous n'avez rien dans votre sac.	*You have nothing in your bag.*
Je ne vais plus à la messe.	*I don't go to church any more.*
N'a-t-il que deux enfants?	*Has he only got two children?*
Elles n'aiment personne.	*They don't like anybody.*
Il n'a aucune idée.	*He hasn't got any idea.*

C **Aucun(e)**, **jamais**, **personne**, **rien**, and **ni ... ni** can stand at the beginning of a clause, with **ne** then following in its usual place.

Personne ne répond.	*Nobody's answering.*
Rien n'est impossible.	*Nothing is impossible.*
Ni Jean ni Hélène ne sont venus.	*Neither Jean nor Hélène has come.*

D **Aucun(e)**, **jamais**, **rien** and **personne** can be used alone without a verb.

Vous buvez de la bière? Jamais.	*Do you drink beer? Never.*
Qui vient à la plage? Personne.	*Who's coming to the beach? Nobody.*

E When an infinitive is being negated it is preceded by the negative, except for those negatives in Group B above, which enclose it.

Je te conseille de ne pas nager ici.	*I advise you not to swim here.*
Je te promets de ne voir personne.	*I promise you not to see anyone.*

> ➤ See indefinite adjectives and pronouns in Units 28 and 29
> and object pronouns (3) in Unit 47.

1 Make the following sentences negative by using *ne ... pas*.

E.g. Il est intelligent. → Il n'est pas intelligent.

a Vous regardez la télévision.

b Il parle espagnol.

c J'aime le vin rouge.

d Elle fait la vaisselle.

e Tu vas au cinéma.

2 Unscramble the following sentences.

E.g. entends je rien n' *I can't hear anything.* → Je n'entends rien.

a pas je comprends ne *I don't understand.*

b au ils pas aller n' cinéma aiment *They don't like going to the cinema.*

c ne personne il voit dans pièce la *He doesn't see anyone in the room.*

d de il plus pain n'y a *There's no bread left.*

e n' je un manteau qu' ai *I've only got one coat.*

f mangez ne rien vous *You're not eating anything.*

3 Match the following sentence halves to make full sentences.

E.g. Pauline n'est + jamais chez elle.

a Sophie ne range	1 personne dans sa voiture.
b Il n'aime	2 jamais gentille.
c Vous ne sortez	3 que des légumes. Elle est végétarienne.
d Il n'y a	4 pas le vin rouge. Il préfère le vin blanc.
e Jean-Paul ne prend	5 rien à voir ici.
f Elle ne mange	6 jamais sa chambre.
g Jeanne n'est	7 pas le weekend.

4 Complete the following conversation.

E.g. Vous voulez un verre de vin? *Say that you never drink wine.* → Je ne bois jamais de vin.

a Vous aimez aller au théâtre?
Say that you never go to the theatre.

b Mais vous aimez le cinéma? Il y a un cinéma près d'ici?
Say that there is no cinema nearby.

c Alors, on peut jouer au tennis?
Say you don't like tennis.

d Vous voulez aller en ville?
Say no, there's nothing to do.

e Qu'est-ce que vous aimez alors?
Say you don't like anything!

83 UNIT | Negatives (2)

A Verbs in compound tenses are made negative by adding **ne** before the auxiliary verb (**avoir** or **être**) and **pas** (etc.) after it: **ne** + auxiliary + **pas** + past participle. If there is an object pronoun it is enclosed within the negative.

J'ai travaillé. → Je n'ai pas travaillé. *I have worked. I have not worked.*
Il est arrivé. → Il n'est pas arrivé.   *He has arrived. He has not arrived.*
Je ne l'ai pas vue.   *I didn't see her.*

B When negating reflexive verbs both the reflexive pronoun and the auxiliary verb are enclosed by the negative.

Je ne me suis pas dépêché.   *I did not hurry.*
Elle ne s'est pas couchée.   *She has not gone to bed.*

C In negative questions where the subject and auxiliary verb are inverted, the negative encloses the auxiliary verb and the subject pronoun, and also any object pronoun. With reflexive verbs the reflexive pronoun is enclosed as well.

N'a-t-il rien dit?   *Didn't he say anything?*
Ne les a-t-elle pas pris?   *Didn't she take them?*
Ne s'est-elle pas annoncée?   *Didn't she say she was there?*

D The negatives in Group B in Unit 82 have a different order in both statements and questions. The order is **ne** + auxiliary + past participle + **pas** (etc.).

Je n'ai vu personne.   *I haven't seen anyone.*
N'as-tu acheté que trois kilos? *Did you only buy three kilos?*

E Negatives can combine in various ways: **ne ... plus rien** *no longer anything*, **ne ... jamais personne** *never anyone*, **ne ... jamais rien** *never anything*, **ne ... plus que** *nothing else but*, **ne ... plus jamais** *never any more*, **ne ... plus personne** *anyone any more*, **ne ... jamais que** *only ever*.

Elle ne fait jamais rien.   *She never does anything.*
Il ne voit plus personne.   *He never sees anyone any more.*
Il ne me donne plus jamais   *He never gives me flowers*
de fleurs.   *any more.*

➤ See the imperative in Unit 56, compound tenses in Units 60–63 (perfect), 66 (pluperfect), 69 (future perfect), 71 (conditional perfect) and asking questions in Units 84–86.

83 UNIT Negatives (2) – Exercises

1 Make the following sentences negative by using *ne ... pas*.

E.g. Je suis allée en ville ce matin. → Je ne suis pas allée en ville ce matin.

a Il a compris le problème.

b Elle s'est levée de bonne heure.

c Il aurait fini le projet.

d Elle avait écrit une lettre.

e J'aurais acheté la robe bleue.

f Nous sommes arrivés à l'heure.

2 Now match the sentences you have written in Question 1 to their English translations below.

a *I would not have bought the blue dress.*

b *We did not arrive on time.*

c *He did not understand the problem.*

d *She did not get up early.*

e *She had not written a letter.*

f *He would not have finished the project.*

3 Answer the following questions in the negative. The answer is given in English to help you.

E.g. Vous avez fini? *Have you finished?* Non, je n'ai pas fini.

a A-t-il vu Pierre? *No, he has not seen him.*

b Tu es parti avant minuit? *No, I did not leave before midnight.*

c Est-ce qu'il sera arrivé à l'heure? *No, he will not have arrived on time.*

d Elle s'est maquillée avant de sortir? *No, she did not put on her make-up before going out.*

e Il avait fini son travail? *No, he had not finished it.*

4 Rearrange the following sentences.

E.g. n'était retournée elle pas *She had not returned.* → Elle n'était pas retournée.

a pas je fini aurais n' *I would not have finished.*

b le elle compris n' problème pas a *She has not understood the problem.*

c vous dit pas auriez cela n' *You would not have said that.*

d t' pas es levé bonne ne de heure tu *You did not get up early.*

e sorti hier je suis pas soir ne *I did not go out last night.*

5 Make the following sentences negative, using the form in brackets.

E.g. Les a-t-il vus? (ne ... pas) → Ne les a-t-il pas vus?

a Y vas-tu? (ne ... pas)

b Me les as-tu donnés? (ne ... pas)

c A-t-il vendu quatre voitures? (ne ... que)

d Avez-vous vu? (ne ... personne)

e A-t-elle laissé un mot? (ne ... aucun)

167

84 | UNIT | Asking questions (1)

A A statement can be made into a question by raising your intonation at the end of the sentence.

Vous aimez le fromage.   *You like cheese.*

→ Vous aimez le fromage?   *Do you like cheese?*

B A statement can also be changed into a question by placing **Est-ce que ...** at the beginning.

Tu as une voiture.   *You have a car.*

→ Est-ce que tu as une voiture?   *Do you have a car?*

Vous avez mangé.   *You have eaten.*

→ Est-ce que vous avez mangé?   *Have you eaten?*

Ils vont partir.   *They're going to leave.*

→ Est-ce qu'ils vont partir?   *Are they going to leave?*

C More formal questions can be formed by reversing (inverting) the subject pronoun and the conjugated verb (in compound tenses the auxiliary verb **avoir** or **être**). This method is not common in informal speech.

Elle fait des études de langues.   *She's studying languages.*

→ Fait-elle des études de langues?   *Is she studying languages?*

Vous voulez manger.   *You want to eat.*

→ Voulez-vous manger?   *Do you want to eat?*

Vous avez fini.   *You have finished.*

→ Avez-vous fini?   *Have you finished?*

Il était déjà rentré quand je suis arrivé.   *He had already gone home when I arrived.*

→ Était-il déjà rentré quand je suis arrivé?   *Had he already gone home when I arrived?*

⚠ When forming a question like this with the third-person singular (**il** or **elle**), and the conjugated verb ends in a vowel, an extra **t** is added to ease pronunciation. This is often necessary in compound tenses.

Joue-t-elle au tennis?   *Does she play tennis?*

Va-t-il finir son travail?   *Is he going to finish his work?*

A-t-elle écrit la lettre?   *Has she written the letter?*

Sera-t-il déjà parti quand j'arriverai?   *Will he have already left when I arrive?*

Form statements from the following questions.

E.g. Est-ce qu'il va à l'école? → Il va à l'école.

a Il parle français?

b Aime-t-elle travailler ici?

c Est-ce qu'ils ont pris le train de huit heures?

d Vas-tu à la conférence cette semaine?

e Vous habitez en ville?

f Est-ce que j'ai assez d'argent?

g Tu prends une photo?

h Faites-vous du ski cette année?

Find three ways of changing each of the following statements into a question.

E.g. Vous avez mangé à midi.

→ Vous avez mangé à midi?

→ Est-ce que vous avez mangé à midi?

→ Avez-vous mangé à midi?

a Tu achètes un ordinateur.

b Il est pharmacien.

c Elle adore le théâtre.

d Vous aimez le vin.

e Ils vont en ville.

What was the question that prompted each of these answers? For each answer give two question forms, as in the example.

E.g. Oui, je suis marié. → Vous êtes marié? Êtes-vous marié?

a Oui, j'ai une voiture.

b Oui, je vais au cinéma ce soir.

c Non, je ne veux pas sortir.

d Non, je ne suis pas agriculteur, je suis pêcheur.

e Non, nous parlons français.

f Oui, je voudrais bien prendre un congé.

85 Unit | Asking questions (2)

There are a number of words you can use to find out what you need to know, for example Why...?, Where...?, When...?, How...?

A There are a number of key words (interrogatives) you can use to find out specific information: **quand?** *when?*, **pourquoi?** *why?*, **où?** *where?*, **comment?** *how?* and **combien (de)?** *how much/how many?*

Ils arrivent quand?	*When do they arrive?*
Pourquoi est-ce que tu pleures?	*Why are you crying?*
Où est la poste?	*Where is the post office?*
Comment voyagez-vous?	*How are you travelling?*
Ça coûte combien?	*How much does it cost?*
Vous gagnez combien (d'argent)?	*How much (money) do you earn?*

B As these examples show, there are three ways of forming questions when using these words, which are broadly in line with the simple question forms seen in Unit 84. You can:

- add the interrogative after the statement (**Ils arrivent *quand*? Tu veux manger *où*?**). (**Pourquoi** however cannot be used this way.)
- add the interrogative at the beginning of a question that uses **est-ce que** (*Pourquoi* **est-ce que tu pleures?** *Quand* **est-ce que tu veux manger?**)
- place the interrogative at the beginning of the question and invert the subject and verb (*Où* **est la poste?** *Où* **est-il?** *Quand* **va-t-elle arriver?**).

C If you want to ask *Which...?* or *What...?* plus a noun, you use the appropriate form of the interrogative adjective **quel?** This agrees in gender and number with the noun that follows it.

	Singular	Plural
Masculine	quel	quels
Feminine	quelle	quelles

Quel livre lisez-vous?	*Which book are you reading?*
Quelle date préférerait-il?	*Which date would he prefer?*

D Some of these interrogatives can be used with a preposition.

D'où est-ce qu'il vient?	*Where does he come from?*
C'est **pour** quand?	*When do you want it?/When is it for?*
Vous venez **avec** quel train?	*Which train will you be coming on?*
Tu arrives **à** quelle heure?	*What time will you arrive?*

> *See prepositions in Units 10–15 and inversion in Unit 97.*

1 **Complete the following questions by selecting an appropriate ending from the right-hand list.**

E.g. Quand est-ce que + vous partez en vacances?

a Quand est-ce que	**1** vont-ils arriver?
b Pourquoi	**2** personnes y-a-t-il?
c Où allez-vous	**3** pleure-t-elle?
d À quelle heure	**4** est-il?
e Combien de	**5** vas-tu faire?
f Quelle heure	**6** vous partez en vacances?
g Quels sports	**7** manger ce soir?

2 **Complete the missing interrogatives in these sentences, using the jumbled answers to guide you. Then match the questions to the answers.**

E.g. _____ heure est-il? Il est huit heures. → Quelle heure est-il?

a _____ est-ce qu'elle habite?	**1** J'ai trente-neuf ans.
b Le train part de _____ quai (*platform*)?	**2** Elle habite près du cinéma.
c _____ allez-vous?	**3** Il a deux frères.
d _____ de frères a-t-il?	**4** Très bien, merci.
e _____ âge avez-vous?	**5** Il part du quai numéro dix.

3 **Which questions would you have asked in order to receive the following replies? Use the *vous* form for 'you' throughout.**

E.g. Je mange à midi.
> → Que faites-vous à midi?
> → Quand est-ce que vous mangez?
> → À quelle heure mangez-vous?

a Je vais à la banque.

b Je quitte le bureau à six heures.

c Je vais au cinéma avec ma sœur.

d J'ai trois frères.

e Il vient du Canada.

f Je préfère la robe bleue.

g Le film finit à dix heures.

h J'aime le foulard jaune.

> *Interrogative pronouns can be used as well to find out specific information.*

A The interrogative pronouns are as follows:

    lequel…? *which (one/ones)…?*   qui…? *who(m)…?*

    quoi? *what?*   que…? *what…?*

B **Lequel** agrees in gender and number with the noun it is replacing, in the same way as the relative pronouns **lequel/laquelle/lesquels/lesquelles**. It also combines with **à** and with **de** to form **auquel**, etc. and **duquel**, etc.

J'ai deux robes du soir – laquelle préférez-vous?	*I've got two evening gowns – which do you prefer?*
Je ne sais pas lequel il choisira.	*I don't know which (one) he'll choose.*
Il y a deux spectacles ce soir – auquel veux-tu aller?	*There are two shows tonight – which one do you want to go to?*

C **Qui** can be used as both the subject and the object of a verb, and can appear after a preposition. In direct questions it can be replaced as a subject by **qui est-ce qui** and, as an object, by **qui est-ce que**.

Qui t'a dit ça?/Qui est-ce qui t'a dit ça?	*Who told you that?*
Qui vas-tu aider?/Qui est-ce que tu vas aider?	*Who(m) are you going to help?*
À qui a-t-il demandé la permission?	*Who(m) did he ask for permission?*
Je n'ai aucune idée qui me l'a donné.	*I've no idea who gave it to me.*

D **Que** is used for things or ideas only and can only be the direct object of a verb. It cannot be used with prepositions. It is often replaced by **qu'est-ce qui** and **qu'est-ce que**, mainly in speech.

Que voulez-vous dire?/ Qu'est-ce que vous voulez dire?	*What do you mean?*
Qu'est-ce que c'est?	*What's that?/What is it?*

E **Quoi** is used instead of **que** (or **qu'est-ce que**) after a preposition and in indirect questions. It can also be used alone, sometimes as an exclamation.

De quoi est-ce que tu parles?	*What are you talking about?*
J'ai une nouvelle pour toi. – Quoi?	*I've got some news for you. – What?*
Quoi?!	*What?!*

⚠ A request for something to be repeated is made by **Comment?** *Pardon?*

> ➤ *See prepositions in Units 10–15, relative pronouns in Units 41 and 43 and inversion in Unit 97.*

1 Match the parts of the sentences, using the English below as a guide.

E.g. Lequel + des dictionnaires veux-tu? *Which of the dictionaries do you want?*

a Lequel   **i** veux-tu prendre?

b Qui   **j** de ces robes veux-tu acheter?

c Il y a deux voitures. Laquelle   **k** veut-il accompagner?

d Qui   **l** vous a donné cela?

e De quoi   **m** est-ce que tu es venu?

f Pour qui   **n** des théâtres préférez-vous?

g Laquelle   **o** travailles-tu?

h Avec qui   **p** parlez-vous?

1 *Which of the theatres do you prefer?*

2 *Who gave you that?*

3 *Who does he want to go with?*

4 *There are two cars. Which one do want to take?*

5 *Which of these dresses do you want to buy?*

6 *What are you talking about?*

7 *Who do you work for?*

8 *Who did you come with?*

2 Complete the following sentences using an interrogative pronoun.

E.g. _____ des enfants joue du piano? → Lequel des enfants joue du piano?

a _____ de ces voitures préfères-tu?

b _____ a oublié son manteau?

c Il a peur de _____ ?

d _____ veux-tu manger?

e _____ avez-vous besoin?

f _____ des ordinateurs est le vôtre?

g Ce plan a été préparé par _____ ?

h _____ est-ce que vous avez oublié?

3 Translate into French

a *What are you afraid of?*

b *Which of the computers do you want?*

c *Who works in this office?*

d *What are you saying?*

e *Who is this document for?*

87 UNIT Numbers (1)

In French a number of patterns are clear in the way numbers (known as cardinal numbers) are formed.

A The numbers 1 to 16 are single words:

0 zéro	5 cinq	9 neuf	13 treize
1 un(e)	6 six	10 dix	14 quatorze
2 deux	7 sept	11 onze	15 quinze
3 trois	8 huit	12 douze	16 seize
4 quatre			

When used as nouns (*the number 4*, *he threw a 9*), the numbers 8 and 11 are never elided with the definite article: **le onze**, **le huit**.

B The numbers 17 to 19 are compounds based on 10:

17 dix-sept	18 dix-huit	19 dix-neuf

C Between 20 and 60, the multiples of 10 are as follows:

20 vingt 30 trente 40 quarante 50 cinquante 60 soixante

D Numbers between these are compounds, and are hyphenated:

22 vingt-deux	35 trente-cinq	48 quarante-huit

However, compounds that include 1 are formed using **et**:

21 vingt et un(e) 51 cinquante et un(e) 61 soixante et un(e)

E The numbers 70, 80 and 90 are compounds of previous numbers:

70 soixante-dix	80 quatre-vingts	90 quatre-vingt-dix
71 soixante et onze	81 quatre-vingt-un	91 quatre-vingt-onze
72 soixante-douze	82 quatre-vingt-deux	92 quatre-vingt-douze

⚠ Quatre-vingts standing alone has an **-s**, but this is dropped when a further digit is added.

F The higher numbers are as follows:

100 cent	101 cent un(e)	102 cent deux
200 deux cents	205 deux cent cinq (no **-s**)	

1 000 mille (invariable, never takes an **-s**)   1 500 mille cinq cent/quinze cents
1 000 000 un million   3 200 000 trois millions deux cent mille
un milliard *a thousand million/a billion*

⚠ Cent and **mille** are not preceded by an indefinite article or *one*, as in English (*a/one hundred*, *a/one thousand*).

➤ See fractions and decimals in Unit 89, dimensions and distance in Unit 90, days, dates and years in Unit 92.

87 Numbers (1) – Exercises

Write out the following drinks order for the interval at a theatre, inserting the written form of the number shown.

E.g. 12 vins rouges → douze vins rouges

2 cafés
1 vin blanc
12 bières
7 jus d'orange
14 limonades
3 panachés (*shandy*)
5 cognacs

Insert the missing numbers in the following sequences.

E.g. un, deux, **trois**, quatre, cinq, **six**, sept

a deux, quatre, six, _____ , dix, douze, quatorze, _____

b un, trois, _____ , sept, neuf, _____ , treize

c dix-huit, _____ , douze, neuf, _____ , trois

d cinq, _____ , quinze, _____ , vingt-cinq

Give the numbers of the reserved rooms in full.

Chambre	Réservée
23	✓
24	
25	
49	✓
50	
51	✓
79	✓
80	✓
81	✓

Complete this list of items by inserting the written form of the appropriate number.

_____ tasses	*42 cups*
_____ fourchettes	*50 forks*
_____ couteaux	*60 knives*
_____ assiettes	*35 plates*
_____ cuillères	*28 spoons*
_____ bols	*53 bowls*

Say each of the following numbers out loud in French.

92, 59, 67, 18, 33, 75, 26, 41, 82, 101, 249, 550, 1 572, 2 500, 1 200 000

> *Ordinal numbers are used to express sequences, for example first, second, third, etc. Collective numbers indicate an approximation.*

A French ordinal numbers are formed by adding the suffix **-ième** to the cardinal number.

3rd (trois) troisième   6th (six) sixième   10th (dix) dixième

- *First* in French has a special form, which must agree in gender with the noun it is referring to.

  1st premier (*m*), première (*f*)
  But when **un** appears in a compound number, the ordinal form is **unième**.
  21st (vingt et un) vingt et unième

- *Second* has two alternative forms in French, the second of which must agree in gender with the noun it is referring to.

  2nd deuxième/second (*m*), seconde (*f*)

- Any number that ends in **-e** drops this **-e** in the ordinal form.

  4th (quatre) quatrième   11th (onze) onzième   12th (douze) douzième

- **Cinq** adds a **-u** (**cinquième**) and **neuf** changes its **-f** to a **-v** (**neuvième**).

- The ordinals **huitième** and **onzième** are never elided with a preceding definite article.

  le huitième jour *the eighth day* la onzième personne *the eleventh person*

B French uses cardinal numbers (not ordinals as in English) in dates.

  le neuf juin, le dix-huit octobre *the ninth of June, the eighteenth of October*

Cardinal numbers are also used with the names of monarchs or popes.

  Louis XIV (*spoken:* quatorze)   *Louis XIV (spoken: the Fourteenth)*
  le pape Jean-Paul II (*spoken:* deux)   *Pope John Paul II (spoken: the Second)*

However, the ordinal number **premier** is used in both contexts.

  le premier septembre   *the first of September*
  François I (*spoken:* premier)   *Francis I (spoken: the First)*

C Collective numbers

- To express an approximate number, there are ten nouns that end in **-aine**.

une huitaine *about eight*	une trentaine *about thirty*
une dizaine *about ten*	une quarantaine *about forty*
une douzaine *a dozen*	une cinquantaine *about fifty*
une quinzaine *about fifteen*	une soixantaine *about sixty*
une vingtaine *about twenty*	une centaine *about a hundred*

➤ *See fractions and decimals in Unit 89, days, dates and years in Unit 92.*

88 UNIT Numbers (2) – Exercises

1 Match items from the two lists to translate the English phrases given below.

E.g. une cinquantaine + d'invités *About fifty guests*

a une vingtaine
b une quarantaine
c une dizaine
d un millier
e une soixantaine
f une quinzaine
g une trentaine
h une centaine

i de lettres
j de livres
k de personnes
l de crayons
m de dépliants
n de brochures
o d'enfants
p de stylos

1 *About thirty children*
2 *About sixty people*
3 *About twenty pencils*
4 *About fifteen books*

5 *About forty pens*
6 *About ten letters*
7 *About a hundred pamphlets*
8 *About a thousand brochures*

2 Insert the appropriate ordinal number into each phrase, using the English as a guide.

E.g. la *soixante-dix-septième* fois *the 77th time*

a la _____ page *the 74th page*
b la _____ voiture *the 95th car*
c la _____ personne *the 76th person*
d le _____ billet *the 100th ticket*

e le __ anniversaire *the 91st birthday*
f la _____ marche *the 80th step*
g la _____ lettre *the 79th letter*
h le _____ vol *the 88th flight*

3 Follow the example to say where the following people live. Use the initials in the diagram to work out who's who.

E.g. Jean habite au _____ étage (*floor/storey*). → Jean habite au troisième étage.

a Cathérine et Pascale habitent au _____ étage.
b Pierre et Sophie habitent au _____ étage.
c Stéphanie habite au _____ étage.
d Henri habite au _____ étage.
e Jeanne habite au _____ étage.
f Jacques habite au _____ étage.

Mr M Gabin (rez-de-chaussée)	
Mr et Mme P Boulanger (1er étage)	
Mlles C et P Durand (2e étage)	
Mr J Dupont (3e étage)	
Mlle S Duplessis (4e étage)	
Mr H Mangin (5e étage)	
Mme J Étienne (6e étage)	

89 Unit | Fractions and decimals

French fractions are formed in a similar way to English fractions, but there are some differences in both formation and usage.

A As in English, French fractions consist of a cardinal (*three, four*, etc.) plus an ordinal number (*third, fourth*, etc.), except for quarters and thirds.

deux sixièmes, trois septièmes	*two sixths, three sevenths*
un quart/trois quarts	*a quarter/three quarters*
un tiers/deux tiers	*a third/two thirds*

In sentences fractions are always preceded by an appropriate article.

Il a perdu les trois quarts de sa fortune.	*He lost three quarters of his fortune.*
J'ai lu un tiers du livre.	*I've read a third of the book.*

B *Half* is expressed using either **demi** or **moitié**, as appropriate:

● **Demi** can be an adjective. It precedes the noun it relates to and is joined to it by a hyphen (and in this position never agrees with it in gender). It may also follow a noun, in which case it is separate and agrees in gender.

une demi-bouteille de whisky	*a half-bottle of whisky*
une demi-heure	*a half-hour*
une bouteille et demie de whisky	*a bottle and a half of whisky*
une heure et demie	*an hour and a half/one and a half hours*

● **Demi** can also be a noun, used only in arithmetic (except for two nouns derived from its use as an adjective: **un demi** *a half (pint/litre of beer)/a glass of beer*, and **la demie** *the half-hour* (on the clock)). In all other uses it is replaced by **la moitié.**

Il a mangé la moitié des biscuits.	*He has eaten half (of the) the biscuits.*

C The word **mi-** is like the English word *mid-* or *halfway*. It is invariable and comes before the noun with a hyphen.

Je l'ai rencontré à mi-chemin.	*I met him halfway.*
Il avait les yeux mi-clos.	*His eyes were half closed.*

D In decimal fractions the decimal point is indicated by a comma (**virgule**).

(3,56) trois **virgule** cinquante-six	*(3.56) three point five six*

E Proportions are expressed using the preposition **sur**:

Un élève sur dix a réussi.	*One out of ten pupils passed.*
Sept jours sur sept.	*Seven days a week.*
Vingt-quatre heures sur vingt-quatre.	*Twenty-four hours a day.*

➤ See agreement of adjectives in Units 17–19 and numbers in Units 87 and 88.

89 UNIT Fractions and decimals – *Exercises*

Match up the figures with the appropriate words.

E.g. ⅝ cinq huitièmes

a ⅞
b 2/9
c ⅓
d ¾
e 4½
f 11/12
g 2¾
h 8¼

i deux et trois quarts
j un tiers
k quatre et demi
l deux neuvièmes
m onze douzièmes
n sept huitièmes
o huit et un quart
p trois quarts

Express the following fractions in words.

E.g. ⅛ un huitième

a ⅜
b ⅙
c ¼
d ⅔
e 9/10
f 7/16
g ⅘
h 3/20

Complete the following sentences by writing out the fractions in full.

E.g. J'ai reçu (¼) de la somme. → J'ai reçu le quart de la somme.

a Il me donne (½) de sa fortune.
b Les enfants ont mangé (⅔) du gâteau.
c Il s'est arrêté à (½) chemin.
d Je prends une livre et (½).
e Je vais acheter un kilo et (½) de fromage.

Complete the following sentences using the information in the graph.

E.g. Cinq pour cent (*per cent*) vont en Allemagne.

De ceux qui ont répondu au questionnaire sur les vacances –

a ______ vont en Espagne.
b ______ vont en France.
c ______ vont en Grande-Bretagne.
d ______ vont en Italie.
e ______ vont aux États-Unis.
f ______ vont ailleurs (*elsewhere*).

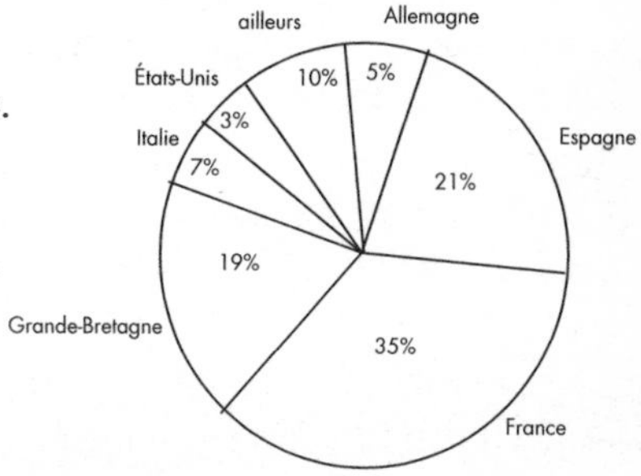

90 UNIT Dimensions and distance

You can use various constructions to give dimensions and distances.

A The most common way to give dimensions is to use the construction **avoir/faire** + (measurement) + **de long/longueur** (*for length*), **de large/largeur** (*for width*), **de haut/hauteur** (*for height*), **de profondeur** (*for depth*), **d'épaisseur** (*for thickness*).

La table a 2 mètres de long.	*The table is 2 metres long.*
Les murs faisaient un mètre d'épaisseur.	*The walls were one metre thick.*

To give a second dimension (*by*) use **sur**:

La pièce a 5 mètres de long sur 4 mètres de large.	*The room is 5 metres long by 4 metres wide.*

B You can also use **être** + adjective + **de** + (measurement). The adjectives are **long** (*for length*), **large** (*for width*), **haut** (*for height*), **profond** (*for depth*), **épais** (*for thickness*). Being adjectives, these must agree with the noun.

Ce chemin est long de 2 kilomètres.	*This path is 2 kilometres long.*
La pièce est longue de 3 mètres.	*The room is 3 metres long.*
L'eau est profonde de 20 mètres.	*The water is 20 metres deep.*

If you wish to give a second dimension simply use **et**:

La tour est haute de 15 mètres et large de 4 mètres.	*The tower is 15 metres high and 4 metres wide.*

C To ask about dimensions use one of the following questions.

Quelle est la longeur/largeur (etc.) de…?	*What is the length/width (etc.) of…?*
(Cette pièce) a/fait combien de long/large (etc.)?	*How long/wide (etc.) is (this room)?*
(Cette pièce) est longue/large (etc.) de combien?	*How long/wide (etc.) is (this room)?*

D To say how far away something is (in distance or time), use the preposition **à**.

On est à un kilomètre de la gare.	*We're one kilometre away from the train station.*
L'hôpital est à 5 minutes d'ici.	*The hospital is 5 minutes from here.*
Le centre commercial est à combien d'ici?	*How far is the shopping centre from here?*

➤ See adjectives (agreement) in Units 17 and 18, avoir in Unit 48, faire in Unit 50, asking questions (2) in Unit 85, numbers (1) in Unit 87.

Give the dimensions of the following monuments using the *avoir* construction.

E.g. **L'arc de Triomphe** *a 50 mètres de haut.*

a *50m high, 45m wide*

la tour Eiffel

b *300m high*

le Sacré-Cœur

c *80m high*

Which questions do you need to ask to obtain the information given in Question 1?

E.g. **L'arc de Triomphe a combien de mètres de hauteur?**

Express the following dimensions using *faire*.

E.g. **Ce livre – 198mm x 129mm → Ce livre fait 198mm sur 129mm.**

a une pièce – 5m x 3m
b une table – 90cm x 45cm
c un jardin – 100m x 80m

Complete these sentences with the missing adjective.

E.g. **Cette rivière est _____ de 40 mètres.** (*wide*) → **Cette rivière est** *large* **de 40 mètres.**

a La rivière est _____ de 3 mètres ici. (*deep*)
b Ce puits (*well*) est _____ de 10 mètres. (*deep*)
c Ces murs sont _____ d'un mètre. (*thick*)
d Le monument est _____ de 20 mètres et _____ de 12 mètres. (*high/wide*)
e Les boîtes sont _____ de 90 centimètres, _____ de 70 centimètres et _____ de 60 centimètres. (*long/wide/high*)

Translate the following sentences into French.

E.g. *I live 10 kilometres from here.* → **J'habite à 10 kilomètres d'ici.**

a *Toulouse is 80 kilometres from here.*
b *We're half an hour away from home* (**de chez nous**).
c *How far is the nearest garage?*
d *It must be at least* (**au moins**) *20 kilometres from here.*
e *The bank is only 5 minutes away.*

91 UNIT | Telling the time

When saying the time, you use the word **heure(s)** *hour(s)*, except for midday and midnight. To ask the time you say **Quelle heure est-il?**

A Times on the hour

Il est une heure/cinq heures.	*It's one o'clock/five o'clock.*
Il est midi.	*It's midday/noon/twelve o'clock.*
Il est minuit.	*It's midnight/twelve o'clock.*

B For times between the hours, minutes are given after the hour:

- *Half past* is **et demie**, except with **midi** and **minuit** when it is **et demi**

Il est six heures et demie.	*It's half past six.*
Il est midi et demi.	*It's half past twelve (noon).*

- *Quarter past* is **et quart**, and *quarter to* **moins le quart**

Je pars à huit heures et quart.	*I leave at quarter past eight.*
Il arrive à neuf heures moins le quart.	*He arrives at quarter to nine.*

- Minutes past the hour are added directly after the hour

Il est trois heures vingt.	*It's twenty past three.*

- Minutes to the hour are expressed by using **moins**

Il est onze heures moins cinq.	*It's five to eleven.*

C Times of the day using the 12-hour clock are indicated by **de …**

Il est dix heures du matin/du soir.	*It's ten o'clock in the morning/evening.*
Il est trois heures de l'après-midi.	*It's three o'clock in the afternoon.*

To indicate the time something happened use **à** (or **vers** for approximate times).

Elle est partie à cinq heures.	*She left at five o'clock.*
Je vais arriver vers quatre heures.	*I'll arrive at about four o'clock.*

To express the idea of *between* two times you say **de … à**, or **entre … et**.

Je serai là de dix heures à midi.	*I'll be there from ten o'clock to midday.*
Je serai au bureau entre dix heures et midi.	*I'll be at the office between ten o'clock and midday.*

D The 24-hour clock is used more widely in French than in English. It works the same way in French except that the word **heure(s)** is included.

08h15 huit heures quinze	*08.15 eight fifteen*
20h45 vingt heures quarante-cinq	*20.45 twenty forty-five*

1 Complete the sentences with the appropriate time.

E.g. Barbara se lève à _____ . Barbara se lève à *sept heures*.

a À _____ elle prend son petit déjeuner. (7h20)

b À _____ elle quitte la maison. (8h10)

c Elle commence son travail à _____. (8h55)

d À _____ elle déjeune. (12h45)

e À _____ elle fait les courses. (18h00)

2 State the following times in full using the 24-hour clock.

E.g. 13h22 → treize heures vingt-deux.

a 17h40   **c** 19h25   **e** 15h15

b 03h35   **d** 12h22   **f** 18h30

3 Match the sentences on the left with those on the right, and insert the appropriate times in full.

E.g. **a + 5, huit heures trente/et demie**

a Il prend le train à _____.

b Nous nous levons à _____.

c J'arrive au bureau à _____.

d À _____ elles regardent la télévision.

e Je me couche à _____.

f Je joue au golf le samedi à _____.

g Ils déjeunent à _____.

h Le musée ferme à _____ du soir.

1 *We get up at quarter past six.*

2 *I play golf at quarter to eleven on Saturdays.*

3 *I go to bed at half past twelve.*

4 *The museum closes at seven o'clock in the evening.*

5 *He catches the train at eight thirty.*

6 *They have lunch at one o'clock.*

7 *At ten past four they watch the television.*

8 *I arrive at the office at nine o'clock.*

92 UNIT Days, dates and years

A Les jours de la semaine

lundi	*Monday*
mardi	*Tuesday*
mercredi	*Wednesday*
jeudi	*Thursday*
vendredi	*Friday*
samedi	*Saturday*
dimanche	*Sunday*

Les mois de l'année

janvier	*January*	juillet	*July*
février	*February*	août	*August*
mars	*March*	septembre	*September*
avril	*April*	octobre	*October*
mai	*May*	novembre	*November*
juin	*June*	décembre	*December*

These are all written without capitals.

B Dates of the month are expressed using cardinal numbers.

le trente décembre   *the thirtieth of December*
vendredi, le quinze août/le vendredi, quinze août   *Friday, 15 August*

The exception is **premier** *first*, as in **le premier mai** *the first of May*.

C The day on which something regularly occurs is given using the definite article, whereas one particular day is given without it.

Je vais à la piscine le samedi.   *I go to the swimming pool on Saturdays.*
Je vais à la piscine samedi.   *I'm going to the swimming pool on Saturday.*

D **En** is used to mean *in* with months or years (also **au mois de** for months).

en avril   *in April*   en 1988   *in 1988*
au mois de janvier   *in January*

E **En** is also used with the seasons, with the exception of spring where **au** is used.

au printemps *in spring*   en automne *in autumn*
en été *in summer*   en hiver *in winter*

F The year can be given in two ways.

en 1999 = en mil neuf cent quatre-vingt-dix-neuf
              en dix-neuf cent quatre-vingt-dix-neuf

G The following phrases are used when talking about days and dates.

Quel jour/Quelle date sommes-nous?   *What day/date is it?*
On est quel jour/quelle date?   *What day/date is it?*
Quelle est la date?   *What's the date?*
C'est/On est jeudi, le 15 août.   *It's Thursday, 15 August.*

 ➤ See asking questions (2) in Unit 85, numbers in Units 87 and 88.

92 UNIT Days, dates and years – Exercises

1 **Look at the following calendar and write down the dates circled.**

E.g. dimanche, le trois janvier *Sunday, 3 January*

2 **Complete the sentences on the left and match them with those on the right.**

E.g. **Je vais au cinéma** *jeudi. I'm going to the cinema on Thursday.*

a Je joue au golf _____.
b Je fais ma correspondance _____.
c Je suis allé au cinéma _____.
d _____ je vais le voir.
e Je vais au cinéma _____.
f J'ai joué au golf _____.
g Je le vois _____.
h J'écrirai la lettre _____.

1 *I will write the letter on Monday.*
2 *On Thursdays I play golf.*
3 *I played golf on Thursday.*
4 *I see him on Sundays.*
5 *I went to the cinema on Friday.*
6 *On Mondays I write letters.*
7 *On Sunday I am going to see him.*
8 *I go to the cinema on Fridays.*

3 **Translate the following into French.**

a *It's my birthday (l'anniversaire (nm)) on Friday, 15 May.*
b *This Sunday I am going to see friends.*
c *Next week I'm on holiday.*
d *He started on 15 April.*
e *In spring we are going to Italy.*
f *Today is 12 January.*
g *In winter she stays in France.*
h *In 1968 I was in Paris.*

185

93 UNIT *Depuis, il y a, venir de*

Depuis, il y a and *venir de generally combine with tenses in ways that are different from English.*

A Depuis

- **Depuis** + present tense means *have been ... for/since*, and describes an action which continues into the present.

  Je travaille ici depuis deux ans.   *I've been working here for two years.*

  Je suis ici depuis lundi.   *I've been here since Monday.*

- **Depuis** + imperfect tense means *had been ... for/since*, and describes an action clearly in the past.

  Elle le connaissait depuis dix ans.   *She had known him for ten years.*

⚠ In the negative you use the perfect and pluperfect tenses, as in English.

  Il n'a pas travaillé depuis des années.   *He hasn't worked for years.*

  Il n'était pas venu depuis longtemps.   *He hadn't been for a long time.*

- When **depuis** is followed by a second verb and subject, you use **que**.

  Elle travaille ici depuis que vous   *She's worked here since you arrived.*
  êtes arrivé.

B Il y a with expressions of time

- **Il y a** (present tense) + a verb in an appropriate tense means *ago*.

  Je suis arrivé il y a trois semaines.   *I arrived three weeks ago.*

  Il y a cinq ans je travaillais.   *Five years ago I was working.*

- **Il y a**, like **depuis**, is also used to indicate the duration of time for something still continuing (*have been ... for*). To indicate this you use **il y a** (present tense) + the period of time + **que** followed by a clause in the present tense. **Voilà que** and **ça fait que** are used in the same way.

  Il y a dix ans que je le connais.   *I've known him for ten years.*

  Voilà/Ça fait dix ans que je le connais.   *I've known him for ten years.*

- When **il y a ... que** and **ça fait ... que** are used with the same structure, but in the imperfect tense, they translate the English *had been ... for*.

  Il y avait/ça faisait dix mois que je   *I had known him for ten months.*
  le connaissais.

C Venir de expresses the English *has just* (when used in the present tense) or *had just* (when used in the imperfect tense).

  Ils viennent de quitter le bureau.   *They've just left the office.*

  Elle venait d'arriver.   *She had just arrived.*

➤ *See all appropriate tense units and conjunctions (2) in Unit 81.*

Match the sentences on the left with their meanings on the right.

E.g. Je suis étudiant ici depuis trois mois. *I've been a student here for three months.*

a Depuis quand lis-tu?

b Je l'ai vu il y a deux jours.

c Elle attendait depuis quinze minutes.

d Ils habitent à Chartres depuis deux mois.

e Ça faisait deux heures qu'il lisait.

f Elles habitaient à Chartres depuis deux mois.

g Je connais Pierre depuis dix ans.

h Il y a une heure qu'il parle.

i Je joue du violon depuis deux ans.

j Voilà un mois qu'elle habite ici.

1 *She had been waiting for fifteen minutes.*

2 *They have been living in Chartres for two months.*

3 *I saw him two days ago.*

4 *I have been playing the violin for two years.*

5 *He has been talking for an hour.*

6 *He had been reading for two hours.*

7 *How long have you been reading for?*

8 *I have known Pierre for ten years.*

9 *She's been living here for a month.*

10 *They had been living in Chartres for two months.*

Insert *depuis* or *il y a* into the following sentences.

E.g. **J'ai appris à nager _____ deux ans.** → **J'ai appris à nager *il y a* deux ans.**

a Il est venu vous voir _____ vingt minutes.

b Je suis en vacances _____ deux jours.

c Je travaille comme institutrice _____ trois ans.

d Elle a vu le film _____ deux semaines.

e Nous sommes rentrés de Grenoble _____ un mois.

f Elles apprennent le chinois _____ un an.

Express each of the following sentences in three ways.

E.g. **J'attends mon ami depuis une heure.**
  → **Il y a une heure que j'attends mon ami.**
  → **Ça fait une heure que j'attends mon ami.**
  → **Voilà une heure que j'attends mon ami**.

a Il fait des études depuis plusieurs semaines.

b Nous attendons le bus depuis quarante minutes.

c Ils travaillaient depuis deux heures.

A Look at the following sentences:

Il y a une boisson dans le frigo.   *There is a drink in the fridge*

Il y a des dossiers sur mon bureau.   *There are some files on my desk.*

As these sentences show, **il y a** is used only in the singular, whether the following noun is singular or plural.

In negative statements, **ne ... pas** enclose the pronoun **y** and the conjugated verb **a**.

Il n'y a pas de place.   *There's no room.*

B **Il y a** can also be used this way in past and future tenses.

- Imperfect tense (*there was/were*):

Il y avait beaucoup de monde   *There were a lot of people at the*
au match.   *match.*

Puis il y avait une discussion.   *Then there was a discussion.*

Il y avait une fois...   *Once upon a time...* (lit. *There was once...*)

- Perfect tense (*there has/have been; there was/were*):

Il y a eu un accident!   *There has been an accident!*

Il y a eu des problèmes.   *There have been/There were problems.*

Il n'y a pas eu de problèmes.   *There haven't been any problems.*

⚠ The past participle **eu** does not agree with any preceding direct object.

Tous les problèmes qu'il y a eu   *All the problems there were have*
ont été facilement résolus.   *been easily resolved.*

- Future tense (*there will be*):

Il y aura un grand repas après   *There will be a big meal after the*
l'exposition.   *exhibition.*

Il y aura des feux d'artifice après   *There will be fireworks after the meal.*
le repas.

C A slightly more formal alternative to **il y a** is **il existe**, also used in the singular only:

Il existe deux cinémas en ville.   *There are two cinemas in town.*

D You can use **il reste** to say *there is/are* **left**:

Il reste du fromage?   *Is there any cheese left?*

➤ *See negatives in Units 82 and 83,* il y a *for time in Unit 93 and all appropriate tense units.*

Match the correct English translation to a French sentence from the box.

E.g. Il y a une boisson sur la table. There was a drink on the table.
There is a drink on the table. ✓

a There has been an accident.
b There will be an accident.

c There will be three people.
d There were three people.

e There's not much to see.
f There wasn't much to see.

g There's a good film at the cinema.
h There was a good film at the cinema.

1 Il y a trop de choses à faire.
2 Il y a un bon film au cinéma.
3 Il y a eu un accident.
4 Il y avait trois personnes.
5 Il n'y a pas grand chose à voir.

i There was too much to do.
j There's too much to do.

Use *il y a* to form a sentence about each illustration.

E.g. Il y a un livre sur la table. (*There is a book on the table.*)

a devant l'école   **b** dans le frigo   **c**

Translate the following sentences using the tense indicated.

E.g. *There are three cars in front of the house.* (present tense) → Il y a trois voitures devant la maison.

a *There will be fireworks in front of the town hall* (**la mairie**). (future tense)
b *There were bottles in the fridge.* (imperfect tense)
c *There are vegetables in the soup* (**la soupe**). (present tense)
d *There has been a mistake* (**une erreur**). (perfect tense)
e *There will be a lot of people* (**beaucoup de monde**) *at the cinema.* (future tense)
f *There were children in the park.* (imperfect tense)
g *There is some money in my pocket* (**la poche**). (present tense)

95 UNIT | Saying yes and no

In French, there are two words for yes, **oui** and **si**. No is translated as **non**.

A In most situations, **oui** is used to mean *yes*.

Tu viens avec nous? Oui.   *Are you coming with us?*
                                      Yes, I am./Yes, I'm coming. etc.

The above response shows that English can sometimes use longer replies than are necessary in French.

Si is needed to answer a negative question, or to contradict a negative statement. **Si** can stand alone for the long English contradiction forms shown here.

Vous ne l'avez pas vu? Si (je l'ai vu).   *Didn't you see him? Yes I did (see him).*
Vous ne le ferez jamais. Mais si!   *You will never do it. Oh yes I will!*

B The English word *no* is translated by **non** (or **mais non** in more exclamatory uses). Often a polite refusal can be given by using **merci** alone. Again, English often uses a longer answer.

Je peux vous offrir un cognac? Merci. *Would you like a brandy? No, thank you.*
Vous voulez un café? Non, merci.   *Would you like a coffee? No thanks.*
Il va pleuvoir? Non.   *Will it rain? No (it won't).*
Vous êtes venu tout seul? Mais non, *Did you come alone? No, I'm*
   je suis avec ma femme!   *with my wife!*

C The word **que** must be added before **oui**, **si** and **non** when used after **peut-être** *perhaps*, **espérer** *to hope* and verbs of saying and thinking.

Est-ce que tu peux venir?   *Can you come?*
  J'ai déjà dit que oui.   *I've already said I can.*
Il a reçu ta lettre? J'espère que oui. *Did he receive your letter? I hope so.*
Il n'arrivera pas aujourd'hui.   *He will not arrive today.*
  Je crois que si.   *I think he will.*
Vont-ils être en retard?   *Are they going to be late?*
  J'espère que non.   *I hope not.*
Il est déjà parti? Je crois que non. *Has he already left? I don't think so.*
Il va pleuvoir? Peut-être que oui, *Will it rain? Perhaps it will,*
  peut-être que non.   *perhaps it won't.*

➤ See conjunctions (2) in Unit 81, negatives in Units 82 and 83, asking questions in Units 84–86.

95 UNIT Saying yes and no – Exercises

1 Read the following questions and choose either (1) or (2) as an appropriate response.

E.g. Il est déjà midi?   1 Oui. ✓
                                2 Si.

a Tu vas venir?   1 Oui, bien sûr!
                                         2 Mais si!

b Vous n'avez pas écrit la lettre.   1 Si, je l'ai écrite.
                                         2 Oui, j'ai écrit la lettre.

c Il ne fera pas ses devoirs avant   1 Oui, il les fera!
    de sortir.   2 Si, il les fera!

d Elle ne parle pas français.   1 Oui, elle parle français.
                                         2 Si, elle parle français.

e Il est déjà arrivé?   1 Mais si!
                                         2 Oui, il est arrivé ce matin.

f Tu n'as pas acheté le pull bleu?   1 Oui, je l'ai acheté.
                                         2 Si, je l'ai acheté.

g Vous avez lu ce livre?   1 Oui, bien sûr!
                                         2 Si, je l'ai lu.

h Elle ne sera pas contente.   1 Si, elle sera très contente.
                                         2 Oui, elle sera contente.

2 Give an appropriate answer to each of the following questions, using the English as a guide.

E.g. Cherche-t-il un nouvel emploi? *I don't think so.* → Je crois que non.

a A-t-il fini son travail? *I think so.*
b Elle ne viendra pas ce weekend. *I hope she will.*
c Il sera en retard? *I hope not.*
d Tu voudrais une bière? *No, thank you.*
e A-t-il reçu mon cadeau? *I don't think so.*
f Va-t-il faire beau? *Perhaps not.*

3 Complete the gaps using *si, oui* or *non*.

E.g. Il n'est pas en vacances. → *Si*, il est en vacances.

a Tu voudrais du vin? _____, j'en voudrais bien.
b Elle ne l'a pas fini? _____, elle l'a fini.
c Il ne t'a pas écrit? _____, il m'a écrit.
d Tu viendras samedi? _____, bien sûr.
e Tu n'es pas content? _____, je suis content.
f Tu l'as vue? _____, elle n'était pas là.

96 UNIT | Countries, nationalities and languages

It is important to know the gender of countries and the rules governing the use of related adjectives and nouns.

A Most countries are feminine; these end in a consonant plus **-e** or **-ie**.

la France *France*	l'Angleterre *England*	la Russie *Russia*
la Norvège *Norway*	l'Espagne *Spain*	l'Italie *Italy*
la Pologne *Poland*	l'Allemagne *Germany*	

⚠ But note *le* **Mexique** *Mexico.*

● Others are masculine.

le Japon Japan   le Canada *Canada*   le Portugal *Portugal*

● A few are plural, as they are in English.

les États-Unis *the United States*   les Caraïbes *the West Indies*

B The definite article (**le, la, les**) is used before names of countries.

Le Maroc est un pays très intéressant. *Morocco is a very interesting country.*

● To say *to* or *in* a country, use **en** for feminine countries, **au** for masculine countries and **aux** for plural countries.

Nous allons en France, puis au Luxembourg et puis aux Pays-Bas. | *We are going to France, then to Luxembourg and then to the Netherlands.*

● To say *from* a country, use **de** for feminine countries, **du** for masculine countries and **des** for plurals countries.

Il est arrivé d'Allemagne ce matin. | *He arrived from Germany this morning.*
Il vient du Canada. | *He comes from Canada.*

C French *adjectives* of nationality are not written with a capital letter.

C'est une voiture italienne. | *It's an Italian car.*
Ils sont canadiens. | *They are Canadian.*

● When using *nouns* of nationality the usual rules of adjectival agreement apply, but the nationality is written with a capital letter.

C'est une Danoise/une Française. | *She's a Dane/a Frenchwoman.*

D When referring to the language, use the masculine noun without a capital. If there is an adverb or other qualifier, insert the masculine definite article.

Parlez-vous français? | *Do you speak French?*
Tu parles très bien le russe. | *You speak Russian very well.*

➤ See genders of nouns (1) in Unit 4, prepositions en, de and à in Units 11, 13 and 14, adjectives (agreement) in Units 17 and 18.

1 Give the gender of the following countries.

a Argentine   b Corse   c Suisse   d Hongrie   e Maroc

f Russie   g Pérou   h Mexique   i Thaïlande   j Tibet

2 Complete these sentences to say where the following people were born. Select from the list and use *en*, *au*, or *aux*.

E.g. François Mitterand est né _____ . | France | François Mitterand est né en France.

a La chanteuse Madonna est née _____ .

b Le cinéaste Kurosawa est né _____ .

c Le chanteur Luciano Pavarotti est né _____ .

d Le révolutionnaire Lénine est né _____ .

e Le peintre Pablo Picasso est né _____ .

> Espagne
> Italie
> Japon
> Russie
> États-Unis

3 Decide where the following people are from. Select from the list and complete with *de*, *du*, or *des*. Then provide the noun of the nationality.

E.g. Mao Tsé Toung était de Chine. C'était un Chinois. *Mao Tse Tung was from China. He was a Chinaman.*

a Bill Clinton est _____ .

b Helmuth Kohl est _____ .

c La reine Elizabeth II est _____ .

d Salvador Dali était _____ .

e Pelé est _____ .

> États-Unis
> Espagne
> Angleterre
> Allemagne
> Brésil

4 Complete the table. One has been done for you.

Country/Continent	Masculine adjective	Feminine adjective
a la France	français	**française**
b		italienne
c	japonais	
d le Canada		
e l'Angleterre	anglais	
f les États-Unis	américain	
g		espagnole
h	luxembourgeois	
i la Chine		chinoise
j l'Afrique	africain	

Inversion

> You need inversion after direct speech and after certain
> expressions. It can also be used for questions.

A When expressing *she said*, *I exclaimed*, *he replied*, etc. after direct speech,
the subject and the verb are inverted (reversed).

    "C'est ridicule", dit-il.   *"It's ridiculous", he says.*
    "Bonjour", a répondu Pauline.   *"Hello", replied Pauline.*

When the third-person singular of the verb ends in a vowel, a **-t-** is inserted
after the verb and before the subject pronoun **il**, **elle** or **on**.

    "C'est combien?" demande-t-elle.   *"How much is it?" she asks.*
    "Bonjour", a-t-il dit.   *"Hello", he said.*

- Any object and reflexive pronouns precede the finite verb.
    "La météo est bonne", nous a-t-il dit.   *"The forecast is good", he told us.*
    "Bonjour!", s'exclama-t-elle.   *"Hello!", she exclaimed.*

- If the verb of saying comes first, word order is normal.
    Elle m'a dit, "Bonjour".   *She said "Hello" to me.*

B The subject and verb are also inverted after the following, when they begin
the sentence.

    à peine … que *scarcely*   encore *nevertheless*
    ainsi *thus*   peut-être *perhaps*
    aussi *therefore* (not when meaning   sans doute *doubtless, no doubt*
      also, as well)

    Peut-être a-t-elle changé d'avis.   *Perhaps she has changed her mind.*
    Ainsi l'avocat a-t-il décidé de   *And so the lawyer decided to give*
      quitter son travail.   *up his job.*
    Sans doute va-t-elle passer la nuit   *No doubt she is going to spend the*
      chez des amis.   *night with friends.*
    Je suis fatigué, aussi ai-je besoin   *I am tired, therefore/consequently I*
      de dormir.   *need to sleep.*

⚠ Peut-être and **sans doute** can be followed by **que**, without inversion.
    Peut-être que tu le verras vendredi. *Perhaps you'll see him on Friday.*

C Remember that one way to ask questions in French is to invert the subject
and verb.

    Avez-vous promis?   *Did you promise?*
    Est-elle à la réunion?   *Is she in the meeting?*

Turn the following sentences round so that the subject and verbs have to be inverted.

E.g. Il a crié, "Courage!" → "Courage!" a-t-il crié.

a J'ai demandé, "Où est la poste?"
b L'agent a répondu, "Continuez tout droit."
c Nous lui avons dit, "Merci bien."
d Il répond, "Bonnes vacances!"
e Elle s'exclama, "C'est impossible!"
f Il s'écriera, "C'est extraordinaire!"

Rewrite the following sentences, starting with the word given in brackets and changing the word order as necessary. Then translate the sentences into English.

E.g. Elle lui avait téléphoné et son fax est arrivé. (à peine … que) → À peine lui avait-elle téléphoné que son fax est arrivé. *She had barely rung him when his fax arrived.*

a Il sera enfin content. (peut-être)
b Le grand homme mourut. (ainsi)
c Il y a encore de l'espoir. (peut-être)
d Elle veut être un jour chef de l'entreprise. (sans doute)
e Elle a besoin d'aide. (aussi)

Rewrite the following as questions, using inversion.

E.g. Il a parlé au médecin. → A-t-il parlé au médecin?

a Il a expliqué le projet.
b Elles sont arrivées à l'heure.
c Nous avons fini notre repas.
d Elle vous a téléphoné ce matin.
e Il a frappé à la porte.

Translate the following into French, looking back at Units 84 and 85 if necessary, and using an inverted form in each.

E.g. Where is my bag? → Où est mon sac?

a What would you like, sir?
b Where's the cinema?
c How are you?
d When are you leaving?
e How much is this coat?
f Which date is the best for you?
g How many people are there?

98 UNIT | Faux amis

These are words that are similar to English words, but which have a different meaning to that which you might expect.

Faux amis literally means *false friends*. The following table gives some examples, followed by a translation into English. It then gives the English word that is similar to the French word, along with its translation back into French.

False friend	Meaning	English	French
actuellement	*at the present time, currently*	*actually*	en fait, à vrai dire, vraiment
assister à	*to be present at, to attend*	*to assist*	aider
l'avis (*nm*)	*notice, option; opinion*	*advice*	le conseil
la banque	*the bank* (for money)	*(money) bank,* but *also riverbank*	la rive, le bord de la rivière
la chance	usual use (*good*) *luck*	*chance*	le hasard
fameux	*notorious*	*famous*	célèbre
l'humeur (*nf*)	*mood*	*humour*	l'humour (*nm*)
la journée	*day(time)*	*journey*	le voyage, le trajet
la librairie	*bookshop*	*library*	la bibliothèque
la monnaie	*currency; small change*	*money*	l'argent (*nm*)
la nouvelle	*piece of news*	*novel*	le roman
passer un examen	*to sit an exam*	*to pass an exam*	réussir à un examen
la pièce	*room; coin; play* (theatre)	*piece*	le morceau
la place	*public square, seat, job.*	*place*	l'endroit (*nm*), le lieu
rester	*to remain, stay*	*to rest*	se reposer
le spectacle	*show, sight*	*spectacles*	les lunettes (*nf*)
user	*to wear out, wear thin*	*to use*	utiliser, se servir de, employer

Some words have two meanings, only one of which is close to the English.

l'histoire	*history/story*
une balle	*ball* (e.g. for tennis)/*bullet*
la campagne	*countryside/(military) campaign*
les parents	*parents/relatives*

➤ *See Unit 6 for words with more than one meaning according to gender.*

98 UNIT Faux amis – Exercises

1 Which is the odd one out? In each case it is the one that means the same in French as in English.

E.g. face   librairie   fameux   **document**

a situation	monnaie	avis	journée
b assister	visiter	rester	user
c pièce	journée	spectacle	panorama
d âge	chance	humeur	actuellement

2 Translate the following sentences into English.

E.g. **Ce roman est intéressant?** → *Is this novel interesting?*

a Par hasard elle a trouvé le document perdu.
b Je vais rester à la maison ce soir.
c La librairie se trouve en face de la gare.
d Ses souliers sont usés.
e C'est une fameuse histoire.
f Il a toujours de la chance.
g Elle est rarement de bonne humeur.
h À mon avis c'est impossible.
i Ils se sont assis dans la banque.
j Une bonne place est difficile à trouver.

3 Translate the following sentences into French.

E.g. *Have you got any change?* → **Tu as de la monnaie?**

a *I am going to the library to choose some books.*
b *Where are my spectacles?*
c *The journey lasted (**durer**) twenty-four hours.*
d *She's a very famous woman.*
e *It's a very interesting place.*
f *Pass me a piece of bread please.*
g *They're going to attend the meeting tomorrow.*
h *I must sit my exams in ten days.*
i *At the moment the news is good.*

99 Unit | Expressions of quantity

Expressions of quantity include terms like a lot of, several, most of, or a packet of.

A Several expressions of quantity are followed by **de**.

Il vend beaucoup de voitures.	*He sells lots of cars.*
Il y a un certain nombre de lettres.	*There are quite a few letters.*
Il y a tant de choses à voir.	*There are so many things to see.*
Il y a énormément d'enfants ici.	*There are loads of children here.*

assez de *enough*	moins de *less, fewer*
autant de *as much, as many*	peu de/un peu de *little/a little*
beaucoup de *much, many, a lot, lots*	plus de *more*
combien de … ? *how much? how many?*	tant de *so much, so many*
énormément de *loads, an enormous amount*	trop de *too much, too many*
	un certain nombre de *quite a few, a certain number*

B Nouns expressing quantity are also followed by **de**.

Vous prenez 200 grammes de champignons?	*Would you like 200 grammes of mushrooms?*
J'ai une bouteille d'eau minérale.	*I've got a bottle of mineral water.*
Je voudrais trois tranches de jambon.	*I'd like three slices of ham.*

C After **la plupart**, **de** combines with the definite article (**le**, **la**, **les**). The verb agrees in number with the noun following **la plupart de**.

La plupart de la collection a été perdue.	*Most of the collection was lost.*
La plupart des clients sont très contents.	*Most of the customers are very happy.*

D Some indefinite adjectives indicate quantity or number. As they are adjectives they do not require **de**.

Il y a **quelques** pots de yaourt dans le frigo.	*There are a few pots of yoghurt in the fridge.*
Il y a **plusieurs** boîtes de sardines dans le placard.	*There are several tins of sardines in the cupboard.*
Certains clients demandent un remboursement.	*Some customers are asking for a refund.*

> ➤ See the preposition de in Unit 13, the comparison of adjectives in Unit 24, indefinite adjectives and pronouns in Units 28 and 29, the object pronoun en in Unit 46.

Complete the following sentences and match them to their English equivalents.

E.g. **Il y a + plusieurs possibilités.** → *There are several possibilities.*

a	Il y a	**i**	francs à dépenser.
b	Ils ont acheté	**j**	quelques légumes.
c	J'ai quelques	**k**	tant de cadeaux.
d	On m'a offert	**l**	journaux à lire.
e	J'ai besoin d'acheter	**m**	plusieurs possibilités.
f	Tu voudrais	**n**	que moi.
g	Il y a plusieurs	**o**	un verre de vin rouge?
h	Il a moins de responsabilités	**p**	six tranches de jambon.

1 *They have bought six slices of ham.*
2 *I have a few francs to spend.*
3 *I need to buy a few vegetables.*
4 *He has fewer responsibilities than I.*
5 *I've been given so many presents.*
6 *Would you like a glass of red wine?*
7 *There are several newspapers to read.*
8 *There are several possibilities.*

Complete the following sentences with an appropriate expression of quantity.

E.g. **J'ai *beaucoup de* cadeaux à acheter.** *I have a lot of presents to buy.*

a Nous avons _____ employés qu'eux. *We have as many employees as them.*
b Vous avez invité _____ personnes? *How many people have you invited?*
c Il a _____ choses à faire. *He has too many things to do.*
d Elle s'est débrouillée avec _____ argent. *She got by on little money.*
e Elle a toujours _____ de projets. *She always has a lot of plans.*
f Vous avez _____ pain? *Have you got enough bread?*
g Il y a _____ choix que je ne peux pas décider. *There is so much choice that I can't decide.*
h Vous avez besoin d'_____ chance! *You need a little luck!*

Translate the following into French.

E.g. *two kilos of flour* → **deux kilos de farine**

a *a bottle of mineral water*	**d** *a tin of peaches*
b *a kilo of apples*	**e** *a cup of tea*
c *a packet of biscuits*	

Verbs followed by à/de

Verbs followed by *à* + infinitive

aider à	*to help to*	s'intéresser à	*to be interested in*
s'amuser à	*to amuse oneself at*	inviter à	*to invite to*
apprendre à	*to learn to*	se mettre à	*to start to*
arriver à	*to manage to*	obliger à	*to oblige to*
s'attendre à	*to expect to*	parvenir à	*to succeed in*
autoriser à	*to authorise to*	penser à	*to think of*
chercher à	*to try to*	persister à	*to persist in*
commencer à	*to start to*	pousser à	*to push to*
consentir à	*to consent to*	se préparer à	*to prepare oneself to*
consister à	*to consist of*	renoncer à	*to renounce something*
continuer à	*to continue to*	réussir à	*to succeed in*
se décider à	*to decide to*	rester à	*to be left to*
demander à	*to ask to*	servir à	*to be used for*
encourager à	*to encourage to*	tarder à	*to delay (doing),*
forcer à	*to force to*		*be late in*
hésiter à	*to hesitate to*	tenir à	*to be keen on*

Verbs followed by *de* + infinitive

accepter de	*to accept to*	s'occuper de	*to deal with*
(s')arrêter de	*to stop doing*	offrir de	*to offer to*
avoir besoin de	*to need to*	ordonner de	*to order to*
cesser de	*to stop*	permettre de	*to allow to*
conseiller de	*to advise to*	persuader de	*to persuade to*
craindre de	*to fear doing*	promettre de	*to promise to*
décider de	*to decide to*	proposer de	*to suggest to*
défendre de	*to forbid to*	rappeler de	*to remind*
demander de	*to ask s.o. to*	se rappeler de	*to remember*
dire de	*to tell to*	recommander de	*to recommend to*
empêcher de	*to prevent from*	refuser de	*to refuse to*
essayer de	*to try to*	regretter de	*to regret doing*
éviter de	*to avoid doing*	remercier to	*to thank for*
finir de	*to finish doing*	se souvenir de	*to remember doing*
interdire de	*to forbid to*	suggérer de	*to suggest doing*

Glossary of grammatical terms

Adjective: an adjective is a word that describes a noun: *a **long** way*, *three **great** and **ancient** buildings*. It can be **descriptive**: *big, loud, green, gentle, contented*, etc. **comparative**: *bigger, older, more/less big than, as big as* **superlative**: *the **biggest** building, the **oldest** house, the most ..., the least...* **demonstrative**: ***this** house, **that** car, **these** shoes, **those** pens* **indefinite**: ***every** person, **some** people, **certain** people, **several** people*, etc. **interrogative**: ***which** car? **what** event?* **possessive**: ***my** office, **his** bike, **her** house*, etc.

Adverb: an adverb modifies a verb, an adjective or another adverb: *He ran **quickly**. This is a **very** interesting book. He writes **very** well.* Adverbs can also have comparative and superlative forms: *He ran **more** quickly (than...) He ran **the quickest**.*

Agreement: this occurs when two words have a form that indicates they have the same gender or number: ***she** talks, **they** run*.

Article: words meaning *the, a* or *an*. The definite article in English is *the*; the indefinite article is *a/an*. *Some* and *any* are partitive articles when used with non-specific nouns: ***some** lemonade. I haven't **any** paper.*

Clause: a group of words that contains one verb. There are main and subordinate clauses. The main clause can stand alone, the subordinate clause is dependent on it. *This is a big city* (main clause) *which I love* (subordinate clause).

Comparative: see **Adverb** and **Adjective**

Compound tense: tense that consists of two verb parts (auxiliary + past participle): *she **has spoken***.

Conjunction: a conjunction can be **coordinating**, **subordinating** or **correlating**. Coordinating conjunctions link sentences, clauses, phrases or words of equal status (two main clauses, two nouns, etc): *and, but, however*, etc. Subordinating conjunctions link main and subordinate clauses: *because, although, when*, etc. Correlating conjunctions balance two or more things: *neither ... nor*.

Consonant: all letters of the alphabet except *a, e, i, o, u* (vowels).

Conjugation: see Unit 30.

Gender: whether a word is masculine or feminine. In French all nouns are either masculine or feminine.

Impersonal verb: verb without a specific subject, used in the third-person singular: *It's lovely outside.*

Imperative: verb form for giving orders, instructions and commands: *Turn left.*

Infinitive: see Unit 30.

Negative: word, phrase or sentence denying or contradicting something. The most common negation in English is *not*: *He couldn't find it.*

Noun: a word used to name a person, an object or an abstract quality: *police officer, bank, honesty*.

Number: this indicates the difference between **singular** and **plural**: *one house, three houses*. In French, articles and adjectives as well as nouns show number: *les vieilles maisons*.

Object: the person, animal or thing that receives the action of the verb. *He ate the **sandwich**. They congratulated **her**. They sought **liberty***.
Objects can be direct or indirect: *I gave the **book*** (direct) ***to he**r* (indirect)

Partitive article: these are *some, any* when used with nouns. ***Some** bread. I haven't **any** money*.

Participle: these are a form of the verb and can be present or past participles. Present participles end in *-ing* in English: *eating*. Past participles are the part of the verb used with *to have* in English: *I have **eaten***.

Passive: form of the verb where the subject of the verb receives the action of the verb. *The day **was chosen**. The animals **will be released***.

Phrase: group of words that has coherence and does not usually contain a subject and verb. It can be part of a sentence: *the way home*; *over the top*; *according to her*.

Plural: see **Number**.

Preposition: word or group of words used before a noun or pronoun to show place, position, time or method: *in, on, to, from*.

Pronoun: word used in place of a noun or noun phrase. A pronoun can be: a **demonstrative** pronoun: *the one, this one, that one, these (ones)/those (ones)*; an **emphatic** (or **disjunctive**) pronoun: *with **me**, for **us***; an **indefinite** pronoun: *something, someone, each one*; an **interrogative** pronoun: *who? whom? what? which one(s)?* a **personal** pronoun (subject or direct object and indirect object pronouns): *I, he, she, it, we, you, they* (subject), *me, him, her, us, them* (direct object and indirect object); a **possessive** pronoun: *mine, his, hers*, etc.; a **relative** pronoun: *who, whom, which, that*; a **reflexive** pronoun: *myself, himself, herself*, etc. These are the object of a reflexive verb: *I wash **myself***.

Relative clause: a clause introduced by a relative pronoun. *These are the friends **who live in America***.

Singular: see **Number**.

Subject: the subject of a verb is the person or object performing the action and can be a noun or pronoun. *The **rain** fell. **They** went for a sail*.

Subjunctive: see Unit 30.

Subordinate clause: see **Conjunctions**.

Superlative: see **Adverb** and **Adjective**.

Tense: see Unit 30.

Verb: see Unit 30.

Vowel: the letters *a, e, i, o, u*.

KEY TO EXERCISES

UNIT 1

1 **a** le **b** la **c** l' **d** la **e** le **f** l' **g** le **h** le

2

3 **a** L'hôtel; la piscine; le petit-déjeuner; Les repas; les vins **4** **a** les journaux **b** les banques **c** les voix **d** les fromages **e** les bateaux **f** les cinémas

UNIT 2

1 **a** un **b** une **c** un **d** une **e** un **f** un **g** une **h** un **i** un **j** un

2

une	voiture (*nf*)	des	voitures
un	bureau (*nm*)	des	bureaux
un	pullover (*nm*)	des	pullovers
une	plante (*nf*)	des	plantes
une	veste (*nf*)	des	vestes
un	journal (*nm*)	des	journaux
une	église (*nf*)	des	églises
un	oeil (*nm*)	des	yeux

3 **a** un; des **b** une; des **c** des; de; des; des **4** **a** des **b** d' **c** des **d** les **e** de

UNIT 3

1 **b** p6 **c** n4 **d** l1 **e** m3 **f** i8 **g** j2 **h** o5 **2** **a** le **b** le **c** le **d** le **e** les **f** la **g** le **h** le **i** le **j** la **k** le **l** la **m** le, le

UNIT 4

1 **a** le **b** l' (le) **c** le **d** le **e** la **f** la **g** la **h** le **i** la **j** le **k** la **l** la **m** la **n** le **o** le **p** le **q** l' (le) **r** le **s** la **t** l' (le) **2** a, b, c, d, f, g **3** a. c. d. e. f. g. h

UNIT 5

1 **a** la **b** le **c** le **d** la **e** la **f** l' (*f*) **g** le **h** le **i** la **j** la **k** la **l** la **m** le **n** la **o** le **2** **a** un **b** la **c** le **d** les **e** la **f** une **g** le **h** une **i** les **j** l' **3** **a** un pied **b** un bras **c** un nez **d** un cheval **e** un livre **f** des téléviseurs **g** des lampes **h** un cinéma **i** une église **j** une docteur

UNIT 6

1 a le **b** Cette, un **c** à la **d** la **2** a le **b** la **c** le, la **d** la **3** a la mémoire **b** un livre **c** un voile **d** la somme **e** un tour **f** le poste **g** une voile

UNIT 7

1 a la **b** le **c** le **d** le **e** le **f** le **2** a les chef-lieux **b** les porte-bagages **c** les timbres-poste **d** les demi-heures **e** les sous-sol **f** les tête-à-tête **g** les vice-présidents **3** a le beau-père **b** le haut-parleur **c** le porte-clefs **d** le chef-d'oeuvre **e** le rouge-gorge **f** l'oiseau-mouche **4** a le beau-frère **b** la belle-fille **c** le beau-fils **d** la belle-mère **e** le beau-père **f** la belle-soeur

UNIT 8

1 1 e 2 a 3 f 4 c 5 d 6 b **2** a C'est **b** C'est **c** C'est **d** Ce sont **e** C'est **f** C'est **g** Ce sont **h** C'est **3** a Il est; C'est **b** C'est **c** est-il; il est **d** il est **e** Ce sont **f** C'est **g** Il est **h** C'est

UNIT 9

1 a *I'd like some ice in my whisky.* **b** *Have you got any cars to hire?* **c** *Give me some coffee, please.* **d** *The computer has a lot of capacity.* **e** *Have you got any/some envelopes?* **2** a de **b** des **c** des **d** des **e** de l' **f** du **g** de l' **3** des champignons; des oeufs; du pain; de la confiture; du lait; du fromage; du poisson; de la soupe

UNIT 10

1 a m **b** l **c** j **d** k **e** n **f** i **g** p **h** o **2** a après, 2 **b** contre, 5 **c** dans, 1 **d** avant, 3 **e** chez; avec, 4

UNIT 11

1 a n1 **b** o2 **c** p3 **d** j4 **e** l5 **f** k6 **g** m7 **h** i8 **2** a entre **b** malgré **c** en **d** en; en **e** en; en **3** a en juillet **b** en avion **c** en voiture

UNIT 12

1 a j4 **b** k6 **c** gl **d** h3 **e** i5 **f** l2 **2** a par **b** par **c** parmi **d** pour **e** vers **f** par **g** par **h** sur **3** a par le train **b** deux fois par semaine **c** par ici **d** arrive vers six heures

UNIT 13

1 a 4 **b** 7 **c** 8 **d** 6 **e** 1 **f** 3 **g** 5 **h** 2 **2** a du **b** de **c** de **d** de l' **e** de **f** de **g** du **h** de l' **3** a Voici la valise d'Hélène. **b** C'est l'appartement de Jean. **c** Le train arrive à six heures du soir. **d** J'aime la couleur des bicyclettes/vélos.

UNIT 14

1 Your sentences should include the following links: à la pâtisserie; à l'école; au cinéma; à la pharmacie; aux magasins; à l'église; au café; à Montpellier **2** a Il mal à la main. **b** Elle a mal aux dents. **c** Il a mal au pied. **d** Il a mal au genou. **e** Elle a mal à la gorge. **3** a Une personne aux cheveux longs et une personne aux cheveux courts. **b** Il va au cinéma. **c** Marie habite au quatrième étage.

UNIT 15

1 a 2 **b** 4 **c** 3 **d** 6 **e** 1 **f** 5 **2** a 4 **b** 1 **c** 5 **d** 3 **e** 2 **3** a en face du **b** d'après **c** à travers **d** près de **e** à cause de

UNIT 16

1 **a** ton; mon; ma **b** ton; mon **c** tes; mes **d** ta; ma **e** ton; mon **f** ton; mon **2** **Vos**, votre, vos; nos; votre, vos; nos; vos. **3** **a** sa; ses; ses; son **b** sa; ses **c** votre **d** tes **e** sa **f** leurs **g** notre **h** ses **4** **a** Vous avez mon stylo. **b** C'est sa veste. **c** Ce sont vos documents. **d** L'hôpital est près de mon église.

UNIT 17

1 **a** petite **b** mignonne **c** rouge **d** active **e** intelligente **f** française **2** **a** courts; verts **b** méchant; timide **c** gris; bleue; jaune; bleues; noires **3** **a** blanches; petite **b** bon; chère; grande **c** espagnole; jolie; long; noirs; bruns

UNIT 18

1 **a** finale **b** vieux; gentil **c** frais **d** heureuse **e** nouvel; beau **f** normal **g** brève **h** inquiète **2** **a** douce **b** gentille **c** belle **d** discrète **3** **a** inférieure **b** extérieurs; anciens **c** heureux **d** vieux **e** vieil **f** brève **g** fatals **h** normaux **i** nouvelles; françaises **4** **a** Les pièces sont grandes. **b** Le fromage est frais. **c** Le nouvel hôtel est ouvert. **d** Cette maison est vieille. **e** La route est très longue.

UNIT 19

1 **a** Elle a un beau costume bleu. **b** C'est une femme riche. **c** C'est un grand bâtiment gris. **d** C'est un bon camarade. **e** Ce vieux monsieur est un écrivain célèbre. **f** Je préfère la longue jupe rouge. **g** C'est le dernier jour du concours. **2** **a** bière française **b** vieil ordinateur **c** rue dangereuse **d** article intéressant **e** Tous les documents; nouveau bureau; **f** crème fraîche **g** beau chemin **h** bonne histoire amusante **3** **a** Ma mère est espagnole. **b** J'ai de la limonade fraîche. **c** C'est un vieil hôtel. **d** C'est une grande pièce. **e** Il a une nouvelle voiture rouge. **f** C'est la dernière bouteille. **g** Le premier car est devant le bâtiment blanc. **h** Tous les enfants sont dans le car.

UNIT 20

1 **a** 3 **b** 6 **c** 7 **d** 2 **e** 8 **f** 5 **g** 1 **h** 4 **2** **a** Ce pantalon coûte 240 F. **b** Ce t-shirt coûte 50 F. **c** Ces chaussures coûtent 350 F. **d** Cette chemise coûte 170 F. **e** Cet anorak coûte 560 F. **3** ces; ces (t-shirts)-là; ces; cette (jupe); cette (jupe)-ci; ce (pull)-ci; ce (short)-ci.

UNIT 21

1 **a** joyeusement **b** vraiment **c** poliment **d** résolument **e** parfaitement **f** profondément **g** malheureusement **h** certainement **i** bruyamment **2** **a** doucement **b** attentivement **c** finalement **d** régulièrement **e** extrêmement **f** complètement **3** **a** confortablement **b** doucement **c** rarement **d** bruyamment **e** lentement **f** sûrement

UNIT 22

1 **a** gentiment **b** sérieusement **c** patiemment **d** peu **e** lentement **f** absolument **g** précisément **h** couramment **i** mal **2** **a** 4 haut **b** 3 mauvais **c** 7 cher **d** 1 bien **e** 6 peu **f** 2 mieux **g** 5 bien **3** **a** bas **b** cher **c** mieux **d** bien **e** bien/mal **f** haut **g** fort **h** net **4** **a** Il travaille peu en ce moment. **b** Elle chante très haut. **c** Il joue bien. **d** Il écrit mal.

UNIT 23

1 **a** Elle est déjà partie. **b** J'ai toujours voulu y aller. **c** Il est arrivé tard. **d** Vous avez bien travaillé. **e** Elle a attendu patiemment. **f** Ils sont arrivés hier. **g** Tu as trop bu. **h** Il est vite parti. **i** C'est absolument impossible. **j** Je suis souvent en retard. **k** Elle va arriver après demain. **l** Je parlais franchement. **m** Vous avez beaucoup mangé. **n** Elle a vite fini. **o** Vous avez rarement tort. **p** Tu as conduis prudemment. **q** Vous êtes parti très tôt. **2** **a** Naturellement il pleut. **b** Il a toujours raison. **c** Elles sont évidemment arrivées. **d** Il a vite fini son travail. **e** Elle va mieux heureusement. *or* Heureusement elle va mieux. **3** **aujourd'hui**; tard; très; lentement; heureusement; à l'heure; déjà; bien; confortablement

UNIT 24

1 **a** plus petite **b** plus de talent **c** plus grand **d** plus chère **e** plus frais **2** **a** plus polie que son frère **b** moins patient que … **c** aussi fort que … **d** moins chic que … **e** plus riche que … **f** aussi active que … **g** moins paresseuse que … **h** n'est pas si intelligent que … **3** **a** meilleur **b** puissante **c** fort **d** bon **e** meilleure **f** chère **4** **a** Cet hôtel est meilleur que l'autre. **b** J-P a plus d'argent que D. **c** S est plus jeune que sa sœur. **d** Ce café est plus fort que l'autre. **e** Jules est plus petit que son frère. **f** La plage est moins bon/pire/plus mauvais que la plage à B. **g** Ce film est plus intéressant que l'autre.

UNIT 25

1 **a** 7 **b** 2 **c** 1 **d** 3 **e** 5 **f** 4 **g** 5 **h** 6 **2** **a** plus sérieusement **b** moins souvent **c** plus prudemment **3** **a** moins régulièrement **b** mieux **c** moins attentivement **d** aussi régulièrement **4** **a** Je vais au cinéma plus régulièrement maintenant. **b** Il joue du piano aussi bien que Charles. **c** Elle parle français plus vite maintenant. **d** Il travaille plus lentement que Jean.

UNIT 26

1 **a** le plus grand festival **b** la plus belle maison **c** la plus haute montagne **d** la plus mauvaise/la pire **e** la meilleure musicienne **f** la plus importante **g** plus stupide **2** **a** le plus grand garçon **b** la fille la plus amusante **c** les enfants les plus intelligents **d** la plus vieille dame **3** **a** le meilleur **b** pire/moins bon/plus mauvais **c** la moindre

UNIT 27

1 **a** j1 **b** h5 **c** g4 **d** l6 **e** i2 **f** k3 **2** **a** le mieux **b** le moins **c** le plus patiemment **d** le plus fort **e** le plus rapidement **3** **a** mieux; le mieux **b** plus mal; le moins bien/le plus mal **c** le plus fréquemment

UNIT 28

1 **a** k2 **b** j3 **c** m1 **d** n7 **e** i8 **f** o6 **g** p5 **h** l4 **2** **a** plusieurs **b** Tous **c** autre **d** Tous **e** certaines **3** **a** autres **b** Certaines **c** plusieurs **d** tous **e** autre **f** Plusieurs

UNIT 29

1 **a** j2 **b** l1 **c** k3 **d** g5 **e** h6 **f** i4 **2** **a** Quelqu'un **b** Chacun **c** Personne **d** Chaque **e** quelques-unes **f** quelque chose **g** Quelqu'un **h** chacune **3** **a** Quelques-uns travaillent dur. **b** Des brochures? Il y a quelques-unes sur la table.

c Chaque jour j'arrive à 6 heures. **d** Chacun mange dans sa chambre. **e** J'ai tous les documents. **f** Elle a plusieurs amies.

UNIT 30

1 *The verbs are*: arrive; go; needs; get; goes off; has; go; is **2** *The verbs are*: commence; (me) lève; pars; prends; mange; finis; mange; regarde; lis; ai; faire **3** **a** manger **b** venir **c** prendre **d** acheter **e** travailler **4** *Elle* s'appelle; *elle* travaille; *le bureau* est; *il* est; *Elle* travaille; *Ils* sont; *ils* s'amusent; *la patronne* s'appelle; *son père* a fondé **5** **a** 3 **b** 1 **c** 4 **d** 2 **6** **a** past **b** future **c** past **d** past **e** present **f** present

UNIT 31

1 **a** il **b** nous **c** vous **d** je **e** tu **2** **a** porte **b** écoutent **c** prépare **d** cherches **e** restez **3** **a** Elle travaille. **b** Ils parlent. **c** Ils jouent au tennis.

UNIT 32

1 **a** vous **b** je/il/elle **c** ils/elles **d** nous **e** j'/il/elle **f** tu **g** vous **h** nous **i** j'/il/elle **j** j'/il/elle **2** **a** appelle **b** nageons **c** essaient **d** manges **e** achète **f** commençons **g** répète **h** envoient **3** **a** Je préfère le théâtre. **b** Je lui achète un livre. **c** Oui, nous mangeons beaucoup au restaurant. **d** J'espère aller en France.

UNIT 33

1 **a** finissons **b** rougit **c** maigris **d** réussissez **e** grandis **2** **a** p5 **b** r8 **c** q7 **d** l2 **e** s9 **f** o4 **g** m1 **h** t6 **i** u3 **j** n10 **3** **a** obéit **b** applaudissent **c** réussissons **d** finit e ouvrez f souffrent g offres h cueille **4** **a** Elle ouvre le cadeau. **b** Il choisit un stylo. **c** Tout le monde applaudit. **d** Ils remplissent les bouteilles. **e** Il/elle souffre. **f** J'y réflechis.

UNIT 34

1 **a** jm **b** in **c** jm **d** o **e** in **f** lp **g** k **h** lp **2** **a** j'attends; ils attendent **b** vous vendez; elle vend **c** je réponds; il répond **d** tu entends; elles entendent **e** ils perdent; nous perdons **f** nous descendons; il descend **g** correspondent; correspond **h** fond; fondent **3** **a** réponds **b** attendent **c** vendez **d** rend **e** correspondons **4** **a** Je vends ce vélo. **b** Ils attendent le train. **c** Il descend la montagne maintenant. **d** Elle répond à la lettre.

UNIT 35

1 **a** Il se lève à sept heures. **b** Elles se brossent les dents. **c** Nous nous couchons à onze heures. **d** Je me lave les cheveux. **e** Vous vous réveillez à six heures. **f** Elle s'habille à huit heures. **g** Ils se promènent ensemble. **h** Le car s'arrête devant le cinéma. **2** **a** Elle s'habille. **b** Je me douche. **c** Il se couche **3** Je me réveille; Je me lève; je me lave; Je m'habille; je me brosse les dents; je me lève; je me promène.

UNIT 36

1 **a** je **b** Elles **c** Nous **d** Elle **e** Il **f** Tu **g** Il **h** Vous **i** Ils **j** Vous **k** On **l** Il/elle **2** **a** *He works/is working* **b** *They carry/are carrying/They wear/are wearing* **c** *You eat//are eating* **d** *I finish/am finishing* **e** *They arrive/are arriving* **f** *We eat/are eating* **g** *You arrive/are arriving* **h** *She changes/is changing* **3** **a** Il mange. **b** Elles changent. **c** Elle finit. **d** Ils vendent. **e** Nous portons. **f** J'arrive. **g** Vous travaillez. **h** Tu travailles. **4** **a** Ils **b** Elles **c** Ils **d** Ils

UNIT 37

1 a 6 b 5 c 1 d 2 e 4 f 3 **2** a on aime b on va c on prend d on fait **3** a fatigués b allé(s) c venu(es)(s) d content/contents/ contentes e arrivé(s) f parti(s) **4** a On va en France à Pâques. b On mange à huit heures. c On se rencontre demain? d Quelquefois on préfère le cinéma au théâtre.

UNIT 38

1 a moi b toi **2** a vous b moi c toi d elle e eux **3** moi; toi; moi; nous; elle **4** a moi; lui; 2 b eux; 1 c nous; 4 d nous; 3 **5** a Moi, je préfère le vin rouge. b Lui, il travaille ici, pas moi. c Elle? Elle a mal à la tête. d Moi, je vais avec eux.

UNIT 39

1 a la tienne; *Here's my cup. Where's yours?* b à la tienne; *She prefers her car to yours.* c le sien; *I've got my purse. She has hers//his.* d aux vôtres; *I'll give the sweets to my children and you give the ices to yours.* e la tienne; *My key is in the car. Have you got yours?* f le tien; *Our garden is smaller than yours.* **2** a les tiens b la sienne c les miennes d à la tienne e les vôtres f la mienne **3** a les miennes b des siens c les vôtres d les nôtres e au tien

UNIT 40

1 a 3 b 5 c 2 d 1 e 4 **2** a h5 b fl c i3 d j2 e g4 **3** a C'est celui de ma sœur. b Ce sont ceux de mon collègue. c … celle de mon père. d … celui du voisin. e … celles de mon épouse.

UNIT 41

1 a que b que c qui d que e qui **2** a qui b que c que d qui e que f qui g qui h que i qu' j que

UNIT 42

1 a i3 b h4 c j1 d g2 e f5 **2** a dont b dont c où d où e dont **3** a Voici les documents, dont il a besoin. b Toutes les personnes, dont nous avons le numéro de téléphone, sont sur la liste.

UNIT 43

1 a laquelle b auxquelles c duquel **2** a laquelle b lesquelles **3** a auxquelles b auquel/à qui c laquelle **4** a de laquelle b desquels c duquel

UNIT 44

1 a ce dont b ce que c ce qu' d ce qui **2** a ce que b ce qu' c ce qui d ce qui e ce que f ce qu' **3** a tout ce que b tout ce qui c tout ce qu' d tout ce qu' e tout ce qu' **4** a Je veux savoir ce qu'elle va faire. b Ce dont il a besoin est un nouveau bureau. c Il n'est pas ici, ce qui est très étrange. d Je mange tout ce qu'il y a.

UNIT 45

1 a la b le c le d les e la **2** a te b vous c me d nous **3** a leur b lui c leur d lui **4** a le b leur c les

UNIT 46

1 **a** Nous y allons. **b** Elle y pense. **c** Il y répond. **d** Il y va souvent. **2** **a** Elle en prend six. *She takes six (of them).* **b** Il en achète quatre. *He buys four (of them).* **c** Nous en avons plusieurs. *We have several (of them).* **d** Elle en met beaucoup sur le bureau. *She puts lots (of them) on the desk.* **3** **a** J'en ai plusieurs. **b** J'y vais deux fois par mois. **c** J'en ai trois. **d** J'y habite depuis trois ans. **4** **a** lui **b** y **c** lui **d** y **e** y

UNIT 47

1 **a** 6 **b** 4 **c** 1 **d** 8 **e** 2 **f** 7 **g** 5 **h** 3 **2** **a** Il les achète. **b** Pouvez-vous l'ouvrir? **c** Les mangez-vous? **d** Prends-la **e** Ne le fermez pas. **f** Elle les aide. **g** Je ne veux pas le boire. **h** Ils ne les cherchent pas. **3** **a** Prends-le/la **b** Donnez-le/la-moi. **c** Écoutez-moi. **d** Achète-le/la. **e** ouvre-les **f** Donne-le/la-lui. **4** **a** la lui **b** les lui **c** les leur **d** le lui

UNIT 48

1 **a** avez; ai **b** avez; a **c** ont; ont **2** **a** J' **b** Vous **c** Il/Elle **d** Ils/Elles **e** Il/Elle **f** Nous **3** **a** Tu as/Vous avez tort **b** Il a peur. **c** Tu as/Vous avez une nouvelle voiture. **d** J'ai faim. **e** Ils ont/Elles ont de la chance. **f** Elle a un rendez-vous. **g** Ils ont trois filles. **h** Nous avons une maison secondaire.

UNIT 49

1 **a** je **b** ils/elles **c** nous **d** il **e** tu **f** ils/elles **2** **1** di **2** gk **3** cj **4** al **5** ho **6** b/en **7** d/fm **8** b/ep **3** **a** Il a 10 ans **b** Je suis ingénieur. **c** J'ai faim. **d** Ils sont espagnols/Elles sont espagnoles. **e** Tu as/Vous avez raison. **f** Elle est heureuse. **g** Tu as/Vous avez/As-tu/Avez-vous soif? **h** Elle est jolie.

UNIT 50

1 **a** Elle va ranger **b** Ils vont jouer **c** Tu vas prendre **d** Nous allons écouter **e** Il va manger **f** Je vais écrire **g** Elles vont choisir **h** Il va acheter **i** Il va faire **2** **a** Ils vont à la piscine/vont faire de la natation. **b** Elle fait du ski **c** Ils font de la voile. **3** **a** vont **b** fais **c** vas **d** vas

UNIT 51

1 **a** 4 **b** 5 **c** 2 **d** 3 **e** 1 **2** **a** 4 **b** 5 **c** 1 **d** 2 **e** 3 **3** **a** mettez **b** surprends **c** comprends **d** prenez **e** promet **4** **a** Apprenez-vous/Vous apprenez l'anglais? **b** Je vais prendre une tasse de thé. **c** Elle prend une douche. **d** Il promet un bon repas. **e** Je vais mettre mon manteau.

UNIT 52

1 **a** 4 **b** 8 **c** 6 **d** 7 **e** 1 **f** 3 **g** 2 **h** 5 **2** **a** Vous voulez prendre une tasse de thé? **b** Pouvez-vous/Est-ce que tu peux ouvrir la porte? **c** Veux-tu/Voulez-vous/Tu veux/Vous voulez sortir ce soir? **d** Je veux acheter une veste. **e** Elle veut aller en France. **f** Puis-je fermer la fenêtre? **g** Je voudrais faire du ski. **3** **a** Elle veut aller à la banque. **b** Tu peux/Vous pouvez manger maintenant. **c** Il veut acheter un vélo. **d** Je voudrais un kilo de pommes. **e** Nous pouvons/On peut entrer maintenant.

UNIT 53

1 **a** 6 **b** 3 **c** 7 **d** 1 **e** 4 **f** 5 **g** 8 **h** 2 **2** **a** Dois-je rentrer avant 10 heures?

b Elle sait faire la cuisine **c** Nous devons finir bientôt. **d** Savez-vous faire du ski? **e** Elle doit aller à Rouen. **f** Sait-il faire de la voile? **3** **a** Je dois aller à Paris. **b** Il doit être dans le salon. **c** Elle doit téléphoner à Rouen. **d** Nous savons faire du ski. **e** Ils doivent promettre. **f** Je connais bien Saumur. **4** **a** pouvez **b** peuvent **c** Savez **d** sait **e** peux

UNIT 54

1 ah5 bk2 cl6 dg4 ej3 fi1 **2** **a** veulent **b** devons **c** nous promenons **d** veulent **3** **a** voulez **b** allons **c** allez

UNIT 55

1 **a** lisant **b** courant **c** mettant **d** prenant **e** regardant **f** voyant **2** **a** Elle se lève en chantant. **b** Elle attend le train en lisant. **c** Il travaille dans le jardin en sifflant. **d** Elle prépare le repas en buvant du vin. **e** Elle fait le ménage en écoutant la radio. **f** Elle travaille en mangeant des bonbons. **3** **a** Elle écoute la radio en se douchant. **b** Il chante en faisant le repassage. **c** Elle mange des chocolats/bonbons en regardant la télévision.

UNIT 56

1 **a** 6 **b** 8 **c** 5 **d** 10 **e** 2 **f** 1 **g** 3 **h** 7 **i** 4 **j** 9 **2** **a** Prends **b** Achetez **c** Jouons **d** Donne **e** Soyez **f** Rentrons **g** va **h** mets **3** **a** Va; Allez **b** aie; ayez **c** Mets; Mettez **d** Prends/Prenez **e** pousse; poussez **f** Pense; pensez **g** Choisis; Choisissez **h** Achète/Achetez **4** **a** Répète/Répétez-le **b** Ne le ferme/fermez pas **c** Donne/Donnez moi un journal. **d** Réserve/Réservez moi deux places, s'il vous plaît. **e** Achète/Achetez-les, s'il vous plaît. **f** Sois patient(e)/Soyez patient(e)(s)(es).

UNIT 57

1 **a** 5 **b** 8 **c** 1 **d** 6 **e** 3 **f** 7 **g** 2 **h** 4 **2** **a** sortir **b** rentrer **c** manger **d** m'asseoir **e** acheter **f** lire; regarder **g** te lever **3** **a** J'aime nager. **b** Je préfère lire. **c** Je dois payer. **d** Je veux aller au lit. **e** J'aime acheter les cadeaux. **f** Je sais nager. **g** Je peux venir. **h** J'espère arriver à quatre heures.

UNIT 58

1 **a** à **b** à **c** d' **d** de **e** à **f** de **g** de **h** de **i** à **j** à **2** **a** Elles continuent à bavarder. **b** Il oublie toujours d'acheter du lait. **c** Il commence à lire le journal. **d** Ils essayent de venir avec nous. **e** Nous allons essayer de revenir bientôt. **f** Elle hésite de partir en vacances. **g** Ils sont contents de rester à la maison. **3** **a** Elle oublie d'acheter le journal. **b** Il est capable de comprendre. **c** Il veut apprendre à faire du ski. **d** Elle continue à essayer. **e** Il part sans payer. **f** Elle est prête à partir.

UNIT 59

1 **a** Philippe aide son ami à écrire la lettre. **b** Nous allons inviter nos amis à déjeuner avec nous. **c** J'encourage mon fils à faire ses devoirs. **d** Marie oblige son frère à faire une décision. **e** Ils aident leur père à laver la voiture **2** **a** à; de **b** à; de **c** d' **d** à; de **e** de **f** de **g** à; de **3** **a** J'attends Jean. **b** Écoute/Écoutez la radio. **c** Veux-tu/Voulez-vous jouer au tennis? **d** Marc aide sa sœur à écrire. **e** Je cherche le plan.

UNIT 60

1 **a** est **b** ai **c** avons **d** as **e** sont **f** avez **2** **a** a écouté **b** a attendu **c** ont travaillé **d** ai rempli **3** **a** visité **b** mangé **c** admiré **d** acheté **e** rencontré

UNIT 61

1 a suis b est c a d avons e ai **2** a sommes b sont c est d est e suis f êtes; est **3** a restée b partis c arrivé d sorti(e)(s)(es) e allé(e)s **4** a Elle est sortie de la gare. b Ils/Elles sont sorties du cinéma. c Elle est tombée du vélo/de la bicyclette. d Il est entré dans la banque. e Elle est née le quatre janvier.

UNIT 62

1 a Tu t'es reposé(e) b Ils se sont arrêtés c Nous nous sommes assis(es) d Vous vous êtes dépêché(e)(s)(es) e Elle s'est ennuyée f Je me suis lavé(e) g Elles se sont promenées **2** a Il s'est mis en route. b L'autobus s'est arrêté devant la banque. c Elle s'est approchée de lui. d Nous nous sommes couchés tard hier soir. e Je me suis reposé dans le jardin. f Vous vous êtes promenés dans le parc. g Tu t'es rasé avant de sortir. h Ils se sont levés de bonne heure ce matin. **3** a S'est-il rasé …? b S'est-elle couchée …? c Se sont-elles rencontrées …? **4** a Non. Elle ne s'est pas habillée. b Non. Je ne me suis pas couché(e) … c Non. Ils ne se sont pas reposés … d Non. Elle ne s'est pas coupé le doigt.

UNIT 63

1 a laissés b achetées c vu d mises e visité f achetée g choisi **2** a donnés b lus c rencontrées d fini e parlé f perdue **3** a Je l'ai visité hier. b Je les ai envoyées … c Je l'ai achetée … d Je les ai perdus … e Je l'ai utilisé … f Je l'ai trouvé … g Je les ai lavées … h Je les ai réparées … **4** a achetées b utilisé c lavés d reçue

UNIT 64

1 ai1 bk4 cn6 dm3 ej2 fl5 gh7 **2** a prenaient b finissiez c jouais d couchais e travaillais f rentraient **3** a Il nageait b Elles regardaient la télévision. c Elle faisait du ski.

UNIT 65

1 a est venue; venait b ont joué; jouaient c est allé; allait d a vu; voyait e a acheté; achetait f a fait; faisait **2** a travaillais; est arrivée b lisais; a sonné c écoutait; a frappé d faisions; ai perdu **3** C'était le … il faisait … Je me promenais … j'ai rencontré … Nous avons décidé … nous buvions … nous avons vu … se sont heurtées … conduisaient … ont commencé

UNIT 66

1 a bu b levés c lu d parties e plu f mangé g expliqué **2** a avait b était c étais d avaient e avais f étions **3** a J'avais déjà préparé b était arrivée c avait perdu d étions réveillé(e)s e avaient écrit f j'avais lavé g étais arrivé(e)

UNIT 67

1 a venir b être c pouvoir d mettre e s'asseoir f lire g revenir h battre **2** a ont frappé b a attendu c j'ai choisi d a perdu e ont acheté f sommes allé(e)s g a fini h ont répondu **3** sonna; entendit; regarda; vit; frappa; dit; prit; lut: écouta; se regardèrent

UNIT 68

1 1a 2d 3c 4b **2** **a** fera **b** louera **c** écrira **d** achètera **e** visitera **f** téléphonera **3** CAPRICORNE: vous vous amuserez; vous recevrez; le 30 sera; vous écrirez; vous achèterez; SCORPION: vous aurez; vous sortirez; dépenserez; vous vous disputerez; vous oublierez; (ils)…/aideront

UNIT 69

1 **a** h **b** f **c** g **d** j **e** i **2** **a** nous serons arrivé(e)s **b** vous aurez déjà mangé **c** tu auras commencé **d** J'aurai acheté **e** aurez reçu **f** vous vous serez reposé(e)s **g** On aura lu **h** tu seras rentré(e) **i** vous aurez fini **3** **a** Quand ils auront fini le repas. **b** Quand il aura fait les courses. **c** Quand j'aurai vu le film. **d** Quand elle sera retournée des vacances. **e** Quand ils auront acheté du vin. **f** Quand elle aura fini son travail. **g** Quand elle se sera réveillée. **h** Quand il aura lu le livre.

UNIT 70

1 **a** 4 **b** 6 **c** 7 **d** 1 **e** 2 **f** 5 **g** 3 **2** **a** il aurait **b** je devrais **c** nous prendrions **d** vous pourriez **e** tu voudrais **f** elle finirait **g** je serais **h** elles feraient **i** vous achèteriez **j** il viendrait **k** nous irions **l** je verrais **3** **a** Je visiterais des musées. **b** J'enverrais des cartes postales. **c** Je mangerais bien.

UNIT 71

1 **a** 6 **b** 4 **c** 8 **d** 1 **e** 3 **f** 7 **g** 2 **h** 5 **2** **a** aurait pris **b** serait partie **c** aurait commencé **d** aurait fait **e** seraient restés **3** **a** Elle aurait dû prendre un parapluie. **b** Ils auraient dû acheter de l'essence. **c** Ils auraient dû partir plus tôt. **d** J'aurais dû porter un anorak.

UNIT 72

1 **a** i2 **b** g4 **c** f5 **d** h1 **e** j3 **2** **a** j'étais, je pourrais **b** sors; verrai **c** avais; aurais **3** **a** avais travaillé; aurais fait **b** avais, achèterais **c** finis; pourrai

UNIT 73

1 **a** Après avoir appris **b** Après être arrivé **c** Après m'être reposé(e) **d** Après être arrivé(e)s **e** Après s'être dépêché **2** **a** Ayant appris **b** Étant arrivé **c** M'étant reposé(e) **d** Étant arrivé(e)s **e** Ayant fini **f** S'étant dépêché **3** **a** Après être arrivée **b** Après avoir dit. **c** Après s'être habillé **4** **a** Après avoir fait le ménage, il a déjeuné… **b** Après s'être levé, il a préparé… **c** Après être rentrée à la maison, elle a écrit…

UNIT 74

1 **a** sont aimés **b** est soigné **c** a été cassé **d** ont été mangés **e** était repeint **f** étaient soignés **g** avaient été servies **h** avait été vendue **i** sera interrogé **j** sera livré **k** serait fermé **l** serait servi **2** **a** On **a** fait le repassage. **b** On a perdu… **c** On vous reconnaîtra. **d** On avait envoyé … **3** **a** s'écrit **b** se dit **c** se boit **d** se mangent

UNIT 75

1 **a** soit **b** puisse **c** vienne **2** **a** que tu parles **b** que nous disions **c** qu'ils mettent **d** que vous vendiez **e** qu' elle choisisse **3** **a** j'apprenne **b** j'aille **c** je choisisse **d** je lise **e** je sois **f** je vienne **g** je prenne **4** **a** je veuille; vous vouliez **b** j'aille; vous alliez **c** je sache, vous sachiez **d** je vienne; vous veniez **e** je boive; vous buviez **f** je sois; vous soyez **g** je prenne; vous preniez

UNIT 76

1 a qu'il ait pris b qu'ils se soient dépêchés c que tu aies lu d qu'elles aient su
e que nous ayons pu f que j'aie eu g que vous soyez allé(e)(s)(es) h qu'elle ait fait
2 a Je regrette que je sois arrivé en retard. b Je suis content que tu sois arrivée. c Je
suis content qu'il soit venu. d Je regrette que vous ayez perdu votre collier. e Je suis
content que tu aies fini ton travail. **3** a qu'il ait gagné le prix. b qu'elle ait appris à
conduire. c que tu te sois reposé(e) un peu. d que vous ayez passé le weekend chez eux.
e qu'elles soient allées en vacances. f qu'il soit parti à l'heure. g que vous ayez parlé au
curé. h que vous ayez écrit la lettre.

UNIT 77

1 a l3 b k2 c j4 d h5 e m6 f i1 g n7 **2** a Il est très content qu'elle …
b Ils/Elles regrettent que … c Paul veut que tu … **3** a écrive b arrives c fassiez
d sache e vienne f veuilles

UNIT 78

1 a soit b comprends c prends d sache **2** a soit b dise c puissions
d aille **3** a Il est important qu'il fasse … b Il faut que vous travailliez. c Il est
impossible qu'il réussisse. d Il se peut qu'elle vienne. e Il est nécessaire qu'il fasse ses
études. f C'est dommage que nous ne prenions pas de vacances.

UNIT 79

1 a sache b puisse c peut d sache e aie **2** a disiez b ailles c soit
d parles **3** a Quelles que b Quoi que c Quoi que d Quelle que

UNIT 80

1 a m4 b l5 c h7 d i6 e j2 f n1 g k3 **2** a au contraire; *Me, I like it, but she on the
other hand/contrary doesn't like it at all.* b donc; *It was snowing so I didn't go.* c mais; *He
wanted to come with us but he didn't have the time.* d puis; *He did the cooking then I
washed up.* e ainsi; *He repaired it so/and so we were able to leave.*
f d'ailleurs; *I don't want to buy it, besides I haven't got enough money.* g c'est pourquoi;
I've lost my passport which is why I can't leave. h ou; *You can come with me or you can stay
here.* i pourtant; *We could go to Canada, however it would be expensive/cost a lot.*

UNIT 81

1 a i3 b h1 c f4 d j2 e g5 **2** a dès que; *We'll start the meeting as soon as you
arrive.* b comme; *I paid by cheque as/because I had no money.* c quoi qu'; *He's here
although he's not very well.* d Depuis qu'; *Since she's worked here our methods have
changed a lot.* **3** Comme; Pendant que; qu'; ou … ou; Donc; s'; aussitôt que **4** a Et
Jean-Pierre et Max ont joué au tennis aujourd'hui. b Comme tu vois/vous voyez la brochure
est prête. c Elle m'a dit qu'elle avait mangé. d On va/nous allons ou en France ou en
Espagne cette année.

UNIT 82

1 a Vous ne regardez pas la télévision. b Il ne parle pas espagnol. c Je n'aime pas …
d Elle ne fait pas … e Tu ne vas pas … **2** a Je ne comprends pas. b Ils n'aiment pas
aller au cinéma. c Il ne voit personne dans la pièce. d Il n'y a plus de pain. e Je n'ai
qu'un manteau. f Vous ne mangez rien. **3** a 6 b 4 c 7 d 5 e 1 f 3 g 2

4 **a** Je ne vais jamais au théâtre. **b** Il n'y a pas de cinéma près d'ici. **c** Je n'aime pas le tennis. **d** Il n'y a rien à faire. **e** Jen'aime rien.

UNIT 83

1 **a** Il n'a pas compris le problème. **b** Elle ne s'est pas levée … **c** Il n'aurait pas fini … **d** Elle n'avait pas écrit … **e** Je n'aurais pas acheté. **f** Nous ne sommes pas arrivés …
2 ac bd cf de ea fb **3** **a** Non. Il ne l'a pas vu. **b** Non. Je ne suis pas parti avant minuit. **c** Non. Il ne sera pas arrivé à l'heure. **d** Non. Elle ne s'est pas maquillée avant de sortir. **e** Non il ne l'avait pas fini. **4** **a** Je n'aurais pas fini. **b** Elle n'a pas compris le problème. **c** Vous n'auriez pas dit cela. **d** Tu ne t'es pas levé de bonne heure. **e** Je ne suis pas sorti hier soir. **5** **a** N'y vas-tu pas? **b** Ne me les as-tu pas donnés? **c** N'a-t-il vendu que quatre voitures? **d** N'avez-vous vu personne? **e** N'a-t-elle laissé aucun mot?

UNIT 84

1 **a** Il parle français. **b** Elle aime travailler ici. **c** Ils ont pris le train de huit heures. **d** Tu vas à la conférence cette semaine. **e** Vous habitez en ville. **f** J'ai assez d'argent. **g** Tu prends une photo. **h** Vous faites du ski cette année. **2** **a** Tu achètes un ordinateur? Est-ce que tu achètes un ordinateur? Achètes-tu un ordinateur? **b** Il est pharmacien? Est-ce qu'il est pharmacien? Est-il pharmacien? **c** Elle adore le théâtre? Est-ce qu'elle adore le théâtre? Adore-t-elle le théâtre? **d** Vous aimez le vin? Est-ce que vous aimez le vin? Aimez-vous le vin? **e** Ils vont en ville? Est-ce qu'ils vont en ville? Vont-ils en ville? **3** (*The following feedback gives all three possible answers in each case. The most likely form of the second-person ('you') is used for each scenario, or both where either is plausible.*) **a** Vous avez une voiture? Tu as une voiture? Est-ce que vous avez une voiture? Est-ce que tu as une voiture? Avez-vous une voiture? As-tu une voiture? **b** Tu vas au cinéma ce soir? Est-ce que tu vas au cinéma ce soir? Vas-tu au cinéma ce soir? **c** Tu veux sortir? Est-ce que tu veux sortir? Veux-tu sortir? **d** Vous êtes agriculteur? Est-ce que vous êtes agriculteur? Êtes-vous agriculteur? **e** Vous parlez (anglais)? Est-ce que vous parlez (anglais)? Parlez-vous (anglais)? **f** Tu voudrais prendre du congé? Est-ce que tu voudrais prendre du congé? (*inversion is not likely for this question*)

UNIT 85

1 **a** 6 **b** 3 **c** 7 **d** 1 **e** 2 **f** 4 **g** 5 **2** **a** 2 Où **b** 5 quel **c** 4 Comment **d** 3 Combien **e** 1 Quel **3** **a** Vous allez où?/Où est-ce que vous allez? Où allez-vous? **b** Vous quittez le bureau à quelle heure? A quelle heure est-ce que vous quittez le bureau? A quelle heure quittez-vous le bureau? **c** Vous allez au cinéma avec qui? Avec qui est-ce que vous allez au cinéma? Avec qui allez-vous au cinéma? **d** Vous avez combien de frères? Combien de frères est-ce que vous avez? Combien de frères avez-vous? **e** Il vient d'où? D'où est-ce qu'il vient? D'où vient-il? **f** Vous préférez quelle robe? Quelle robe est-ce que vous préférez? Quelle robe préférez-vous? **g** Le film finit à quelle heure? A quelle heure est-ce que le film finit? A quelle heure finit le film? **h** Vous aimez quel foulard? Quel foulard est-ce que vous aimez? Quel foulard aimez-vous?

UNIT 86

1 **a** n1 **b** l12 **c** i4 **d** k3 **e** p6 **f** o7 **g** j5 **h** m8 **2** **a** Laquelle **b** Qui **c** quoi **d** Que **e** De quoi **f** Lequel **g** qui **h** Qu' **3** **a** De quoi as-tu/avez-vous peur? **b** Lequel des ordinateurs veux-tu/voulez-vous? **c** Qui travaille dans ce bureau?

d Qu'est-ce que tu dis/vous dites? Que dis-tu/dites-vous? **e** Pour qui est ce document? Ce document est pour qui?

UNIT 87

1 deux cafés; un vin blanc; douze bières; sept jus d'orange; quatorze limonades; trois panachés; cinq cognacs **2** **a** huit, seize (*two-times table*) **b** cinq, onze (*odd numbers*) **c** quinze, six (*subtract*) **d** dix, vingt (*five-times table*) **3** 23 vingt-trois; 49 quarante-neuf; 51 cinquante-et-un; 79 soixante-dix-neuf; 80 quatre-vingts; 81 quatre-vingt-un **4** quarante-deux tasses; cinquante fourchettes; soixante couteaux; trente-cinq assiettes; vingt-huit cuillères; cinquante-trois bols **5** quatre-vingt-douze; cinquante-neuf; soixante-sept; dix-huit; trente-trois; soixante-quinze; vingt-six; quarante et un; quatre-vingt-deux; cent un; deux cent quarante-neuf; cinq cent cinquante; mille cinq cent soixante-douze (*or* quinze cent soixante-douze); deux mille cinq cents (*or* vingt-cinq cents); un million deux cent mille

UNIT 88

1 **a** 13 **b** p5 **c** i6 **d** n8 **e** k2 **f** j4 **g** o1 **h** m7 **2** **a** soixante-quatorzième **b** quatre-vingt-quinzième **c** soixante-seizième **d** centième **e** quatre-vingt-unième **f** quatre-vingtième **g** soixante-dix-neuvième **h** quatre-vingt-huitième **3** **a** deuxième **b** premier **c** quatrième **d** cinquième **e** sixième **f** troisième

UNIT 89

1 **a** n **b** l **c** j **d** p **e** k **f** m **g** i **h** o **2** **a** troix huitièmes **b** un sixième **c** un quart **d** deux tiers **e** neuf dixièmes **f** sept seizièmes **g** quatre cinquièmes **h** trois vingtièmes **3** **a** la moitié **b** les deux tiers **c** à mi-chemin **d** une livre et demie **e** un kilo et demi **4** **a** Vingt-et-un pour cent … **b** Trente-cinq pour cent … **c** Dix-neuf pour cent … **d** Sept pour cent … **e** Trois pour cent … **f** Dix pour cent …

UNIT 90

1 **a** L'arc de Triomphe a 50m de haute/hauteur sur 45m de large/de largeur. **b** La tour Eiffel a 300m de haut/de hauteur. **c** La basilique du Sacré-Coeur a 80m de haut/de hauteur. **2** **a** Quelle est la hauteur et la largeur de l'arc de Triomphe? L'arc de Triomphe a/fait combien de haut/de hauteur et combien de large/de largeur? L'arc de Triomphe est haut de combien? **b** Quelle et la hauteur de la tour Eiffel? La tour Eiffel a//fait combien de haut/de hauter? La tour Eiffel est haute de combien? **c** Quelle est la hauteur de la basilique du Sacré-Coeur? La basilique du Sacré-Coeur a/fait combien de haut/de hauteur? La basilique du Sacré-Coeur est haute de combien? **3** **a** Cette pièce fait 5m sur 3m. **b** Cette table fait 90cm sur 45cm. **c** Ce jardin fait 100m sur 80m **4** **a** profonde **b** profond **c** épais **d** haut; large **e** longues; larges; hautes **5** **a** Toulouse est à 80 kilomètres d'ici. **b** Nous sommes à une demi-heure de chez nous. **c** Le garage le plus près est à combien d'ici? **d** Il doit être à au moins 20 kilomètres d'ici. **e** La banque est à 5 minutes (d'ici) seulement.

UNIT 91

1 **a** sept heures vingt **b** huit heures dix **c** neuf heures moins cinq **d** une heure moins le quart **e** dix-huit heures **2** **a** dix-sept heures quarante **b** trois heures trente-cinq **c** dix-neuf heures vingt-cinq **d** douze heures vingt-deux **e** quinze heures quinze **f** dix-huit heures trente **3** **a** 5 huit heures et demie **b** 1 six heures quinze/et quart **c** 8 neuf heures **d** 7 quatre heures dix **e** 3 minuit et demi/douze heures et demi **f** 2 onze heures moins le quart/dix heures quarante-cinq **g** 6 une heure **h** 4 sept heures du soir

UNIT 92

1 **a** vendredi, le 22 janvier **b** samedi, le 13 février **c** mardi, le 9 février **d** lundi, le 15 mars **e** mercredi, le 17 mars **2** **a** 2 le jeudi **b** 6 le lundi **c** 5 vendredi **d** 7 dimanche **e** 8 le vendredi **f** 3 jeudi **g** 4 le dimanche **h** 1 lundi **3** **a** C'est mon anniversaire (le) vendredi le 15 mai. **b** Ce dimanche je vais voir des amis. **c** La semaine prochaine je suis en vacances. **d** Il a commencé le 15 avril. **e** Au printemps nous allons en Italie. **f** Aujoud'hui c'est le 12 janvier. **g** En hiver elle reste en France. **h** En 1968 j'étais à Paris.

UNIT 93

1 **a** 7 **b** 3 **c** 1 **d** 2 **e** 6 **f** 10 **g** 8 **h** 5 **i** 4 **j** 9 **2** **a** il y a **b** depuis **c** depuis **d** il y a **e** il y a **f** depuis **3** **a** Il y a plusieurs semaines qu'il fait des études. Ça fait plusieurs … Voilà plusieurs … **b** Il y a 40 minutes que nous attendons le bus. Voilà 40 minutes que nous … Ça fait 40 minutes que nous … **c** Il y avait deux heures qu'ils travaillaient. Voilà deux heures qu'ils travaillaient. Ça faisait deux heures qu'ils travaillaient.

UNIT 94

1 **a** 3 **d** 4 **e** 5 **g** 2 **j** 1 **2** **a** Il y a deux voitures devant l'école. **b** Il y a des sandwichs dans le frigo. **c** Il y a des documents sur la table. **3** **a** Il y aura des feux d'artifice devant la mairie. **b** Il y avait des bouteilles dans le frigo. **c** Il y a des légumes dans la soupe. **d** Il y a eu une erreur. **e** Il y aura beaucoup de monde au cinéma. **f** Il y avait des enfants dans le parc. **g** Il y a de l'argent dans ma poche.

UNIT 95

1 **a** 1 **b** 1 **c** 2 **d** 2 **e** 2 **f** 2 **g** 1 **h** 1 **2** **a** Je crois que oui. **b** J'espère qui si. **c** J'espère que non. **d** Non merci. **e** Je crois que non. **f** Peut-être que non. **3** **a** Oui **b** Si **c** Si **d** Oui **e** Si **f** Non

UNIT 96

1 **a** f **b** f **c** f **d** f **e** m **f** f **g** m **h** m **i** f **j** m **2** **a** aux États-Unis **b** au Japon **c** en Italie **d** en Russie **e** en Espagne **3** **a** des États-Unis. C'est un Américain. **b** d'Allemagne. C'est un Allemand. **c** de France. C'était un Français. **d** d'Angleterre. C'est une Anglaise. **e** d'Espagne. C'était un Espagnol. **f** du Brésil. C'est un Brésilien. **4** **a** française **b** L'Italie; italien **c** le Japon; japonaise **d** canadien; canadienne **e** anglaise **f** américaine **g** Espagne; espagnol **h** Luxembourg; luxembourgeoise **i** chinois **j** africaine

UNIT 97

1 **a** ai-je demandé **b** a répondu l'agent **c** lui avons-nous dit **d** répond-il **e** s'exclama-t-elle **f** s'écriera-t-il **2** **a** Peut-être sera-t-il … **b** Ainsi mourut le grand homme. **c** Peut-être y a-t-il encore … **d** Sans doute veut-elle être … **e** Aussi a-t-elle besoin … **f** Encore vous faut-il le faire. **a** *Perhaps he'll be happy at last.* **b** *Thus died the great man.* **c** *Perhaps there is still hope.* **d** *Without doubt she wants to be boss of the company.* **e** *So/therefore she needs help.* **f** *Nevertheless you have to do it.* **3** **a** A-t-il expliqué …? **b** Sont-elles arrivées …? **c** Avons-nous fini …? **d** Vous a-t-elle téléphoné …? **e** A-t-il frappé …? **4** **a** Que voulez-vous/prenez-vous, monsieur? **b** Où est le cinéma? **c** Comment vas-tu/allez-vous? **d** Quand pars-tu/partez-vous? **e** Combien est ce manteau? **f** Quelle est la meilleure date pour vous? **g** Combien de personnes y a-t-il?

UNIT 98

1 **a** situation **b** visiter **c** panorama **d** âge **2** **a** *She found the lost document by chance.* **b** *I'm going to stay at home this evening.* **c** *The book shop is opposite the station.* **d** *His/her shoes are worn (out).* e *It's a notorious story.* **f** *He's always lucky.* **g** *She's rarely good tempered.* **h** *In my opinion it's impossible.* **i** *They sat down in the bank.* **j** *A good job is hard to find.* **3** **a** Je vais à la bibliothèque choisir des livres. **b** Où sont mes lunettes? **c** Le voyage/trajet a duré vingt-quatre heures. **d** C'est une femme très renommée. **e** C'est un endroit/lieu très intéressant. **f** Passe-moi/Passez-moi un morceau de pain, s'il te/vous plaît. **g** Ils vont assister à la réunion demain. **h** Je dois passer mon examen dans dix jours. **i** En ce moment la nouvelle est bonne.

UNIT 99

1 **a** m8 **b** p1 **c** i2 **d** k5 **e** j3 **f** o6 **g** l7 **h** n4 **2** **a** autant de **b** combien de **c** trop de **d** peu d' **e** beaucoup **f** assez de **g** tant de **h** un peu de **3** **a** une bouteille d'eau minérale **b** un kilo de pommes **c** un paquet de biscuits **d** une boîte de pêches **e** une tasse de thé